Defending
Intellectual
Freedom

Defending Intellectual Freedom

The Library and the Censor

Eli M. Oboler

Contributions in Librarianship and Information Science, Number 32

GREENWOOD PRESS
Westport, Connecticut
London, England

Library of Congress Cataloging in Publication Data

Oboler, Eli M
    Defending intellectual freedom.

    (Contributions in librarianship and information
science ; no. 32 ISSN 0084-9243)
    Bibliography: p.
    Includes index.
    1. Censorship.   2.   Libraries—Censorship.
I. Title.   II. Series.
Z657.O23   0.25.2'1   79-8585
ISBN 0-313-21472-7 lib. bdg.

Library of Congress Catalog Card Number: 79-8585
ISBN: 0-313-21472-7
ISSN: 0084-9243

First published in 1980

Greenwood Press
A division of Congressional Information Service, Inc.
88 Post Road West, Westport, Connecticut 06881

Printed in the United States of America

10 9 8 7 6 5 4 3 2 1

Acknowledgments

The articles, talks, editorials, reviews, and letters which appear in this book and have been previously published are reprinted with permissions and copyright acknowledgment as indicated hereinafter.

"The Free Mind," from *Library Journal* 101 (1 January 1976): 237-42.
"The Freedom to Choose," from *Intellect* 103 (January 1975): 263-64.
"Congress as Censor" [I], from *Library Journal* 77 (15 November 1952): 1927-30.
"Congress as Censor" [II] from *Library Trends* 19 (July 1970): 64-73.
"The Politics of Pornography," from *Library Journal* 95 (15 December 1970): 4225-28.
"The Grand Illusion," from *Library Journal* 93 (15 March 1968): 1277-79.
"Everything You Always Wanted to Know about Censorship (But Were Afraid to Ask), Explained," from *American Libraries* 2 (February 1971): 194-98.
"Just Like the Child in the Family," from *Library Journal* 98 (1 September 1973): 2395-98.
"Public Relations and Intellectual Freedom," from *PNLA Quarterly* 38 (Spring 1974): 17-21.
"The Purpose of a Librarian," from *Utah Libraries* 22 (Spring 1979): 21-24.
"Idaho School Librarians and Salinger's *Catcher in the Rye*," from *Idaho Librarian* 15 (October 1963): 137-39.
"Idaho Libraries and Intellectual Freedom," from *Idaho Librarian* 17 (July 1965): 101-4.

"Pornography in Modern America," from *Idaho State Journal* (2 June 1972), section C, p. 5.

"Obscenity and Pornography: The Legal Question," from *Idaho State Journal* (28 June 1974), section C, p. 15.

"Thoughts Concerning Censorship Disputes," from *Idaho Librarian* 27 (October 1975): 138-39.

"The First Amendment: The Growing Affronts on Free Speech," from *Idaho State Journal* (4 June 1978), section A, p. 5.

EDITORIALS:

"Three and Four Letter Words," from *PNLA Quarterly* 26 (July 1962): 235-36.

"All or Nothing at All," from *Newsletter on Intellectual Freedom* (July 1969): 20.

"Viewpoint: The Case Against 'Liberal' Censorship," from *NOIF* 21 (January 1972): 30.

"Post July 4th Thoughts: A View of American Patriotism," from *Idaho State Journal* (23 July 1971), section D, p. 5.

"The Old Man on the Hill," from *NOIF* 25 (January 1976): 7.

LETTERS:

From *Commentary* 52 (July 1971): 33-34; *Library Journal* 98 (1 January 1973): 29-30; 98 (15 November 1973): 3324-25; 101 (1 March 1976): 643; *Intellect* 105 (September-October 1976): 59; *Library Journal* 101 (1 November 1976): 2203; *Library Journal* 102 (1 February 1977): 299; *Wilson Library Bulletin* 52 (November 1977): 227; The Norman-Oboler Joust in *Library Journal* 101 (1 June 1976): 102 (15 January 1977), and 102 (1 April 1977).

REVIEWS:

From *PNLA Quarterly* 24 (October 1959): 102-3; 30 (October 1965): 88-90; 31 (July 1967): 277-78; *NOIF* 21 (May 1972): 79-81, 95; 21 (November 1972): 166, 170; *Library Journal* 98 (15 January 1973): 166; *NOIF* 22 (September 1973): 120-21; 23 (September 1974): 110; 24 (March 1975): 40, 64-65; 25 (January 1976): 6; 25 (July 1976): 83; *College and Research Libraries* 37 (November 1976): 566; *Library Quarterly* 47 (January 1977): 85-86; *Journal of Library History* 12

(Fall 1977): 423-24; *NOIF* 26 (November 1977): 154, 175-76; *Journal of Academic Librarianship* 4 (March 1978): 34; *NOIF* (July 1978): 108; 28 (March 1979): 26; 28 (May 1979): 47; "The Pleasures of a Reviewer," *NOIF* 28 (July 1979): 74.

READING LISTS:

"The Freedom to Read: A Selected Reading List," revised in 1979 from Idaho State University Library List No. 76-7 (1976).
"The Censor's Library," *NOIF* 26 (May 1977): 68, 89.

To my sister, Dr. Minnie Oboler Perlstein,
and my brother, Arch Oboler—
exemplars of courage and independence

Outside of the prison cell in a state of freedom there are certain problems, yes. They are not prison misfortunes. They are misfortunes of freedom. These are liberty's burdens, which are not easy but cannot be compared to the heavy weight of unfreedom.

Alexander Ginzburg and four other
freed Russian dissenters, in a joint
statement released to the world press
28 April 1979.

79-80

Contents

Foreword

Eli M. Oboler, university librarian at Idaho State University for over three decades, has been an exemplar of service to his profession. In addition to his contributions to higher education, he has been one of librarianship's most persistent critics of censorship and one of its most vocal proponents of intellectual freedom.

Mr. Oboler has not only spoken for intellectual freedom on behalf of librarianship and the American Library Association, he has been our loyal gadfly, constantly demanding the dismantling of barriers to freedom of expression and freedom of inquiry.

In urging the American Library Association not to follow but to lead in social movements advancing freedom, Mr. Oboler was one of ALA's premier advocates of the removal of racial restrictions in library services during the early civil rights movement in America. Later, as one of the essays in this volume shows, he called for the elimination of restrictions on library services to youth.

In 1961, the *Library Bill of Rights*, ALA's basic statement on intellectual freedom in library services, was amended to oppose abridgment of the right to use a library based on "race, religion, national origins or political views." In 1967, the word "age" was added to this article against discrimination. On both occasions, the forceful voice of Eli Oboler was heard.

In the jargon of First Amendment debates, Mr. Oboler has been a purist. But purists have never had an easy time of it.

In the not-too-distant past, the term "purist" was applied to idealists striving for a world that was not and, in the views of most, never would be. The term often prompted a disbelieving shake of the head.

Today, the word "purist" sometimes carries with it the hint of a taint. Purists believe that the First Amendment applies to the expressions of the views of both civil rights advocates and neo-Nazis. Fortunately for his colleagues, Mr. Oboler has not been deterred by those who would tar the purist with the brush of the hated dogmas of speakers whose First Amendment rights he defends.

Of all the issues raised in this volume, perhaps none will be more vexatious in the next decade than the defense of purism. In the years ahead, I hope we can use the bench mark presented in these pages.

But the urgency of this question of purism should not hide from readers the fact that some of today's popular views on intellectual freedom were once regarded as extremely odious by many influential people, both within and without librarianship. Thus, the elaboration of a consistent and comprehensive philosophy of freedom of expression is not the easy task that it sometimes appears in retrospect.

In 1922, in a series of articles on "questionable" books in libraries, *Library Journal* condemned "salacious" works which supposedly appealed to the "prurient" interest. The editors refused to name specific publications, fearing that a demand would be created for them. The conversion of most librarians to the philosophy of the *Library Bill of Rights* did not occur overnight. Those who join the profession of librarianship today, and perhaps even more all those who use library services, owe a debt of gratitude to Eli Oboler.

Judith F. Krug, *Director*
OFFICE FOR INTELLECTUAL FREEDOM
AMERICAN LIBRARY ASSOCIATION

Preface

Alfred North Whitehead defined *dogma* as "the product of mere abstract thought elaborating its notions of the fitness of things"— what a minor American philosopher, Henshaw Ward, described as "thobbing: *th*inking out *b*eliefs." Although I am sure I shall be deemed both a dogmatist and a "thobber" in at least some of the pages that follow, my honest intention has been to follow Whitehead's advice concerning research methodology: to ". . . pay full attention to the empirical evidence, and to the whole of that evidence."

There is a great deal of evidence that intellectual freedom in America these last thirty years has been in constant danger of diminution, if not extinction. The Joe McCarthyism of the 1950s that hinged on the belief that America was in extreme danger from an internal pro-Communist conspiracy and the Gene McCarthyism of the 1960s that claimed the existence of an equally dangerous plot against democracy by American ultrarightists both had their effects on libraries and librarianship. Through both periods I was involved in the efforts of some—and eventually a majority—of the library profession to give full professional rights to all librarians within the American Library Association and to minimize the censorial ventures of those in and out of our profession who neither believed in nor practiced the freedom to read.

This volume includes previously published articles, editorials, letters, and reviews, as well as new material, that expatiate on a theme. That theme—which, I suppose, is that of my professional life and career—is that man is by nature free in mind as well as body, and that librarians, of all mankind, are (or *should* be) the leaders in explanation, defense, promulgation, and practice of intellectual freedom. This book is, I hope, not my last word on either intellectual freedom or censorship, but I think it says some things worth preserving and noting as reflections of the embattled state of the freedom of the mind in America, and particularly in American libraries, in the mid-years of the contentious twentieth century. It will be successful if it reminds its readers that what the Russian dissenters have described as "liberty's burden" is a universal, continuing, and bearable load that all who love freedom must be prepared to assume when the occasion arises.

My previous volume in the *Contributions in Librarianship and Information Science* series, *Ideas and the University Library*, was criticized by some readers and reviewers because its contents— mostly previously printed articles, as in this volume—had not been updated and revised. However, I cling to the obviously outdated and ridiculously old-fashioned notion that intellectual honesty is as important as, or perhaps more important than, timeliness. So, once again, these products of my pen are republished as they first appeared, warts and all.

I owe particular thanks to the many editors and publishers (all noted on the acknowledgments pages) who have graciously permitted me to reprint what they first found worthy of publication. Those items not listed as previously published are otherwise acknowledged.

Finally, let me offer due appreciation to my colleagues, in and out of Idaho State University, who helped me toward reasonable views on some highly charged, emotion-filled issues. The ALA Office of Intellectual Freedom (and especially Judy Krug, who speaks for herself elsewhere in this book), the ALA Intellectual Freedom Committee in the 1960s, the Freedom to Read Foundation, and especially my fellow members of the Idaho Library Association's Intellectual Freedom Committee—all are owed thanks for their special shares in this work, for the imperfections of which, of course, I take full responsibility.

And, as with all my writings, the Muse Polyhymnia made her tuneful contribution—via flute, oboe, and violin, especially.

E.M.O.

Pocatello, Idaho
Idaho State University
August 1979

Defending
Intellectual
Freedom

The free mind: Intellectual freedom's perils and prospects *

1

(This article, which formed part of Library Journal's *1976 100th Anniversary issue whose theme was "Libraries in America's Future," was perhaps a little more euphoric than the grim facts of the struggle against censorship in America really justified; but it was intended to be, even if somewhat rhetorical, a reminder to experienced librarians and a stimulus to library neophytes to engage, personally and directly, in the necessary battle to save intellectual freedom. After several years, about the only additions I believe needed are to underscore its perhaps prescient comments on the inchoate dangers to libraries in the commercial information industry and once again to ask vehemently for strong measures by the library profession to prevent the spreading contagion of censorship [whether conscious or unconscious] by librarians themselves.)*

THE FREE MIND: INTELLECTUAL FREEDOM'S PERILS AND PROSPECTS

"Let us look forward to the future with that salutary fear which makes men keep watch and ward for freedom, not with that faint and idle terror which depresses and enervates the heart."[1]

When de Tocqueville wrote this ringing exhortation, nearly 150 years ago, he was convinced that "the press is the chiefest (sic)

*Reprinted from *Library Journal*, January 1, 1976. Published by R. R. Bowker Co. (a Xerox Company) Copyright © 1976 by Xerox Corporation

democratic instrument of freedom." He saw no way for the preservation of individual independence in democracies without the
most absolute freedom of the press possible. Indeed, he went so far
as to assert that ". . . the liberty of the press. . .is the only cure for
the evils which equality may produce."[2] In his utterly commenda-
tory review John Stuart Mill proclaimed that in a democracy ". . .
the superior spirits and the government, so far as it is permitted,
should devote their utmost energies . . . to vindicate and protect the
unfettered exercise of reason, and the moral freedom of the individual . . ."[3]

These are noble, ringing sentiments, which are good backgrounds
for the expression of some simple truths which those who believe in
the bright future of the free exercise of the free mind should find
agreeable. First, there is no good reason to assume that the free
flow of ideas and argument will *not* result in a better life for the
individual and nation. Secondly, those few who advocate suppression, restriction, and censorship are in no way, as Zechariah
Chafee, Jr., has written, ". . .so much wiser than the masses that
they can safely regulate their views for them."[4] Finally, the usual
argument for denial of argument is a belief in the not-to-be-ques-
tioned virtues of tradition and the obvious evils of any and all
change. I agree with Chafee that the best cause for all is: "Let us
have enough faith in our institutions to believe that they can safely
withstand voice and paper. . . ."[5]

Graham Wallas had an interesting theory: ". . . the great periods
of intellectual activity are apt to follow the coincidence of the discovery of important new facts with the wide extension of a sense of
personal liberty."[6] Assuming this to be true—and both logic and
history indicate its likely validity—then surely the cause of intellectual freedom has one more strong justification. If the individual
who *could* help human progress advance is more likely to do so if
he has "a sense of personal liberty," then it is clearly up to us to
help give him that "sense." Censorship—legal or extra-legal—is
thus (among other things) a barrier to the great breakthroughs to
more and better civilization.

OPINION AND INNOVATION

De Tocqueville saw the greatest potential danger to that democracy which he admired as America's greatest contribution to civili-

zation not in either political or even intellectual revolutions; he feared that ". . . modern society . . . will ultimately be too invariably fixed in the same institutions, the same prejudices, the same manners, so that mankind will be stopped and circumscribed; that the mind will swing backwards and forwards forever, without begetting fresh ideas; that man will waste his strength in bootless and solitary trifling; and, though in continual revolution, that humanity will cease to advance."[7]

This grim prospect of frustratingly Sisyphean "progress" seems only too possible in 1976. Whether it becomes likely, or even an accomplished fact, depends on how those who really are concerned about the freedom of the mind face up to that prospect. It is surely not pre-ordained or otherwise inevitable—but it can more likely become a reality if what de Tocqueville describes as the "empty phantom of public opinion" is permitted to become, as he warns, ". . . strong enough to chill innovators, and to keep them silent and at a respectful distance."

We who are the inheritors of the tradition of free opinion and who have the opportunity and responsibility to fight for that tradition will deserve the opprobrium of untold generations if we, in our professional groups and in the performance of our daily duties, do not, collectively and severally, fulfill our obligations. It is not merely rhetoric to say that the battle for the free mind, never-ending, is one battle that must always be fought and yet can never be completely won. The free mind is an ideal; so is true democracy; but democracy and intellectual freedom, even *with* imperfections, are certainly better than their antitheses.

FREEDOM IS THE PURSUIT OF TRUTH

There is a great temptation for any believer in intellectual freedom to equate the belief in and practice of freedom of expression with some kind of perfect state, perfect world, perfect life. It is, of course, only a means toward a highly desirable end, the self-realization of man and the democratization of nations. It is also a manifestly unattainable ideal, which in no way affects its practical and immediate value as the only way to come even close to that essential of a livable life, Truth.

To escape the restrictive bonds of government and society and the all-too-human limitations of individual prejudice and intolerance in regard to thought and its expression is a goal set by idealists throughout civilized history. Whether complete intellectual freedom for everyone is a reasonable aim or simply a chimera—an idealistic will-of-the-wisp that will help in the achievement of lesser, but more attainable, goals—is hardly worth arguing; the very act of working toward absolute individual intellectual freedom is a highly motivated, assuredly widely acceptable activity which merits even wider support.

It is not enough to be released from the restraints of tradition-tied church and state, of psyche and conscience, of political control and moral rectitude; it is vital that intellectual freedom, once achieved at whatever quantitative or qualitative level, be *used*, be *exercised*, to avoid atrophy. The power of the free mind is hardly a true power if it is kept in reserve for some possible future moment of extreme need. The point-counterpoint of human dialogue, whether in print, on the platform, or on film, is truly a potent force which will achieve its highest level of power only if constantly and consistently practiced.

When Thomas Jefferson contrasted the status of physical liberty with what he called "moral emancipation," this nation was a long way from the Emancipation Proclamation, and it, in turn, was only at the merest beginning of a process not yet complete—the removal of racial discrimination from American life. But the act of Jefferson's publicly stating the importance of this problem contributed its share to the ever-ongoing process of seeking human freedom. The Word has been, is, and will be as mighty a weapon as shot and shell.

John Dewey deplores the fact that ". . . men may be brought by long habit to hug their chains"; this is true of both physical and mental slavery. Where the chains are self-imposed and there is only apathy restraining manumission, mankind suffers the most. The intellectually free individual is the product of a long and distinguished line of fighters for the mind's freedom. In the Anglo-American tradition John Locke, John Milton, Roger Williams, Benjamin Franklin, Thomas Jefferson, Ralph Waldo Emerson, John Dewey, and Zechariah Chafee, Jr. are only a few obvious individuals among those theorists and practitioners of intellectual freedom who deserve the gratitude of any sincere truth-seekers. But all their efforts will have been wasted if each generation does not fight its own battle against the ever-present forces of repression and restraint. From the lawyers and judges and legislators, the librarians and teachers and professors, the journalists and authors and media-men and publishers must come the leadership, the willingness to engage in even the less publicized skirmishes, often resulting in only minutely incremental gains, to keep the mind free. No single facet of human existence in society is as likely to lose its always tenuous standing, to be taken for granted, even to be nearly forgotten, as man's right to free expression, to speak and listen and read and view, to argue and debate, to have as free access as possible to the widest possible reaches of knowledge and opinion.

FREEDOM IS INDIVIDUAL

In the vital and abiding concerns of mankind, intellectual freedom may seem to some less important than physical freedom, or economic freedom, or equality and justice. But none of these or the other highly regarded human freedoms can endure without the first freedom, the freedom of the intellect.

There is a continuous struggle going on for the minds and hearts of men and nations. On the one extreme are those who call for a "dictatorship of the proletariat"; on the other, the individuals and groups who, in one way or another, subscribe to fascist principles. They both desire the muzzling of their opponents. Only the intellectually free will listen to both. The automatized, "nickel-in-a-slot" reaction that any risk to security justifies the denial of liberty is just not acceptable; history and reason alike are on the side of those who see freedom of speech and press as basic to any form of truly democratic government, to a self-improving, renewing, and renewable society. (As a case in point, consider India's current situation.)

To be genuinely intellectually free is to be a paragon of paragons, a "never-was" and "never-will-be." But this is one contest where only the non-competitors lose. It is as impossible to achieve perfect intellectual freedom as it is to achieve perfection in any human effort. That this particular effort is among the most significant and important ones that an individual or nation can make clearly justifies whatever reasonable risk is taken, whatever sensible program be followed to achieve as near a perfect result as possible.

Putting it most directly, the intellectually free are those who honestly try to find out the truth on any issue as dispassionately, objectively, and fully as human failings of the mind and body permit. Any barriers to threading the maze of opinion and argument and agreement and disagreement are only achievable hurdles, not impassable walls or blind alleys . . . to the intellectually free.

Self-knowledge leads to self-realization. The intellectually free face up, not only to what A. E. Housman called "man's bedevilment, and God's," but also to their own inadequacies. No one claims that intellectual freedom equates with individual or social perfection—only that it will by definition permit a greater likelihood of both. In agreeing with Pascal when he said that thought makes the whole dignity of man, one does not have to forget that there is no more basic attribute of man the thinker than uncertainty and instability. The restless mind of man is both his badge of distinction and his primal curse. From his creation, man has been unsatisfied and insecure. And intellectual freedom is the source of his greatest pride and greatest conflict.

THE FUTURE OF INDIVIDUALISM

There is ample evidence, historical and experimental, of the fact that man is basically a social being . . . and this fact certainly affects any attempt to predict how man as an individual will do in the years, the decades ahead, so far as the freedom of his mind is concerned. Where society, in its basic urge toward self-preservation, toward continuity, toward the maintenance of traditional patterns and values, tends toward requiring conformity and decrying dissent, the individual is paramount in fighting for freedom. The great breakthroughs in invention, in truly creative matters, have always been the product of the individual, not of society. Out of this dichotomy of the society and the individual, the tension between the many and the one, must come whatever success there really is, what progress is possible in the future, as in the past.

The question is, of course, how these forces—both complementary and opposing—of society and of the individual will in fact operate tomorrow. Granted that man is, as Herbert Muller says, ". . . free to make his own history . . ."[8] (whether for better or worse), it is only a tentative, "iffy" series of guesses we can make on this topic. But we can at least attempt to make these guesses more informed than apocalyptic.

A time-traveler, capable of omniscient spatial and temporal perspective, would be utterly perplexed by the erratic ups and downs of the fortunes of the freedom of the mind of the individual from century to century—and, in this seemingly most unpredictable century (the one we live in), almost from year to year. The Victorian ideal of progress, so eloquently voiced by Tennyson, ". . . that somehow good will be the final goal of ill . . ." was not exemplified before, during, or after the good Queen's reign.

TECHNOLOGY VS. FREEDOM

We are, if anything, slipping back into medieval, perhaps even primitive, beliefs and practices as regards to the opportunity and willingness to let man's mind run free. The baleful spectre of utter denial of privacy—via interconnected data banks and computers, in a wired nation—daily becomes more corporeal. Advances in communications technology are certainly no guarantee of equal advances toward intellectual freedom; they are more likely to have just the reverse effect, from all we can see at present.

Where the librarian of the first decades of this past 100 years was mostly preoccupied with the minutiae of publication-organization, today's librarian is confronted by Big Government that self-confessedly has come about as close to Orwell's "Big Brother" as reality —not fiction—could permit, as well as by a new nemesis in the form of a self-labeled "information industry." How the free exchange of ideas and facts and opinions can survive this double onslaught is the problem librarians must do their full share to solve, if intellectual freedom itself is to survive.

PROPERTY AND FREEDOM

To elaborate on this rather new and even startling concept of "the information industry," it is certainly related to the current (yet long-lasting) conflict between the authors and publishers of print and nonprint materials and those who make use of them, such as educators and libraries. Is copyright a form of control of intellectual property whose value transcends the rights of students and researchers to "reasonable" (whatever that is!) use of published materials in copied format? Is it fair to the freedom of the mind and its wide and general exercise to bottle up facts in Lockheed's computer system or in the New York Times' data bank or elsewhere, where it costs thousands upon thousands of dollars to get these facts for a single corporation or library or school?

These are not academic, theoretical questions. Upon their answers depends, it may well be, the future of any property system in information. Gene Wunderlich has recently put the modern theory behind the concept of the relation between property and information as follows:

There is only one privacy—the free mind. Therefore, privacy depends on education, and education is the product of information. All information . . . is potentially an invasion of privacy. It can be considered an invasion of privacy, however, only if it is accepted without evaluation. . . . If information does pass through the gate of evaluation, it becomes a quality of the mind to be used, in turn, for growth and extension—toward a direction of freedom.
. . . information that is withheld may also affect the free mind. . . . Property in information connotes a control of information antithetical to freedom. The price of freedom is the cost of search for information and its intent, knowledge.[9]

Mr. Wunderlich enlarges on these basic points most ingeniously —but I leave his elaboration to concerned researchers. His main insight is as outlined above: we cannot have any true freedom of the mind and treat the source and the product of the mind's ratiocination as a property right. It is fully as censorious to deny the mind its sustenance—information—because the individual cannot pay for it, as because of any religio-political-legalistic bar. When Emily Dickinson wrote a century ago that "There is no frigate like a book / To take us lands away / . . . This traverse may the purest take / Without oppress of toll . . . ," obviously she hadn't heard of today's "information industry." They certainly demand ". . . oppress of toll"!

What this bodes for the future is difficult to judge . . . but clearly it is a problem which librarians cannot leave for a fortuitous solution. It is their concern, their problem—and, like the related problem of copyright, may very well be solved by the rush of technological advance and the power of law rather than by the librarian's sole criterion—the absolute necessity for the free flow of information if democracy itself is to survive.

Or, as Donald M. Lamberton has (rather ponderously) put it, "Those responsible for shaping information policy must determine the appropriate mix of information inputs to achieve social objectives, while at the same time they must have regard for equity considerations."[10]

What helps make difficult dealing with the profit-motive as concerns information and with an all-powerful Peeping Tom of a government is that a great many self-constituted Cassandras and nay-sayers are denying that we have any hope at all. We are, they say, like the Gadarene swine, rushing down the slopes into the abysm of inevitable destruction.

But there are more hopeful voices. The ringing rhetoric of the Universal Declaration of Rights, as proclaimed by the General Assembly of the United Nations in 1948, is still, of course, more honored in the breach than the observance—but it *does* articulate—among its long catalog of the important (indeed, the *vital*) political and civil rights for all societies and all men—the rights to freedom of thought and of opinion and of expression. It is true that the Universal Declaration is not yet more than a pious hope—but a pious hope is certainly better than impious despair.

Santayana once wrote that he, for one, believed in ". . . discourse, in experience, in substance, in truth, and in spirit." He felt that these beliefs ". . . express a rational instinct or instinctive reason, the waxing faith of an animal living in a world which he can observe and sometimes remodel."[11]

NO UTOPIAS AHEAD

In whatever technological form the library of the future emerges, it will still have the double function of acting as a repository and a communicating agent. It will be a storehouse for information and culture and a conveyor of what its public needs and wants, whether in literature, art, music, science, or any other part of knowledge and the arts. Within these known parameters, there are many improbables and unknowns. But whoever makes the decisions on *what* is to be stored, *what* is to be communicated, and *how*, must, if the free mind is to remain free, be equally free.

Whether it is restrictive government, censorious extra-legal groups, or self-censorship, it is clear that there will always—short of Utopia—be *some* barriers to true and complete intellectual freedom. But because there can never be perfection is no argument for not working to achieve as near to it as possible. Acceptance of bondage is rarely a conscious, deliberate act—but torpor and sloth are certainly among the enemies of freedom. Without continual, planned, reasonable action we may all be slaves of tradition, habit, and the easy way.

THE LIBRARY OF ROSNEC

Yet even good intentions may not prevent one possible future, which must be explained (if only briefly). The Library of Rosnec will come into existence at a certain time which cannot be specified, and in a certain place uncharted on any map. But if its latitude, longitude, and chronology are impossible to state with exactitude, its main outlines as an institution are clear. Here will be the ideal of all librarians, the place where *no* censorship exists. Here there will be found no barriers of funding or staffing, of space or control, to the purchase, preparation for use, and making openly available all the knowledge, entertainment, the fact and fiction, wanted by the library's users. Whether in print or near-print, on paper, film, or disc, in the depths of a data-bank or freshly painted on canvas, all the treasures and despairs of man, his prides and his disgusts, will be on record in the Library of Rosnec.

But there still will remain one insoluble dilemma—the books and the facilities and the staff will all be there, but will the individual or individuals who have to make the selection of the books and the films and the records not still have to be *human*? Being human, will they not have prejudices? And will not the librarians' prejudices, somewhere along the line, lead to censorship—overt or covert—but still censorship?

THE LIBRARIAN-CENSOR

Whether in the Library of Rosnec (the library where all the standard excuses and alibis for not having books are absent) or in *your* library, are not all (or at least, all but the most saintly and near-perfect) susceptible to the temptations afforded by the combination of maximum opportunity and expectable human fallibility? Rationalize, as you will, most of you will surely find some occasion in your professional history when you indubitably, clearly, were more of a censor than a book-selector. It does not take a Fiske-model study[12] to verify this obvious statement. Librarians are not paragons, no matter how astute and convincing their professional education, how ethically instructional their professional experience.

This situation will not change with the passage of time, so the only service a prophet on intellectual freedom can offer, in this instance, is to advise acceptance of the perdurability of prejudice in all time to come. Whoever expects censorship to vanish entirely must, of course, reckon with the sheer cussedness of human nature. And unless the future of library service lies entirely with push-buttons and wires, we must allow for some small percentage of the group who handle library service to be *censor*-librarians, contradictory as those two linked appellations are. Our task is to keep that percentage to its irreducible minimum.

The library trustee and the library administrator (at whatever level), the library educator and the library association, all can and should work constantly and unceasingly to root out the *consistently* censorious from our profession. It will never be possible to eliminate the librarian-censor completely—but we must keep on trying.

But enough of self-castigation; we must give up the sceptic's role and retain and put into practice that "waxing faith" in discourse and truth for which the philosopher fought and argued. It is a battle which we cannot, we *must* not lose. Freedom of the mind is so absolutely basic that the battle for it—whether against tyrannical government, censorious minorities, or within our own minds and hearts—is too important ever to give up. The censor may always be a part of life—but so is man's indomitable will to freedom of choice, to decide for himself what he wants to say, to read, to view, to hear, to think. The library profession in 2076—it is earnestly to be hoped—will be able to look back on a century of victory over the powers of ignorance, obfuscation, and deceit.

It is also to be hoped that in *Library Journal*'s bicentennial issue of January 1, 2076 someone may be able to look back with pride on the library profession's valiant leadership in this never-ending war. It cannot happen in a series of spectacular, pyrotechnical battles; it can only happen in the convictions and opinions of the American public, with the continuing help of day-to-day exemplary efforts by all members of our profession. This may bring about as near to a true freedom of the mind as is humanly possible. It certainly will not happen without this continuing effort.

A NEW ATTITUDE

To win the battles of the next generation in this area will require a whole new attitude by the library profession. Bills of Rights and Statements and Codes and all the current paraphernalia of the American Library Association and the Office for Intellectual Freedom and state and regional library associations are good beginnings —but they are only beginnings. The very limited resources of the presently sparsely-membered Freedom to Read Foundation, for example, as at present funded, cannot possibly win more than a few of the to-be-expected legal cases which must be won on a state and national basis before librarians can really practice intellectual freedom.

Just as it was the rank and file of the big unions who financed and won legal battles of the 1930s and 1940s, who persuaded the legislators and paid the lawyers to argue the court cases, so must librarianship's upcoming generation realize they cannot give only lip-service to their desire, their need for freedom of the mind. It will cost more than words. But the time and the dollars and the inevitable sacrifices along the way will be well worth it.

Without intellectual freedom a librarian is only a book-keeper, a storer, a book-handler. With it he can fulfill his rightful function as truly a guardian of the truth. Tomorrow's librarian, like today's and yesterday's, will use all of the knowledge and technical developments currently available in the world of information—but, if our profession is to survive and keep its integrity, it can never be their servant. It is more important to make available all possible shades of opinion and varieties of creative effort than to have the widest possible range of gadgets and gizmos connected by the fanciest and longest possible networks, but including only a restricted, censored, limited range of topics and their interpretations. Tomorrow's library will be a haven for the accepted and the non-accepted; indeed, if some present trends continue, it may be the only such haven!

Two scenarios seem likely possibilities for the futurologist who attempts the admittedly difficult task of forecasting what the year 2000 will bring in the way of mind-control over literary creativeness. One can, of course, in the Tennysonian kind of vision, see a world where authors will continue to "paint the mortal shame of nature with the living hues of Art," to "rip your brothers' vices open, strip your own foul passions bare." Or, at the other extreme, the censors may have once again taken over, and Elsie Dinsmore, rather than Lady Chatterley, may be fiction's exemplar. But both scenarios, like most over-simplifications of situations which involve both human emotion and reason, are not really that likely.

Somewhere between the spate of perhaps over-freely expressed description of the physiology and physical mechanics of sexual activity and the repressions of a Henry James or a William Dean Howells will emerge the fiction of the future. As librarians, our only obligation is to give all the voices every possible chance to speak.

It is doubtful that America can even keep its present freedoms, let alone improve in them in the future, without the most open society possible. We must maintain a society where all the significant issues can be discussed openly and rationally, with a solid background of both information and informed opinion. If the opportunity for promulgating possible error is not given equal scope to whatever is currently accepted as incontrovertible truth, then we are never going to know all that we should.

Every new idea is usually the result of the denial of an old truth— and we must stimulate the freedom of choice or suffer the consequences of stagnation. We who are celebrating this year the bicentennial of our political independence can best do our share toward its continuance if we remember, and prove by our actions, that political freedom can only survive if it is bolstered by independence of the mind.

NOTES

1. Tocqueville, Alexis de. *Democracy in America.* Schocken, 1961. (Reprint of 1840 Edition). Volume II, p. 395.

2. *Ibid.* pp. 388-89.

3. Mill, John Stuart. "Introduction," in: *ibid.* p. xl.

4. Chafee, Zechariah, Jr. *The Inquiring Mind.* Da Capo Pr., 1974. (Reprint of 1928 Edition), p. 30.

5. *Ibid.* p. 36.

6. Wallas, Graham. *The Great Society.* Macmillan, 1923. p. 196.

7. Tocqueville, Alexis de. *Op. cit.* pp. 315-16.

8. Muller, Herbert. *Issues of Freedom: Paradox and Promises.* Harper, 1960. p. 16.

9. Wunderlich, Gene. "Property Rights and Information," *Annals of the American Academy of Political Science and Social Science*, March 1974, p. 96.

10. Lamberton, Donald M. "National Information Policy," *Annals of the American Academy of Political Science and Social Science*, March 1974, p. 151.

11. Santayana, George. *Skepticism and Animal Faith: Introduction to a System of Philosophy.* Dover, 1955. (Reprint of 1923 Edition), p. 308-09.

12. Fiske, Marjorie. *Book Selection and Censorship.* Univ. of California Pr., 1959.

(This article was, surprisingly, one of the few things I have written which brought reaction from nonlibrarians. The audience for Intellect *[now* USA Today*], composed, I would suppose, mainly of "intellectuals"—or at least of college professors—reacted quite favorably to my call for the American's right to choose what he or she reads, and not to have the Mrs. Grundys [or Mr. Grundys] decide for him. The readers of* Intellect *[if letters to me are any indication] lean toward the so-called purist side in support of the First Amendment. Now, if we could only get all the librarians to do as much . . .)*

THE FREEDOM TO CHOOSE: A REPLY TO "FREEDOM FROM FILTH"

In December, 1973, *Intellect*'s editor, William W. Brickman, presented as his opinion an editorial entitled "Freedom from Filth." His statement approves of the June, 1973, Supreme Court majority obscenity decisions as not a "limitation on liberty, but rather . . . an effort toward justice for a wider multitude." He suggests that the use of "contemporary community standards" as a criterion for permissibility should not bother any individual who feels his constitutional freedom has suffered. After all, he says, such an individual "could obtain relief by travel to another area." He recommends what he calls a Fifth Freedom—"the freedom for the individual not to be overwhelmed by obscenity."

Superficially, this may seem like a pretty good case for censorship. What Dr. Brickman has overlooked (or forgotten)—in a magazine called *Intellect*! is the sheer, overwhelming importance in, and to, a democracy of the freedom of the mind. Without the kind of freedom denied by the Supreme Court decisions (just some more in a long series of obviously futile attempts to undermine the First Amendment and to define the indefinable), how can that reasonably acceptable goal of *any* society—truth—be known? One man's truth can be another man's obscenity—and vice versa.

The democratic philosophy is based on man's ability to reason and decide for himself his own best interests, on his educability, and on his conscience. Obviously, censorship denies each one of these. Regardless of the issue of what is true and what is false, of what is dangerous or what may be considered obscene, completely free expression is invaluable for progress. Censorship—*any* censor-ship—can not be justified in a democracy if we really believe in man's freedom to choose for himself, in man's God-given right to motivation by his own conscience, and, finally, in the ability of man to learn only when he is given an opportunity to learn by see-ing all knowledge spread out before him.

In this time of Watergate and its repercussions, we should be more than ever aware of what suppression of the facts of life—particularly in political life—can mean to all of us. However, it is simply not enough to say that it is certainly wrong to censor anything which involves knowledge and ideas, but it is perfectly proper to censor various forms of artistic or literary expression. It very well may be that particular words and particular incidents and particular situations irritate, annoy, even oppress some particular individuals, but why should those particular individuals have the right to decide for others how the latter should react?

Nobody says that the local public library should become what has come to be known as a "porn" shop. Surely, one can trust the good taste and professional abilities of a library head and of the board of trustees which goes along with that individual to see to it that there is a reasonable balance and no excesses. However, if a particular novel appears in a library and the book bothers a few individuals in the community, should those individuals be entitled to deny access to that novel for all the other residents of that com-munity?

When a public library finds itself concerned with what *not* to include, with what *not* to have on its shelves, in what to hide and conceal, in what it can "get away with," it really is not doing the job it is supposed to be doing. The public library should be basically concerned with making worthwhile, constructive, useful reading available for its entire community. Obviously, public li-braries do not, and never will, approve of commercial exploitation of the meretricious and sleazy by both authors and publishers, and they do appreciate, and even ask for, honesty and sincerity in literary expression. Yet, with all this, they still feel that the adult reader, as an adult, as a citizen, and as a reader, has the full power of the *only* necessary censorship—the individual right to selective reading, within a library, within a book. None of this is to imply that someone else should decide what he should read inside the library, or even within the book, or on a page. That is *his* business, and *only* his business.

The Freedom to Read Statement, issued in 1972 by the American Library Association and the Association of American Publishers, includes this statement: "Parents and teachers have a responsibility to prepare the young to meet the diversity of experiences in life to which they will be exposed, as they have a responsibility to help them learn to think critically for themselves." Think about that a minute. Are the parents and teachers of the U.S. meeting their vital responsibility to "prepare the young to meet the diversity of experiences in life to which they will be exposed, as they have a responsibility to help them learn to think critically for themselves?" As the statement further says, "These are affirmative responsibilities, not to be discharged simply by preventing them from reading works for which they are not yet prepared. In these matters, taste differs, and taste cannot be legislated; nor can machinery be devised which will suit the demands of one group without limiting the freedom of others."

One suggested expedient is that books should be labelled, so that one would know in advance whether the book or author is dangerous or subversive. This is to presuppose that there are individual groups with sufficient wisdom to determine what is good or bad for the citizen, and, further, that each individual has to have his mind made up for him about the ideas he examines.

Archibald MacLeish, who is still writing, but is not as well-known as he used to be, once proposed what he called "the American Proposition."[1] In his words, "the American Proposition is the proposition that if men are free to think for themselves and to believe as they think and to say as they believe—if men, all men, are free to make their own way by their own means to the truth which is true for them, each one of them—the world in which they live and which together they compose will be a better world: juster, stronger, wiser, more various." He called this "the most courageous, the most high-hearted of all propositions: the most daring, the most revolutionary of earthly acts of faith." He continued, "it is, indeed, the one new and wholly revolutionary idea the world we call the modern world has produced, for it affirms the maturity of man as mind and spirit and rests its hopes for the future upon man's will.'' In other words, as he titled the book in which this statement appeared, freedom is the right to choose.

There are laws to cover overt action, but there are none to affect —and there should not be any laws to cover—the thoughts of the individual. Without reading, how empty those thoughts must be. Without exchange of ideas—which is what reading really is—how can different ideas come into one's mind? How can different times and places and the kinds of people be made known to the vast majority of us—who can not join ''the jet set'' and travel the world over? Even the jet-setters can not travel in time—unless our science fiction books are really more than fiction! Only books can permit this in the fullest sense.

I hold no brief for what is in bad taste, but I do think that the decision as to what is good taste and what is bad taste is much more than a matter of the kind of decision that says that everyone must have his or her taste modified to suit a particular faith, a particular concept of life, or a particular style of life. The books should be there, and then it should be up to the individual to decide for himself or herself what he or she will read. If making the decision is a matter of pressure by extra-legal groups of people who are trying to impose their own measure of morality on everyone else, who could possibly benefit—except those particular individuals? Democracy, the basic concept of Americanism, will certainly be the loser.

NOTE

1. Archibald MacLeish, *Freedom Is the Right to Choose* (Freeport, NY: Books for Libraries Press, 1971), pp. viii-ix.

(Never before printed, this brief essay deals with a rather unusual intellectual attack on intellectual freedom. Dr. Tussman's book was widely reviewed, though not always favorably; but it did elicit a good deal of respectful attention. My rejoinder is to only a portion of his reasoned argument, which, as a whole, goes beyond the direct interests of libraries and librarians. The pages herein printed will best be understood if the reader first reads the whole Tussman volume.)

DOES AND SHOULD GOVERNMENT CONTROL THE MIND?
A BRIEF REPLY TO TUSSMAN

Several years ago Dr. Joseph Tussman, chairman of the Department of Philosophy at the University of California, Berkeley, wrote a book[1] whose major thesis was, to quote him, "... the necessity and legitimacy of governmental action in the various provinces of the domain of mind." This brief article will not attempt to take up seriatim all of his detailed discussions of the appropriate role of the government in dealing with the university, mass media, the Artist (that is Dr. Tussman's capitalization), the school, and the forum. Of most importance for those concerned with defending the always frail and beset image of intellectual freedom in our society, it seems to me, is to refute the Tussman attack on the very basis of our long established, hard won, and constantly embattled freedom of communication. His self-styled "free-speech primer" is definitely not for children; it is rather a highly sophisticated, deceptively simplistic, and, as I shall attempt to prove, entirely erroneous disquisition in both its pronunciamentos and their implications.

Tussman begins by asserting that words are acts, that "... saying, which is essential to thinking, is a kind of public doing: it is action which has consequences for others."[2] This is, of course, not exactly a novel way of looking at the relationship of words and actions. Even the Supreme Court, in its well-known *Chaplinsky* v. *New Hampshire* (1942) decision, defined some kinds of expression as essentially "fighting words." But Tussman goes far beyond this; indeed, he seems to look at all public speech in a militant way.

In discussing freedom of speech, Tussman, rather surprisingly, defines speech as "... a generally aggressive form of action, almost, by its very nature, a form of assault."[3] This antagonistic type of definition, if accepted and acceptable (which I believe is not the case for most of us), naturally leads to his next formulation, that of a "... catalog of crimes." This begins to sound like Madame Roland's antirevolutionary, "O Liberty, what crimes are committed in thy name!" Among these so-called crimes Tussman includes the following: "verbal assault (oral or written) against public authority ... ," "verbal assault" against religion (blasphemy), and, finally, "verbal violations of social taboos."[4]

Most American democratic theory would probably rename "verbal assault . . . against public authority" as simply "public opinion." Surely to accept Tussman's theory on this would really create a one-voice dictatorship. Tussman seems to recognize this in calling his own views ". . . that archaic, anti-American point of view." It is a fact, however, that we no longer genuflect to aristocracy; we do not see, as Tussman does, "respect [as] the alternative to violence."[5] Kipling once saw the American as an individual who does not fear "to match with destiny for beers." Tussman seems more inclined to see that our citizens wait for sure things.

The Puritan concept of the government's responsibility to guard against blasphemy seems to Americans in 1980, too much of the established church as part and parcel of the state to accept. Tussman says it would take "a special effort of the imagination"[6] for us to find defense against blasphemy as requiring a "sense of urgency. . . ." I believe it would take not only a special effort of the imagination but also a revocation of the First Amendment and perhaps even a new American revolution before we would return to the days of the Mathers, the ducking-stool, and the stocks.

I find Tussman's definition of obscenity nothing less than amusing. He describes obscenity as "a kind of blasphemy about a central value."[7] This rhetorical flourish, combined with his statement about "irreverence," should place his views on sex and its discussion in proper perspective. (In discussing verbal taboos in general Tussman shows a rather broad ignorance of the literature on this topic. He says, for instance, that he is "unaware of any serious psychological or anthropological analysis of . . . the verbal taboo." Immodestly, may I refer him to my own book, *The Fear of the Word*, which, in addition to its basic content, does include a very comprehensive bibliography on this significant topic. As far back as 1962 Edward Sagarin wrote *The Anatomy of Dirty Words*, and his predecessors in dealing with verbal taboos include such worthies as Vance Randolph, Allen Walker Reed, Weston LaBarre—indeed, so many that even a Berkeley philosopher *should* have caught at least a glimpse of them from his ivory tower.) Tussman claims "there is . . . a perfectly reputable case for the enforcement of linguistic taboos. . . ."[8] Maybe so—but he certainly doesn't make that case in this book.

As is his habit throughout this work Tussman sets up a straw man on the subject of the freedom of speech as a natural right. He says that "the claim that freedom of speech is a time-honored natural right is a fraudulent claim with a frayed pedigree."[9] Alexander Meiklejohn, among many other political science theorists who have written on this very point, has written, "The principle of the freedom of speech springs from the necessities of the program of self-government. It is not a Law of Nature or of Reason in the abstract." It is, he goes on, rather ". . . a deduction from the basic American agreement that public issues should be decided by universal suffrage."[10]

Tussman ends this particular section with a paragraph on slander and libel, notable chiefly for its statement that "there are some attempts to extend this protection to groups." Thus, we readily see where Tussman would stand in considering such touchstones of the defense of freedom of speech as the previously cited *Chaplinsky* case or *Terminiello* v. *Chicago* (1949),[11] in which Justice Douglas, speaking for the minority, stated,

. . . speech is often provocative and challenging . . . freedom of speech, though not absolute, is nevertheless protected against censorship or punishment when shown likely to produce a clear and present danger of a serious substantive evil that rises far above public inconvenience, annoyance, or unrest.

And, perhaps even more pertinent to refutation of the Tussman thesis, Douglas stated, "There is no room under our Constitution for a more restrictive view. For the alternative would lead to standardization of ideas either by legislatures, courts, or dominant political or community groups."

Tussman, it appears, is not very happy with the whole idea of government's standing as a protector of speech or of discussion. His lengthy[12] discourse on the relation of government to the forum (which he defines as "the whole range of institutions and situations of public communication"), deals principally with the theory of prior restraint, as opposed to the use of subsequent punishment. Here is where Tussman makes his sole reference[14] to the public library.

In this connection he makes what seems like an absolutely un-
deniable point, "every item in the library is put there by a positive
decision of government. Some bureaucrat decides to order this and
not that." Then he asks the rather amusing (to knowledgeable librarians and library trustees, at least) rhetorical question, "According to what policy?" And he answers himself in a manner which
can only be called ignorant: "That is really an important question,
but we seldom ask it." Somewhere there is a gap in the good
professor's information on this matter; one must presume he has
never heard of the Library Bill of Rights, the Freedom to Read
Statement, or the many, many individually written and board
approved book-selection statements of policy which govern public,
school, and even many academic libraries.

I do agree, finally, with Tussman's conclusion, which is that "to
be granted the freedom of speech . . . is to be given a place in a rule-
governed forum, the institution within which and under whose
protection the citizen may share in the reflective and deliberative
process by which the community seeks to govern itself." That
sounds fine. Where I differ, and where I believe most contemporary
exponents of intellectual freedom may also differ, is in Tussman's
general attitude, which appears elitist, Platonic, and even anti-
democratic.

I agree with John Stuart Mill that "liberty, as a principle, has no
application to any state of things anterior to the time when mankind have become capable of being improved by free and equal
discussion." Intellectual freedom—which includes freedom from
governmental controls of the mind—must exist, or no one is really
free. Tussman seems to follow William Butler Yeats's advice, based
on complete lack of faith in either government or the press: ". . . stay
at home and drink your beer/And let the neighbors vote." Tussman is also in the tradition of Pope Leo III, who, in his encyclical
Immortale Dei (1885), stated that "the liberty of thinking and of
publishing whatever one likes . . . is the fountain-head of many
evils." With all due respect to the pontiff, the freedom of the mind
is the only possible source of *fighting* as many—or probably more
—evils. I guess it all depends on what one sees as "evils"!

NOTES

1. Joseph Tussman. *Government and the Mind* (New York: Oxford University Press, 1977).

2. *Ibid.*, p. 88.

3. *Ibid.*

4. *Ibid.*, pp. 89-92.

5. *Ibid.*, p. 89.

6. *Ibid.*, p. 91.

7. *Ibid.*

8. *Ibid.*, p. 169.

9. *Ibid.*, p. 170.

10. Alexander Meiklejohn. *Political Freedom* (New York: Harper & Row, 1960), p. 27.

11. Both decisions reprinted in full in: Haig A. Bosnijian, ed., *The Principles and Practice of Freedom of Speech* (Boston: Houghton Mifflin, 1971), pp. 166-91.

12. Tussman, *Government and the Mind*, pp. 95-126.

13. *Ibid.*, p. 95.

14. *Ibid.*, p. 111.

The politics of censorship

2

(The first two sections of this chapter, both published under the title of "Congress as Censor," were among a very few in the whole literature of librarianship to single out the legislative branch of our government as an actual or prospective censor. The first article was a call to action, as well as a recital of censorship threats. The second, published nearly two decades after the first, was itself a witness to the statement contained therein, "the threat of censorship from Congress is perennial, and seemingly will continue to be so.")

CONGRESS AS CENSOR—1952*

During the second session of the 82nd Congress, a total of 4,549 measures were introduced. Of these, only a very few concerned librarians who are becoming increasingly aware of the post-war censorship that is seemingly inevitably descending upon us. A total of less than ten bills and resolutions from more than 4,500 possibilities would seem like a not too worrisome proportion. Yet the danger in these censorship measures far exceeds their insignificant number.

*Reprinted from *Library Journal*, November 15, 1952. Published by R. R. Bowker Co. (a Xerox Company). Copyright © 1952 by Xerox Corporation.

Congressional activity aimed at books and libraries began only a few weeks after the solons assembled. On January 30, 1952, Representative Harold Velde (Rep., Ill.) offered H.R. 6335, "a bill to provide that the Librarian of Congress shall mark all subversive matter in the Library of Congress and compile a list thereof for the guidance of other librarians in the United States." This bill was referred to the Committee on House Administration and was never reported out. In a strongly worded editorial, which appeared on February 24, *The New York Times* described the task proposed for the Librarian of Congress as "a presumptuous one to undertake in a society where freedom of choice in most things has been one of the cardinal tenets of a successful way of life." *The Times* felt that "it would be no different from what is being done in totalitarian countries, where so little faith is held in the people's ability to discriminate that it is felt necessary to bar all possible avenues for deviation." The editorial concluded: "The bill itself is not so much a matter of concern as is the thinking which prompted it. Fear has allowed good sense to be tossed out of the window to be replaced by a jittery tension which demands authoritarian action. Fear of communism is justified, but communism cannot be fought by going into hiding. The battle must be fought with full knowledge of what is being fought."

Representative Velde is a former F.B.I. agent and a member of both the House Un-American Activities Committee and the House Education and Labor Committee.

Representative Ernest K. Bramblett (Rep., Cal.) introduced H.R. 6523 on February 11. This was "a bill to prohibit the transmittal of communistic propaganda matter in the United States mails or in interstate commerce for circulation or use in public schools." The bill has not yet emerged from the Committee on Post Office and Civil Service. Any individual or organization violating this rule would, if the Bramblett bill were to become law, be guilty of a felony punishable by 5 years imprisonment and $10,000 fine.

Emerging victorious in a scramble among several legislators who wished to be in charge of a Congressional investigation into the state of morals of our literature, Representative Ezekiel C. Gathings (Dem., Ark.) was appointed on July 2 as chairman of a "Select

Committee on Study of Current Pornographic Materials." By the terms of H. Res. 596 this committee is to "conduct a full and complete investigation and study (1) to determine the extent to which current literature—books, magazines, and comic books—containing immoral, obscene, or otherwise offensive matter, or placing improper emphasis on crime, violence, and corruption are being made available to the people of the United States through the U.S. mails or otherwise; and (2) to determine the adequacy of existing law to prevent the publication and distribution of books containing immoral, offensive, and other undesirable matter."

During debate on this resolution on May 12, Representative Chet Holifield (Dem., Cal.) stressed that "there will devolve upon the members of this special committee a great obligation to keep in mind the constitutional safeguards on individuals, and, while being in opposition of (sic!) some of the material that they will have to permit to be printed under the existing laws on free speech, I am predicting that they will have a hard time writing legislation which will protect the people from literature which they may think undesirable but which, if attempts are made to legislate against it, they may find that it will have an overlapping effect upon the privileges of free speech and free press." Representative Eugene J. McCarthy (Dem., Minn.) warned that "when Government goes to extremes the effect is to violate fundamentally the right of the individual and person to think for himself and to choose for himself." The select committee has $25,000 to spend; results are to be reported "as soon as practicable."

On May 19 the House of Representatives passed H.R. 5850, "an Act to authorize the Postmaster General to impound mail in certain cases." Representative Tom Murray (Dem., Tenn.) was the bill's sponsor. Although approved by the Senate Committee on Post Office and Civil Service, on July 3 the bill failed to pass in the Senate, mainly because of objections by Senator George Smathers (Dem., Fla.) and Herbert Lehman (Dem., N.Y.). Senator Lehman quoted one of his constituents as saying ". . . if the Department independently determines that a book is obscene, and institutes proper administered proceedings, all mail addressed to the publisher may be impounded until final decision of the issues, which may be a matter of years, and which may ultimately establish that the book is in fact not obscene. . . . This is in fact the power to control the industry by precensorship in violation of the Bill of Rights and of the basic tenets of democracy."

Another bill proposing to use the U.S. Post Office as a punitive agent was H.R. 7434, presented by Representative Abraham Multer (Dem., N.Y.) on April 7. This bill was aimed to bar from the mails "all papers, pamphlets, magazines, periodicals, books, pictures, and writings of any kind, containing any defamatory and false statements which tend to expose persons designated, identified, or characterized therein by race or religion, any of whom reside in the United States, to hatred, contempt, ridicule, or obloquy or tend to cause such persons to be shamed or avoided or to be injured in their business or occupation. . . ." It is specifically left to "the court" to determine whether the matter . . . is in fact defamatory and false." The bill was pigeonholed by the House Committee on Post Office and Civil Service.

Just before the end of the session, on July 5, Senator Joseph McCarthy (Rep. Wis.) introduced S. 3491, "a Bill prohibiting the exhibition in educational institutions, or the use by departments or agencies of the Government, of motion pictures based upon script written by persons having Communist or Communist-front connections." Senator McCarthy's bill proposed a licensing system, supervised by the Secretary of Commerce. The Secretary would be required to issue a license unless he were to find that the picture in question had been "written in whole or in part by any person who (1) has Communist or Communist-front connections, or (2) has had such connections and (A) has not publicly repudiated them, (B) has not consistently refrained from any association with any Communist or Communist-front organization since such repudiation, and (C) cannot affirmatively show that he no longer believes in the principles advocated by Communist and Communist-front organizations." To find out just how tinged with red the suspected scriptwriter is, the Secretary is told to "consider any information possessed by the Federal Bureau of Investigation, Civil Service Commission, Office of Naval Intelligence, and Army Intelligence and any other information possessed by any investigative agency of the executive branch of the Government." Licensed films would be required to be labeled with official signs of their approval; anyone sending or exhibiting unlicensed films would be liable to a $10,000 fine and/or a one-year prison term.

Senator William Benton (Dem., Conn.) and Senator McCarthy engaged in spirited debate on the Senate floor concerning this bill. Senator Benton deplored "the increasing tendency toward censorship in this country, sponsored at private levels and by public officials at the public level." He termed the McCarthy bill "a very dangerous proposal." He suggested that rather than bar possibly Communistic films, we should "in the traditional American way by exposure to them allow our citizens and young people better to understand their fallacies and the falseness of their doctrine."

Senator McCarthy replied (in part): "I think it would be a mistake to try in any way to prevent anyone from saying and thinking what he pleases, regardless of how cockeyed his thoughts or sayings might be. But when we are dealing with the Communist Party, we are not dealing with freedom of thought or freedom of speech. I repeat, the loyal members of the Communist Party have no freedom of thought and no freedom of speech now, and they never had. . . . If any Senator thinks that we must give Communists the right to go into our colleges, high schools, and grade schools to twist, distort, and pervert the minds of our young people, then that Senator is either so stupid that he knows nothing about the Communist movement, or worse."

The McCarthy bill was referred to the Senate Committee on Interstate and Foreign Commerce.

Senators Bronson Cutting of New Mexico and Reed Smoot of Utah engaged in a somewhat similar debate during the consideration, in 1929, of a measure to extend the censorship powers of the U.S. Bureau of Customs. On October 11, 1929, Senator Cutting made this memorable statement: "In my opinion, the only policy we can accept in this matter is the belief that the American people in the long run can be trusted to take care of their own moral and spiritual welfare; that no bureaucratic guardian is competent to decide for them what they shall or shall not read."

The representatives of the people have spoken; what is the responsibility of American librarians? The librarian's responsibility does not end with accepting what censors condescend to permit him to keep and make available in his library. The librarian as citizen must get out of his ivory tower and use the techniques of public relations, which his profession has taught him, to fight the enemy at the gates. Mere talk, even on the level of the recent ALA Conference on Intellectual Freedom, is not sufficient.

There must be persuasive activity to acquaint all of those engaged in communicating ideas—the educators, the journalists, the radio-film-TV people, the lecturers—with the real and urgent nature of the dire threat to freedom of speech which a censorship-minded Congress presents. It is fully as important to let legislators know the stand on the question of censorship as it is to inform them of the position on taxation, controls, or any of the more highly publicized national issues.

Talk to the local civic groups; alert the local editors; start a "grass-roots" campaign which will effectively convince Congress that censorship is *not* what America wants. This is the very moment when the librarian must use his well-merited reputation as a selfless, objective individual in his community to the best advantage. What use will a Library Services bill be if political censors select the books, the films, and other materials to be made available?

CONGRESS AS CENSOR—1970*

In May 1969, President Richard Nixon sent Congress the first message on obscenity ever directed by a President of the United States to the Congress of the United States. During the first session of the Ninety-first Congress over a hundred bills dealing with the subject of obscenity were introduced in both the House and Senate as part of Congress' continuing effort to keep America pure.

For the first time in our history, the chief executive of our country thought that "new measures . . . to crack down on . . . peddlers of obscenity" were so important that they justified a special message to Congress requesting specific legislation. His message requested these laws: "To make it a Federal crime to use the mails or other facilities of commerce to deliver to anyone under 18 years of age material dealing with a sexual subject in a manner unsuitable

*Reprinted from *Library Trends*, vol. 19, no. 1, pp. 64-73. © 1970 by the Board of Trustees of the University of Illinois.

for young people . . . to make it a Federal crime to use the mails, or other facilities of commerce, for the commercial exploitation of a prurient interest in sex through advertising," and "to extend the existing law to enable a citizen to protect his home from any intrusion of sex-oriented advertising regardless of whether or not a citizen has ever received such mailings."[1] He said further, concerning this third proposal, that "this new stronger measure would require mailers and potential mailers to respect the expressed wishes of those citizens who do not wish to have sex-oriented advertising sent into their homes. These citizens will put smut-mailers on notice simply by filing their directions with the designated postal authorities. To deliberately send such advertising to their homes could be an offense subject to both civil and criminal penalties."

In this instance the President òf the United States was definitely not attempting to lead congressional opinion or voiced desire. He was, rather, following it. As an indication of just how significant such items seem to be to Congress, it might well be noted that on November 10, 1969, Senator Mike Mansfield (Dem., Mont.), majority leader, referred to three of the most pressing matters facing this country. These three were, respectively, drugs, crime, and obscenity. Through the years other congressmen have also indicated that to them the matter of dealing with so-called obscene literature is of prime importance—certainly more important in many respects than dealing with such comparatively minor matters as poverty, racism, and even misplaced national priorities.

For over half a century after the country began, there was no law put on the books of the federal government by Congress concerning censorship. In 1842, a law was passed stating that "the importation of all indecent and obscene prints, paintings, lithographs, engravings, and transparencies is hereby prohibited." It is clear that the law in no way concerned books, unless those books were collections of "indecent and obscene prints, paintings"[2] and so on.

But in 1873, under the influence of Anthony Comstock and the then-prestigious and powerful New York Society for the Suppression of Vice, Congress passed its first omnibus anti-obscenity law. This law included sections barring importation of obscene material from abroad, outlawing distribution of obscene materials in federal territories, and making it a felony to send or receive such materials through the mails. Actually, a postal statute on obscenity, which was intended to keep lewd materials from the hands of soldiers in the field, was enacted in 1865. The so-called "Comstock Act," as it has come to be known, is still a part of the law as it stands in the United States Code, but the effect of this has been greatly diminished by various court decisions.

Throughout the latter part of the nineteenth century and the early years of the twentieth century, Congress found little occasion to do more than touch up various sections of the Comstock Act and the postal statutes, as was felt to be necessary. But there was no real hassle in Congress about obscenity and pornography until the famous Smoot-Cutting set-to which took place in 1929. This was memorialized for all time, by Ogden Nash's poem about "Senator Smoot of Ut," with its rousing refrain of "Smoot fights smut." In more prosaic fashion, what actually happened was that Senator Reed Smoot (Rep., Utah) and Senator Bronson Cutting (Dem., New Mex.) had a prolonged debate in the Senate on the subject of a proposed section of the Smoot-Hawley tariff bill of 1929.

According to the original bill, section 305 stated the following:

Immoral articles—importation prohibited: (a) prohibition of importation: All persons are prohibited from importing into the United States from any foreign country any book, pamphlet, paper, writing, advertisement, circular, print, picture, drawing, or other representation, figure, or image on or of paper or other material, or any cast, instrument, or other article of an immoral nature, or any drug or medicine, or any article whatsoever for the prevention of conception or causing unlawful abortion, or any lottery ticket, or any printed paper that may be used as lottery tickets, or any advertisement of any lottery. No such articles, whether imported separately or contained in packages with other goods, should be admitted to entry; and all such articles, unless it appears to the satisfactions of the collector that the obscene articles contained in the package were enclosed without the knowledge or consent of the importer, owner, agent, or cosignee, the entire contents of the package in which such articles are contained shall be subject to seizure, forfeiture under the customs law.[3]

The fine imposed upon any government officer who helped such items to be smuggled in was not more than $5,000 or imprisonment at hard labor for not more than ten years or both. Senator Cutting pointed out that such a sweeping disposal was something new in American legislation, and deserved more than a cursory study and approval by the Senate.

Cutting made a number of memorable statements during the debate, but perhaps the most important for indicating at least one trend in Congressional thinking was his defense of the rights of books, as well as men, to have a hearing before decisions were made. He strongly criticized the idea that the average customs clerk could decide whether or not a book was obscene, because, he stated, "a clerk, in order to make a correct decision, must necessarily read the book as a whole. Many books of highly moral tendency would be excluded if a man's attention were confined to one page, one paragraph, or one sentence, or one word." He said "there are two entirely incongruous ideas of what constitutes obscenity. One is the idea that something is obscene which has the capacity to shock the sensitive mind; that is interpretation that is carried out in these decisions about words, phrases and sentences. The other idea of obscenity is that it is something which has general tendency to corrupt public morals."[4]

He went on, "The more a book tends to shock an individual, the less apt it is to do him any damage. If it shocks him enough, he will throw it in the fire or the waste basket, and it will not damage his morals at all. The books which are apt to do a man harm are books which do not shock him, but which in various insidious ways may tempt him to read a little further from page to page, and in the long run may undermine the whole moral fiber of his being." He stressed that "the fundamental trouble in this whole thing is that we cannot say what is decent and what is indecent. No human being is infallible in those respects. Every generation and every century changes its standards of decency, and even of morality."

It was at this point that Smoot got into his long debate with the Senator from New Mexico. Senator Smoot said, "I hope that the Congress of the United States will not serve notice to the world the bars are down, so far as our customs laws are concerned, to all the obscene, indecent, and salacious matter that may be published abroad. I know it is said that much of the so-called obscene matter is literature, classical literature, and that foreign classics die along with the matter immoral in purpose, use, and tendency. Well, Mr.

President, let the dead bury the dead. It would be better, to my mind, that a few classics suffer the application of the expurgating shears than that this country be flooded with the books, pamphlets, pictures, and other articles that are wholly indecent both in purpose and tendency, and that we know all too well would follow the repeal of this provision.''*

Senator Cutting's reply to this was that "the only policy we can accept in this matter is the belief that the American people in the long run can be trusted to take care of their own moral and spiritual welfare; that no bureaucratic guardian has competence to decide for them what they shall or shall not read." He added, "I admit there be those among us who occasionally abuse those privileges; but I insist that the same men who would abuse those privileges would abuse the privileges of franchise. If a man is not capable of deciding what he may or may not read without injury to himself, then that man is not fit to be entrusted with the right to select his own representatives in the government."

Among the others who got into the discussion were such people as Senators Norris, Borah, Black, Robert M. LaFollette, Jr., Tydings, Wheeler, and other well-known liberals of the time on one side, and Heflin and other conservatives on the other.** When the Cutting amendment came to a vote, it was defeated. But finally Cutting did get through a revised amendment to the section (which omitted any reference to "books" or "literature") by the narrow vote of 38 to 36.

Then, for a number of years there was very little, if any, censorship activity on the part of Congress. In 1944 Congressman Samuel Dickstein (Dem., N.Y.) recommended "that in addition to the matter described as non-mailable pursuant to Section 211 of the Criminal Code as amended (USC, Title 18, Section 33404), all

---

*Ezra Pound, in a brief article entitled "Honor and the United States Senate," *Poetry* (June, 1930), pp. 150-52, commented: "Smoot is a gratuitous insult offered by the state of Utah to any school-child in the country." He added, "We pay heavily for official lowbrows." And finally, "no one has made a clear case *against* having high officials possessed of some sense of history and literature."

**Ezra Pound, *ibid.*, "Cutting has put New Mexico on the map."

papers, pamphlets, magazines, periodicals, books, pictures, and writings of any kind, and every article and thing designed or intended to cause racial or religious hatred or bigotry or intolerance are hereby declared non-mailable matter."[5] Most surprisingly to Congressman Dickstein, the National Association for the Advancement of Colored People, the American Civil Liberties Union, and many representatives of religious groups indicated their opposition to such a measure. Ultimately, it failed to pass.

In 1952, came the first all-out Congressional attack on obscenity in this century, under the auspices of Representative Ezekiel C. Gathings (Dem., Ark.), Chairman of the House of Representatives Special Committee on Current Pornographic Materials. The committee, after lengthy hearings (with most witnesses from the censor ranks), recommended legislation to widen postal censorship powers, tighten loopholes in the law against interstate shipment of obscene materials, and to favor what might be called "censorship by police pressure." A minority report of this committee warned against censorship of ideas and defended the paperback book industry's general performance. (This industry had been the principal target of the Gathings committee).

During the debate in Congress on the resolution to establish the Gathings committee, Representative Chet Holifield (Dem., Cal.) stated that "there will develop among the members of this special committee a great obligation to keep in mind the constitutional safeguards on individuals, and, while being in opposition on some of the material that they will have to permit to be printed under the existing laws on free speech, I am predicting they will have a hard time writing legislation which will protect the people from literature which they may think undesirable but which, if attempts are made to legislate against, they may find that it will have an overlapping effect upon the privileges of free speech and free press."[6] During the same debate Representative Eugene McCarthy (Dem., Minn.) warned that "when Government goes to extremes the effect is to violate fundamentally the right of the individual person to think for himself and to choose for himself."[7]

One of the most extraordinary bills ever to come out of Congress was presented by Representative Harold Velde (Rep., Ill.) in 1952, when he offered "a bill to provide that the Librarian of Congress shall mark all subversive matter in the Library of Congress and compile a list thereof for the guidance of other libraries in the United States." Fortunately, this bill was referred to the House Committee on Administration and never reported out. Representative Velde was a former F.B.I. agent and a member of both the House Committee on Un-American Activities and the House Education and Labor Committee. A few days after Velde's bill, Representative Ernest K. Bramblett (Rep., Cal.) introduced a "bill to prohibit the transmittal of Communistic propaganda matter in the United States mails or in interstate commerce for circulation or use in public schools." This bill also died in committee.

In 1953, Senator Joseph McCarthy (Rep., Wisc.) held hearings on the Senate Subcommittee to investigate the U.S. Information Agency's Service Libraries in foreign countries. Combining hearings with a sending out of emissaries for on-the-spot investigations, his committee's activities resulted in the barring—at least temporarily, and in some cases permanently—of many books, the actual burning of a few books in one library, and, in general, great damage to the prestige of the United States as an advocate of freedom throughout the world.

The year 1954 was highlighted by another attack on the USIA libraries, this time by a House subcommittee on appropriations, headed by Representative John J. Rooney. They "thought pictures of a little red school-house, an elderly teacher, a dust storm, and a pair of jitter-bugs might give comfort to the Kremlin," so Congress, in appropriating funds for the USIA that year barred the use of any part of such funds to purchase copies of Emily Davie's *Profile of America.*

In 1955, Congress passed a law prohibiting interstate transportation of "obscene" matter by common carrier. Senator Estes Kefauver (Dem., Ark.) held three days of hearings on the relationship between juvenile delinquency and so-called "objectionable literature." The senator called for stiffer anti-obscenity laws—which were not immediately forthcoming.

The next year Congress passed a law which permitted the Post Office to impound mail suspected of promoting fraud, obscenity, and gambling—but excepted from this stricture were books and publications with second-class mail privileges. In 1959, the House

passed a bill submitted by Representative Kathryn E. Granahan
(Dem., Pa.) allowing the Postmaster General to issue an impound-
ing order effective up to forty-five days (an extension of the existing legal twenty-day limit). In 1960 Representative Granahan
toured the United States to investigate the distribution of pornography. She stated that there was definitely a causative connection
between such material and juvenile delinquency, and told the press
that "distribution of smut was part of the Communist conspiracy."
When she came back to Washington she introduced a bill to broad-
en the Postmaster General's powers to impound mail, and the bill
was finally passed by Congress in a re-written form assigning im-
pounding power and time limits to the jurisdiction of the U.S.
district courts.

In the same year constitutional amendments to give the states
jurisdiction over "questions of decency and morality" and to
remove so-called "hard-core" pornography from First Amendment protection were introduced, but died. A group of twenty-five
U.S. senators called for a national conference, which was never
held, to consider what to do about fighting the traffic in obscene
matter and materials in this country.

In 1958, Congress passed a "venue" law which extended the
jurisdiction for prosecution of all allegedly obscene material from
the point of mailing, where prosecution had formerly been limited
to any place which was passed by the challenged matter on its way
through the mails. Thus, for example, a publisher might be prosecuted in a place which was deliberately selected because its community standards and mores were much narrower and more rigid
than, say, those of Los Angeles or New York. Another reason for
selecting a different place might be because it lacked one or more
local attorneys familiar with the laws of censorship. This law also
provided much stiffer penalties for second offenders convicted of
mailing obscene matter, provided for a greater latitude in the
varieties of obscene matter the post office could seize, and made it
a violation to send matter adjudged to be obscene to anyone under
nineteen years of age.

In 1961, the Senate voted to create a commission on "noxious"
and obscene matters and materials. This bill was introduced by
Senator Karl Mundt (Rep., S. Dak.), but did not have any effect at

the time, because the House let the bill die. In 1962, Representative Glenn Cunningham (Rep., Neb.) managed to convince Congress to pass the Cunningham amendment to the general postal law, whereby for the first time a mail-screening provision was placed on federal statute books. This dealt with so-called "Communist propaganda." This year Congress did pass a wide-sweeping censorship bill for the District of Columbia, but the bill was vetoed by President Kennedy. Several years later, in 1964, the House passed a bill giving every postal patron the right to complain to the postmaster about any material received through the mails which he considered "morally offensive." According to this law the postmaster, after receiving notice from the postal patron, would be empowered to stop the mailer from sending further such material to the complainant through the U.S. mails. This law was approved by the Senate and signed by the President in 1968.

Previous to this, the bill which had gotten through the Senate in 1961, concerning a national commission on obscenity, was finally passed by both houses and signed by the President in 1967. This bill created a National Commission on Obscenity and Pornography, which was to report to the President and Congress no later than January 31, 1970. This commission was assigned four specific duties:

1) with the aid of leading Constitutional law authorities, to analyze the laws pertaining to the control of obscenity and pornography and to evaluate and recommend definitions of obscenity and pornography; 2) to ascertain the methods employed in distribution of obscene and pornographic materials and to explore the nature and volume of traffic in such materials; 3) to study the effect of obscenity and pornography upon the public, and particularly minors, and its relationship to crime and other antisocial behavior; and 4) to recommend such legislative, administrative, or other advisable and appropriate action as the commission deems necessary to regulate effectively the flow of such traffic, without interfering with constitutional rights.[8]

The commission included, as the law stated, "persons having expert knowledge in the fields of obscenity and anti-social behavior, including but not limited to psychiatrists, sociologists, psychologists, criminologists, jurists, lawyers, and others who have special competence with respect to obscenity laws and their application to juveniles."[11] There was even one librarian among the membership; Frederick H. Wagman, former president of the American Library Association and the director of the University of Michigan Library. Its chairman was William B. Lockhart, dean of the University of Minnesota School of Law, and a recognized authority in the field of obscenity and its legal implications and handling.

The Ninety-first Congress, as mentioned earlier, saw many new anti-obscenity bills. When the first session ended in December, 1969, no bills had passed but several sets of hearings had been held by both the Senate and the House. Senator Everett Dirksen (Rep., Ill.) had proposed a bill designed to protect children from receiving pornography through the mails. It was intended to place federal enforcement powers regarding obscenity in the Justice Department. Senator Dirksen's bill, which Senator Barry Goldwater later took over, was intended to deny federal courts; including the Supreme Court, jurisdiction over lower court rulings on obscenity cases.

In 1969, Senator Goldwater came forth as more or less the leader of those who were trying to strengthen the laws against pornography. A statement which he issued on December 17, 1969, said that "common sense will tell most people that exposure of young children to material promoting sexual promiscuity or abnormal behavior might undermine their normal development." He admitted that "not much research exists to show what effect pornography has on the social life of the individual," but he stressed what he called "the wealth of expert testimony that is available from psychiatrists, law enforcement officers, and other professionals who have had contact with consumers of obscenity."[9] He agreed that there is no scientific proof one way or the other, but he says that Congress has two bases on which to act on legislation for the protection of children. He put it this way: "Whether or not we conclude that pornography is harmful to children, there is a second concept which I believe has a strong basis for enacting a special law with respect to minors. This is the power of Congress to protect the Constitutional guarantee of freedom of privacy." He said, "There is no question that indiscriminate distribution of smut to minors is undermining the ability of parents to try to educate their children in a decent way as to the purpose and meaning of sex."[9]

Clearly, laws based on this kind of thinking could well affect book selection and the operation of libraries, and could ultimately lead to prior restraint of a nature never conceived of before in this country as a responsibility of Congress. In sum, the threat of censorship from Congress is perennial, and seemingly will continue to be so. Though laws are not actually always passed, at the very least sensational hearings are held which get national publicity, and are often reflected in state and local laws and more rigid administration of laws already on the books.

NOTES

1. Nixon, Richard M. "Text of President's Message on Obscenity" (*Congressional Quarterly,* May 9, 1969), p. 701.

2. Lowman, Seymour. "The U.S. Customs Service and Its Censorship of Foreign Publications: Existing Laws and Procedure Covering the Prohibition of Importation of Immoral Books and Articles" (*Congressional Digest,* v. 9, no. 2, February, 1930), p. 48.

3. "The Pending Tariff Bill" (*Congressional Digest,* v. 9, no. 2, February, 1930), p. 48.

4. *Congressional Record,* October 11, 1929, pp. 4432-39.

5. *Congressional Record,* January 12, 1943, p. 139.

6. *Congressional Record,* May 12, 1952, p. 5063.

7. *Ibid.,* p. 5065.

8. Krug, Judith F. "Intellectual Freedom" (*ALA Bulletin,* April, 1968), p. 365.

8. *Ibid.*

9. (*Congressional Record,* December 17, 1969), pp. S 17054-56.

9. *Ibid.*

ADDITIONAL NOTES

"Annual Book-Industry Summary Numbers" (Usually in a January issue of *Publishers' Weekly*), vols. 179-195, 1961-69.

McIntyre, William R. "Control of Obscenity" (*Editorial Research Reports,* July 29, 1959), pp. 555-72.

(This rather impassioned piece was written at white heat after the Senate refused to accept the 1970 findings of the majority of the President's Commission on Obscenity and Pornogra-

phy. The fall of both Agnew and Nixon within a very few months after they so cavalierly dismissed the Commission Report was, of course, simply a coincidence. Nixon did leave an abiding ultraconservative legacy in his four U.S. Supreme Court appointees, who, in 1973, with their utterly confusing and retrograde Miller *and related decisions, ended a ten-year period during which obscenity had essentially been declared dead as a legal concept in American jurisprudence.)*

THE POLITICS OF PORNOGRAPHY*

On October 13, 1970, just 13 days after the issuance of a voluminous report (an 824-page majority report, 171 pages of minority opinion, and 10 as yet unreleased supporting volumes), the U.S. Senate, in its Capitoline majesty, voted 60-5 (with 35 abstentions), in favor of a resolution presented by Senator McClellan of Arkansas and co-sponsored by 25 other Democratic senators and 24 Republican senators "declaring that the Senate rejects the findings and recommendations of the Commission on Obscenity and Pornography." Just 41 years before that, almost to the day, on October 11, 1929, an amendment by Senator Bronson Cutting of New Mexico, removing books from the purview of the obscenity clause (Section 305) of the then new tariff bill, passed the Senate by a vote of 38-36.

So, in a little more than a generation, the U.S. Senate, generally considered to be one of the greatest deliberative bodies on the face of the earth, had moved forward with civilization and culture to a stage where as one of the nay-voters in 1970 (Senator Mondale of Minnesota) said, they were trying to deal "with an issue that perhaps cannot be grappled with in light of the current temperament of this country." The fact that the 1970 vote was just three weeks before a Congressional election *certainly* could not have been related to the way our august delegates to the Senate expressed their opinions.

*Reprinted from *Library Journal*, December 15, 1970. Published by R.R. Bowker Co. (a Xerox Company). Copyright © 1970 by Xerox Corporation.

It may be of interest to look into some of the political backgrounds of this Commission, rather than its factual achievements or lack of them. The President's Commission on Obscenity and Pornography was established by Congress in October, 1967. Its membership was appointed by President Johnson in January, 1968. The final report was originally scheduled for January, 1970, but the Commission received extensions, first to July 31 and then to September 30.

Although the Commissioners were named in January, Congress did not vote any actual funds until July 1, 1968. At that time they were allotted $643,000. For the remainder of its existence, the Commission received an additional $1,100,000. This means that the total cost of the Commission has been within $1,743,000 and not anywhere near the excessive "millions" charged by those who oppose its activities and its results.

As required by the bill signed by President Johnson on October 3, 1967, the Commission has had 18 members, appointed solely by the President. Of the original 18 members, all served to the end of the Commission's existence, with the exception of Judge Kenneth Keating, who was appointed Ambassador to India by President Nixon, and who was replaced by Charles A. Keating, Jr., a Cincinnati lawyer and the head of the Citizens for Decent Literature. The other members of the Commission are the following: William B. Lockhart, Dean of the University of Minnesota Law School (Chairman); Edward Ellis, president of an Atlanta, Georgia, news agency; Thomas D. Gill, Chief Judge of the Connecticut Juvenile Court; Dr. Edward D. Greenwood, Child Psychiatrist, Menninger Foundation, Topeka, Kansas; Morton A. Hill, S.J., President of *Morality in Media*, New York City; Dr. G. William Jones, Assistant Professor of Broadcast-Film Art, Southern Methodist University; Dr. Joseph T. Klapper, Director of Social Research for the Columbia Broadcasting System; Dr. Otto M. Larsen, Professor of Sociology, University of Washington; Dr. Irving Lehrman, Rabbi of Temple Emanu-El, Miami Beach, Florida; Freeman Lewis, Vice-President, Simon & Schuster; Reverend Winfrey C. Link, of the Methodist Church Tennessee Annual Conference; Dr. Morris A. Lipton, Professor of Psychiatry, University of North Carolina Medical School; Attorney General Thomas C. Lynch, Attorney

General, State of California; Barbara Scott, attorney for the Motion Picture Association of America; Mrs. Cathryn A. Spelts, Instructor in English, South Dakota School of Mines; Dr. Frederick H. Wagman, Director of Libraries, University of Michigan (Vice-Chairman); and Dr. Marvin E. Wolfgang, Professor of Sociology, University of Pennsylvania.

Certainly this is as "representative" a group as could have been put together for such a difficult set of purposes as were those set forth for the Commission. These purposes were, according to the bill which put the Commission into existence, ". . . after thorough study which will include a study of the causal relationship of such materials to anti-social behavior, to recommend advisable, appropriate, effective, and constitutional means to deal effectively with such traffic in obscenity and pornography." The actual bill had an interesting misprint of "casual" for "causal." There may have been some subconscious, Freudian slip involved in this error, so clearly not intended, which, in the eventual long run, might have had some effect on the Committee's conclusions.

Incidentally, in establishing the Commission, it was required that the members "shall include persons having expert knowledge in the fields of obscenity and antisocial behavior, including but not limited to sociologists, psychologists, psychiatrists, criminologists, jurists, lawyers, and others from organizations and professions who have special and practical competence or experience with respect to obscenity laws and their application to juveniles."

In its more detailed statement of what the Commission was to do, the law says "it shall be the duty of the Commission 1) with the aid of leading constitutional law authorities, to analyze the laws pertaining to the control of obscenity and pornography; and to evaluate and recommend definitions of obscenity and pornography; 2) to ascertain the methods employed in the distribution of obscene and pornographic materials and to explore the nature and volume of traffic in such materials; 3) to study the effect of obscenity and pornography upon the public, and particularly minors, and its relationship to crime and other antisocial behavior; and 4) to recommend such legislative, administrative, or other advisable and appropriate action as the Commission deems necessary to regulate effectively the flow of such traffic, without any way interfering with constitutional rights.'' The law also authorized the Commission to ''make contracts with universities, research institutions, foundations, laboratories, hospitals, and other competent public or private agencies to conduct research on the casual (*sic!*) relationship of obscene material and antisocial behavior.'' Once again, there is what seems to be obviously a typographical error, but the fact that it is used twice in the enabling law would seem to cast doubt on this.

Throughout its existence, the Commission was constantly under the critical view of Congress, and more or less involved in politics. The fact that, for the first time in the history of the United States, a President of the United States sent a major message to Congress on the subject of dealing with pornography (as President Nixon did in 1969) certainly made it clear that pornography, these days, is in the forefront of politically useful issues.

During the debate in the Senate on October 13, Senator McClellan managed to include as part of his speech on his resolution a lengthy report on the minority views of Commissioners Hill and Link, but nowhere in his statement was there any clear presentation of the *results* of the Commission's labors. Without a single minute of hearings on his resolution, McClellan asked for immediate approval, which is not exactly normal in Senatorial practice on this kind of item, particularly in discussing the findings and recommendations of a Commission, duly voted in by Congress, with members appointed by the President of the United States, which conducted hearings and did research over a period of several years. Without in any way *proving* his point, except by simple statement of opinion, he called upon the Senate to reject what obviously the Senate as a whole knew very little about—that is, what was really in the report and what were the recommendations of the Commission.

The matter of dealing with obscenity and pornography has been in American politics for many years. The story of Senator Cutting and his supporters and their valiant efforts to keep Senator Smoot of Utah from deciding on barring smut from our shores for all time to come is told—and well told—in Paul Boyer's *Purity in Print: The Vice-Society Movement and Book Censorship in America.* Mr. Boyer devotes some 25 pages to his detailed story of this most important episode in the history of American Congressional censorship, which should be read for full background on the recent Senate action. Boyer's conclusion is of immediate significance in 1970, when he says that "the contrast between the caliber of the senators who rallied behind Cutting and those who were attracted by Smoot's position was not lost on the public." One wonders if the American people today will take cognizance of the interesting fact that more than one-third of the Senate actually did not stand up even to be counted on this important issue, and that those who did, did so without any real debate or discussion worth counting as such.

Pornography is a valid topic for discussion by the U.S. Senate or any other legislative group, but one questions whether it is appropriate, some three weeks before an important election, for the most significant single study of obscenity and pornography in our generation, if not in this century, to be so cavalierly dismissed and to suffer the kind of abuse evidenced in most public reaction, both in the pages of the *Congressional Record* and elsewhere. One statement which perhaps best sums up the feelings of most of us who are concerned with the search for truth in this matter appeared in the *St. Louis Post-Dispatch*. Its editorial comment was that "except for off-campus riots, there is really nothing a candidate bent on diverting attention from real issues would rather run against than smut. It's wonderful. Smut can't talk back. You run against smut, you've got every right-thinking, decent citizen running with you.

"And so the pornography report will be buried under an avalanche of angry cries from self-appointed guardians of other people's morals. There is (a) little of the censor in nearly everybody. Nearly everybody knows just what is fit for somebody else to read, and all he needs to decide any particular case is a quick look at the material itself.

"But we do not despair. Despite all the uproar, the Presidential Commission on Obscenity and Pornography was composed of men like Dean Lockhart of the Minnesota Law School whose conclusions are worthy of respectful attention. That such citizens found it possible to be honest enough, and receptive enough to scientific evidence to bring in a finding that challenges folk wisdom encourages us to believe that, in due time, other citizens may summon equal honesty and equal receptivity to objective facts. And who knows?—maybe some people will actually read the report in addition to denouncing it."

As the *Post-Dispatch* said, there is hope. The "folk wisdom" is not always going to be accepted as either wise or prevalent. The very fact that 60 U.S. Senators . . . in these days when domestic and foreign violence and dissension are seemingly on the verge of tearing our country and our world apart . . . thought pornography an important enough issue to necessitate their going on record as being its basic opponents is proof enough of the political value of pornography—or rather *anti*-pornography—today.

Vice-President Agnew has proclaimed that "as long as Nixon is President, Main Street will never be Smut Alley." He forgot to mention that the nearly two years since January 20, 1969, have witnessed the greatest freedom of expression, in all mass media, in our history. If smut must be stopped—although the majority of the President's Commission felt it was unnecessary—maybe it will take more than a Senatorial vote to do so.

The fear of science: Back of *the speaker* controversy

3

(This is an article with an interesting, even curious, history. It was rejected by the editors of Library Journal, Wilson Library Bulletin, *and* American Libraries—*for various reasons or no reason. But its author believes it has something rather special to say, perhaps even to ordinary citizens concerned about freedom to think, to speculate, and to do research, no matter whose toes are stepped on in the process. It appears here without apology or further explanation; as our legal friends say, ipse dixit.)*

THE FEAR OF SCIENCE: BACK OF *THE SPEAKER* CONTROVERSY

. . . Of all the vulgar modes of escaping from the consideration of the effect of social and moral influences upon the human mind, the most vulgar is that of attributing the diversities of conduct and character to inherent natural differences.

—John Stuart Mill

. . . I have reached the inescapable opinion that a major cause of American Negroes' intellectual and social deficits is hereditary and racially genetic in origin. This is not remediable to a major degree by practical improvements in environment.

—William B. Shockley

At least one of the above epigraphs should make everyone who reads it indignant. If it happens to be the quotation from a *New York Times* interview with Dr. Shockley,[1] it may make you even more indignant to find out that—according to the *Times*—Dr. Shockley's genocidal "research" in the field of genetics (he won a 1956 Nobel Prize in Physics for his development of the transistor) was financed by private foundation grants of "at least" $179,000 during the last decade. Dr. Arthur R. Jensen, a University of California educational psychologist who revived the old arguments about whether or not there was such a thing as race-linked intelligence level with a 1969 article in a Harvard magazine, has been a "major beneficiary" of the $2 million Pioneer Fund, a tax-exempt foundation which was begun in 1937 for, they said, ". . . research into racial betterment . . . ."

But the same article quotes leaders in the Genetics Society of America and the American Society of Human Genetics as being ". . . in principle in favor of any legitimate genetics research, even when it encourages what some feel is an extreme point of view." Dr. Hope Punnet, ASHG secretary, said, "If you really believe in open research you've got to let those people do their 'research' and then let the rest of us question it."

Is this what was behind *The Speaker* controversy?

When Chaucer wrote ". . . out of olde bookes, in good feyth/ Cometh al this newe science that men lere . . . ,"[2] he was as much ahead of his time about the relationship of learning and books as he was about the connection between manners and morals in what he wrote in *The Canterbury Tales*. Even today, however, there are those who feel otherwise. Sometimes it would seem some are inclined to bar the library to much of "this newe science."

What *is* the proper place of the librarian and the library in facilitating or impeding scientific research? The answer to this increasingly important question can, conceivably, make quite a difference in the progress of mankind; very little scientific advancement happens serendipitously, without reference to "olde bookes." What comes out of the library often—*very* often—is the product of the book or the journal article, fully as much as of the test tube or the retort.

The problem is that much of today's scientific research is more and more meeting with what might be called "social opposition." The antitechnology movement characteristic of the early industrial revolution in the beginnings of the nineteenth century—the Luddite movement, as it has been named—has become an antiscience movement in the latter years of the twentieth century. From recombinant DNA to experimental surgery to nuclear fission to—you name it, some group or groups are against studying it.

And their activities are not confined to parades and picketing, letters to the editors in newspapers, or speeches in friendly and unfriendly forums. The newest manifestation of the enemies of science has emerged just recently among librarians, the group which one might, offhand, believe to be the *least* likely to be trying to inhibit free inquiry.

Superficially the long drawn-out controversy over the production and distribution of *The Speaker* might seem to be a battle for power in ALA, or an aesthetic disagreement over filming quality, or any one of a dozen possible nodes of dispute. But it is hard to evade what looks like the basic cause—an attempt by librarians, among others, to bar research, scientific inquiry into the inequalities seen by some scientists among the levels of intelligence of various racial groups.

At the January 1978 Midwinter Conference, the Black Caucus of ALA issued a statement which said, among other things,[3] "The subject of race is not sheltered and forbidden by frightened, super-sensitive black librarians. *Every subject under the sun*[4] is fair game for open-minded investigation. The problem of race and all its aspects cries out for both scholarly and popular study and discussion, at all levels." This sounds like a clear, strong call for intellectual freedom.

Unfortunately, two paragraphs later *in the very same statement,*[5] these paragraphs appear:

Periodically, the subject of the inferiority of black people is revived in the popular forum, after the manner of Shockley and Jensen today, each time with supposed new and more scientific proof. This theory was out of keeping with the spirit of democratic idealism that characterized the civil rights protest movement of the 1950's and early 60's. However, as the moral fervor of those years began to wane in the face of the frustrating task of building new patterns of human relationships after the official end of segregation, the black inferiority rationale, always lurking in the wings, now is reasserting itself and finding new acceptance.

It might well be said that some subjects are as painful or offensive to other people as the charge of mental inferiority is to black people, but there is a unique ingredient affecting the black person. The supreme personal insult, added to all other human burdens and possible degradation, is to judge a race of people as inherently inferior in mentality to others, for that denies their very humanity. Many men believe women to be physically and mentally inferior to themselves, but there is never any challenge to white women's humanity or to their inclusion in the presumed superior race. A murderer has degraded himself in the worst way possible, but he is a fallen human being and his birthright remains intact—unless he is black. The arrogance of this attitude is unspeakable and is one of the most hateful of all problems to cope with, even when it is an unconscious assumption.

There is an unwholesome emphasis in the film, and especially in the "Discussion Guide," on "tolerating ideas we detest." The spirit of the First Amendment is more like the popular saying, "I disagree with what you say, but I will fight to the death to defend your right to say it." Democracy does not require "tolerance of ideas we detest." This nation was founded by people who would not tolerate "ideas they detested." Slavery in this country would not have ended if tolerance of the detested idea had prevailed, nor would Hitler have been stopped. There should be closer study of this phrase before it is used in the name of the American Library Association, either by inference as a cardinal principle, or aligned with a twisted perception of the First Amendment.

All this seems to add up to, at the very least, inconsistency, and, to this writer, rather clear contradiction. If *"every subject under the sun* is fair game for investigation," clearly *every subject* includes the Shockley-Jensen revival of the old racist claims of the mental inferiority of blacks—no matter how hateful or hurtful the idea may be to blacks and/or others. Despite the Black Caucus' claim that the ending of slavery and the stopping of Hitler would not have happened if there had been "tolerance of the detested ideas," I remind the Black Caucus that they also claim to feel that "the subject of race is not sheltered and forbidden by frightened, supersensitive black librarians."

Will the *real* ALA Black Caucus please stand up and be heard? Do they *really*, as they say at one point, have their ". . . quarrel . . . with the irresponsible method of presentation . . ." or, even if there had been complete control by them of the *way* the film was done, would they have refused to permit filming of the particular theme of the necessity of giving free speech to a racist speaker, because (a) this was ". . . the supreme personal insult" to all blacks, and (b) because they do *not* favor ". . . tolerance of ideas we detest . . ."?

There is one added bit of evidence. Clara Jones, spokeswoman for the Black Caucus and former ALA president, wrote an article for the *Wilson Library Bulletin*,[6] which appeared in print several months before the Black Caucus statement was delivered in January. In this article she referred to ". . . the subject of the inferiority of black people" as *not* being ". . . an open question."[7] She said she challenged the assertion that this *is "an open question"*; indeed she refers to it as a "spurious" subject. In fact, at another point she says, "I challenge and protest the arrogance of identifying the subject [of the mental inferiority of the black] as an open question." And then, in language very similar to Position B (if I may so designate it, in terms of the discussion heretofore), she says, "Our humanity is not debatable!" How on earth can anyone say this is a position in consonance with the Library Bill of Rights, with the First Amendment, or even with Position A of the Black Caucus?

Of course, the Black Caucus and/or Ms. Jones are far from being the first or the only individuals or groups to try to stop discussion, investigation, or even research into the question of "Is intelligence race-linked?" In 1967, when William Shockley pressed the National Academy of Sciences to sponsor research in this area, the Academy responded as follows: "We certainly need to know more about human genetics; as to the desirability of further research there can be no serious question."[8] But, on the specific questions relating to the relationship of race and intelligence, the statement said (in part), ". . . we question the *social*[9] urgency of a greatly enhanced program to measure the heritability of complex intellectual and emotional factors. This is not to say such works should not be done. But we would not, for example, urge that work in other parts of genetics be reduced in order to supply trained personnel to study this area more intensively." They went on, ". . . we question

the social urgency of a crash program to measure genetic differences in intellectual and emotional traits between racial groups."
They concluded by saying that ". . . no promising new approach to
answering these questions should be discouraged . . . the best strat-
egy would be to support the basic research from which such insights
may arise."

In recent years a great (even international) controversy has developed over the propriety of studying the differences, especially in
intelligence, among various races. On a nonscientific basis, this has
been promulgated by sensational novelists—Thomas Dixon, for
example, in *The Leopard's Spots* and *The Klansman*—and quasi-
scientists from Madison Grant to Houston Stewart Chamberlain.
And there is absolutely no question that this view of the reported
inferiority of one race to another contributed to the century-long
post-Civil War dominant racist philosophy in the United States.
Even the Supreme Court, in its infamous *Plessy* v. *Ferguson* (1896)
decision, said, "Legislation is powerless to eradicate racial instincts
or to abolish distinctions based upon physical differences. . . . If
one race is inferior to the other socially, the Constitution of the
United States cannot put them upon the same plane."[10]

But times and philosophies have changed. In an official statement on *Scientific Freedom and Responsibility*, the American Association for the Advancement of Science, in a section devoted to
"The Legitimacy of Research on the Role of Genetic and Environmental Factors in Human Behavior,"[11] said, "We reaffirm the
view that inquiry into genetic difference between racial groups is a
thoroughly legitimate field of research, and we condemn the
emotional attacks and personal threats that thave been made against
such persons as Arthur Jensen and R. S. Herrnstein, because of
their views concerning the importance of genetic factors in human
intelligence." The report goes on, "Their views are, of course,
open to critical debate and challenge on scientific ground, as long
as the debate is conducted on an objective scientific level." The section concludes, "Here, as elsewhere, unceasing critical examination
of hypotheses is the lifeblood of science."

On this same topic Loren R. Graham, Columbia University
history professor, writing on what he calls "prejudicial science" in
a very recent symposium on the "Limits of Scientific Inquiry,"[12]

pointed out that "there are governments today which ban such research on principle." For example, he cites the fact that by the constitution of Communist Germany (the German Democratic Republic) neither freedom of speech nor research on the relationship of race and intelligence are legal. Graham states that he personally would not be in favor of funding research projects for studies of race-intelligence, but yet, he stresses, "a social environment so hostile to research of this type that no research could be done would pose, in fact, a true limit to inquiry of a sort that could be a dangerous precedent. . . ." To the contrary, he also points out, ". . . a social environment in which certain political groups eagerly seized and successfully exploited arguments linking intelligence and race would present an extreme threat to society of another sort."

As part of the same symposium Nobel Laureate David Baltimore, a nuclear biologist, talks of the "necessity of freedom." He says that if the question is asked as to whether or not limits should be placed on biological research because of possible threats which knowledge so discussed might present to the Establishment, there can be only ". . . two simple, and almost universally applicable, answers." These, he writes, are:

First, the criteria determining what areas to restrain inevitably express certain sociopolitical attitudes that reflect a dominant ideology. Such criteria cannot be allowed to guide scientific choice. Second, attempts to restrain directions of scientific inquiry are more likely to be generally disruptive to science than to provide the desired specific restraints.[13]

Why? Because, he says, ". . . science should not be the servant of ideology, because ideology assumes answers, but science asks questions." His other argument is that making science a servant of ideological philosophies ". . . will merely make science impotent," but cannot make *certain* that the only questions studied are those which ideology wants studied.

He concludes by stressing the "disastrous" possibilities implicit in sociopolitical limits to science's efforts. Just as believers in intellectual freedom have always argued for the importance of looking at free expression as a whole, Baltimore argues that "a social system that leaves science free to explore, and encourages scientific discoveries rather than trying to make science serve it by producing the truths necessary for its stability, transmits to the members of that society strength, not fear, and can endure."

Baltimore adds a coda to his own research by citing what Dr. Lewis Thomas, president of the Memorial Sloan-Kettering Cancer Center, wrote on this topic:

This is the greater danger for our species, to try to pretend that we are another kind of animal, that we do not need to satisfy our curiosity, that we can get along somehow without inquiry and exploration, and experimentation, and that the human mind can rise above its ignorance by simply asserting that there are things it has no need to know.[14]

Other prestigious national and international scientific groups have expressed themselves quite forthrightly on this issue. For example, at its 1971 meeting the National Academy of Sciences voted to accept that part of a report by its Ad Hoc Committee on Genetic Factors in Human Performance (including such internationally known biologists and geneticists as Theodosius Dobzhansky, Ralph W. Gerard, and H. Bentley Glass) which contained this strong statement:

The freedom to pursue scientific thought and investigation without hindrance because of fear that results may be misused or because the conclusions may be unpalatable to any is a right that ought to be upheld by every individual scientist and every organized body of scientists. Investigation of the nature and significance of individual, populational, and racial heredity differences in the human species is a proper and socially relevant scientific subject. The freedom to pursue such investigation should be protected, and, to the extent to which methodology gives promise of reasonable progress, the investigation itself should be encouraged.[15]

Unfortunately, the members present voted to reject the Ad Hoc Committee's recommendation that a study should be made of "the feasibility of an effective, long-range program of coordinated research into the interaction of genetic environmental factors and the development of individual human capacities, and to outline such a program if one is found feasible."

In 1972 thirty distinguished American, British, Canadian, and French scientists—including Nobel Laureates Crick, Kendrew, Monod, and Northup (as well as such noted adherents of the prohereditarian view as Eysenck, Herrnstein, and Jensen)—proffered a statement on "Behavior and Heredity" to the American Psychological Association, which included the following "beliefs and principles":

... We wish strongly to encourage research into the biological hereditary basis of behavior, as a major complement to the environmental efforts at explanation.

... We strongly defend the right, and emphasize the scholarly duty, of the teacher to discuss hereditary influences on behavior, in appropriate settings and with responsible scholarship.

... We call upon liberal academics . . . to insist upon the openness of social science to the well-grounded claims of biobehavioral reasoning, and to protect vigilantly any qualified faculty members who responsibly teach, research, or publish concerning such reasoning. We so urge because as scientists we believe that human problems may best be remedied by increased human knowledge, and that such increases in knowledge lead much more probably to the enhancement of human happiness than to the opposite.[16]

The APA, like the NAS with a similar committee, did not vote its approval (or disapproval, for that matter).

The Genetics Society of America, in 1975, considered by mail a 796-word draft resolution on heredity, race, and IQ. Of the 1,088 respondees, from 88.4 percent to 96.1 (962 to 1,046) stated ". . . they agreed with the substance" of various parts of the resolution.[17] The final draft of the resolution was approved by a majority of GSA members in 1976. The resolution, in addition to some statements on the problems of intelligence and factors influencing IQ, said, ". . . there is no convincing evidence as to whether there is or is not an appreciable genetic difference in intelligence between races," and that ". . . whether or not there are significant genetic inequalities in no way alters our ideal or political equality nor justifies racism or discrimination in any form." They concluded that "although the application of the techniques of quantitative genetics to the analysis of human behavior is fraught with complications and

potential biases, well-designed research on the genetic and environmental components of human psychological traits may yield valid
and socially useful results, and should not be discouraged."

Dr. Charles W. Thomas of the University of California, San
Diego, writing in 1973, questioned whether white psychologists can
possibly do a fair job of research in this area because, he says, ". . .
the scientific methods employed are entrenched in institutionalized
perspectives laced with cherished, pathological notions regarding
race." He finds that "research finds based on these assumptions
perpetuate an ideology which is grounded in a belief that the white
North American represents the highest end of the evolutionary
scale." In conclusion, he says that "the role of the white researcher
in black communities will remain ambiguous until the moral and
political issues surrounding their presence are clarified to the satisfaction of community members." I read this as being along the
same line—perhaps even a little more so—as the Black Caucus'
view which seems to say, "Whites can never understand blacks."
This I see as a counsel of despair.

The main point here is that there are some who are very deliberate,
even blatant, in their call to stop science when it seems to them
science is getting into the "wrong" field or fields—whatever they
may be at the moment.

In 1973-74 *Phylon* (a "review of race and culture" published by
Atlanta University and founded by Dr. W. E. B. Du Bois) published
a series of articles all calculated to explain the black viewpoint on
the race/intelligence matter. Edgar E. Epps, writing on "Race,
Intelligence, and Learning: Some Consequences of the Misuse of
Test Results," refers negatively to ". . . a 'market' for a racist
pseudoscience in this country," but he also says that "the highest
priority for social scientists should be to develop the knowledge
needed to make policy decisions effective."[19] A related paper, on
"Sociology and Racism: An Analysis of the First Era of American
Sociology," said that American sociologists had only three choices
in dealing with racism, either to be for it, be against it, or else "to
claim neutrality."[20] The author sees ". . . a non (value-free) position
at best as dangerous as overt racism." And in March 1974, Grace
Rubin-Rabson concluded that "comparing group intelligence ac-

cording to racial or geographical origin has neither social nor scientific value. Investigators would do well to invest their talents in more rewarding areas."[21]

There have been others to belittle the merits of scientific research on race. A British physics professor (Shockley is obviously not the *only* scientist to speak outside of his expertise on the issue of racism), John Ziman, sees so many, such "formidable" barriers ". . . to the 'scientific' study of the relations between race and intelligence that one must begin to question the motives of those who advocate such a program." Like the ALA Black Caucus, he says that ". . . the whole investigation is offensive, by implication, to those who might thus be deemed inferior; why should their sensibilities be ridden over in the name of research when the most likely outcome is continued doubt."[22] Even a nonscientist could ask the obvious question: Since when is scientific research justified *only* if it seems likely to give absolute certainty?

One of the most interesting discussions of the quandary in which scientists have been placed in regard to these matters is by the white authors of a recent volume[23] on *The IQ Controversy*. They state that ". . . at this time, in this country, in this political climate individual scientists should voluntarily refrain from the investigation of genotypical racial differences in performance of IQ tests."[24] But they stress that ". . . nothing we have said implies that it is legitimate to interfere with the teaching, research, or speaking activities of researchers who act responsibly." They never do explain just who decides what is and is not responsible in scientific research. Perhaps we will eventually have some kind of an overall Supreme Court of Science which will make these determinations: neither the American Association for the Advancement of Science nor the National Academy of Sciences nor any other similar group seems inclined to set itself up in this way.

In fact, a philosopher of science named Imre Latakos has proposed that there be so-called universal criteria to help differentiate between what he calls "progressive" and "degenerating" scientific research programs.[25] Latakos singles out "environmentalist theories of intelligence" as one of the programs that might not meet such criteria and so be regarded as "degenerating." He calls for "statute law of rational appraisal" to help a lay jury to pass judgment on such programs. If the program is found wanting, he suggests no scientific journal should publish papers in this field, nor would research groups or foundations be justified in financially supporting such programs.

Dr. Edwin Wilson, of Yale, who has faced his share of public obloquy because of his views on what he calls "sociobiology," wrote a factual, dispassionate article recently on the current efforts to suppress ". . . any kind of study that touches on the genetic evolution of human behavior."[26] He documents his charges quite extensively. He cites, in particular, the efforts of *Science for the People*, which he describes as ". . . the principal . . . activist organization . . . now promoting politically radical approaches to scientific ideology and practice." Taking the offensive himself, Wilson says that

. . . rather than classifying biologists into hereditarians and environmentalists, and judging them on the basis of the supposed political implications of their results, we should distinguish between those who wish to politicize science and those who wish to depoliticize it. Opprobrium is more justly placed on those who attempt to impose their political convictions on the primary process of research itself.

I agree with Dr. Wilson—not necessarily in his point of view on sociobiology, on which I certainly profess no expertise—but on the point of view of ideological politicization. To paraphrase Dr. Wilson's statement, in terms of intellectual freedom (about which I'll be vain enough to claim I *do* have a little expertise!), my conclusion is this: Rather than classifying librarians into freedom-lovers and freedom-haters, and judging them on the basis of the supposed political implications of their results, we should distinguish between those who wish to politicize librarianship and those who wish to depoliticize it. The idea that "opprobrium is more justly placed on those who attempt to impose their political convictions on the primary process of research itself" applies to librarians as well as biologists.

Along the same line, Walter F. Bodmer and Luigi Luca Cavalli-Sforza, two geneticists, writing in the *Scientific American* a few years ago, stated that ". . . there is no good case for encouraging the support of studies of this kind [IQ, race, and intelligence] on either theoretical or practical grounds.''[27] They agree with the National Academy of Sciences and the Block/Dworkin views, stating that "in the present racial climate of the U.S. studies on racial differences in I.Q., however well-intentioned, could easily be interpreted as a form of racism and lead to an unnecessary accentuation of racial tensions." We do have to live together, work together, research together. Apartheid is bad whether inspired by blacks *or* whites. And I agree unequivocally with a recent *New York Times* editorial, which contained this very basic statement on intellectual freedom:

The right of free speech rests on the premise that the airing of obnoxious speech is more beneficial to society than its suppression; that it is better for citizens to choose among contending ideas than for the state to do the choosing for them; that minority voices must be protected against the power of prejudice of the majority.[28]

And so it goes. One can find "authorities" on either side of this argument, and it really depends on your own *Weltanschauung* how you feel about this. If you are basically an all-out believer in intellectual freedom, you will overlook the predicted horrors of social consequences in favor of the equally likely good social consequences from taking away *any* restrictions from scientific inquiry. If you believe that the social consequences of scientific inquiry are more important than intellectual freedom as such, you will certainly plump on the side of the Black Caucus and the others who feel as they do.

The Galileos of tomorrow should not have to face library inquisitors today. I, for one, cannot see how we who are members of a profession that is basically aimed at the widest possible distribution of information and knowledge can possibly support—even assist in raising!—barriers to such distribution or, more particularly, barriers to the discovery of knowledge. Whether or not this knowledge turns out to be "pseudoscientific" or "scientific," I believe, is none of our business. Just as we have both the writings of the accepted astronomers and of Velikovsky in our libraries, so we should have the writings of the Arthur Jensens and the Shockleys, as well as those with whom the majority seems to agree.

And let *The Speaker* speak!

NOTES

1. *New York Times*, 11 December 1977.
2. Geoffrey Chaucer, *The Parliament of Fowls* in *The Complete Works of Geoffrey Chaucer* (Boston: Houghton Mifflin Co., 1933), p. 363.
3. ALA Black Caucus, "The Speaker Statement," *American Libraries* (March 1978), pp. 152-54.
4. Emphasis in original.
5. Author's emphasis.
6. Clara S. Jones, "Reflections on *The Speaker*," *Wilson Library Bulletin*, 52 (September 1977), pp. 51-55.
7. Emphasis in original.
8. National Academy of Sciences, "Racial Studies: Academy States Position on Call for New Research," *Science* 158 (November 1967), pp. 892-93.
9. Emphasis in original.
10. Cited in: Richard Bardolph, ed., *The Civil Rights Record: Black Americans and the Law* (New York: Thomas Y. Crowell, 1970), p. 150.
11. AAAS Committee on Scientific Freedom and Responsibility, *Scientific Freedom and Responsibility* (Washington, D.C.: AAAS, 1975), pp. 14-16.
12. Loren R. Graham, "Concerns about Science and Attempts to Regulate Inquiry," *Daedalus* 107 (Spring 1978), pp. 1-21.
13. David Baltimore, "Limiting Science: A Biologist's Perspective," *Daedalus* 107 (Spring 1978), pp. 37-45.
14. Lewis Thomas, "The Hazards of Science," *New England Journal of Medicine* 296 (10 February 1977), p. 328. (Cited in: Baltimore, op. cit.)
15. "Recommendations with Respect to the Behaviorial and Social Aspects of Human Genetics," *National Academy of Sciences Proceedings* 69 (January 1972), pp. 1-3.
16. "Behavior and Heredity," *American Psychologist* 27 (July 1972), pp. 660-61.
17. "Genetic Differences in Intelligence," *Intellect* 105 (January 1977), pp. 214-15.
18. Charles W. Thomas, "The System-Maintenance Role of the White Psychologist," *Journal of Social Issues* 29, no. 1 (1973), pp. 57-65.
19. Edgar E. Epps, "Race, Intelligence, and Learning: Some Consequences of the Misuse of Test Results," *Phylon* 34 (June 1973), pp. 153-59.
20. James R. Hayes, "Sociology and Racism: An Analysis of the First Era of American Sociology," 34 *Phylon* (December 1973), pp. 330-41.
21. Grace Rubin-Rabson, "Nature-Nurture and the Intelligence Issue," *Phylon* 35 (March 1974), pp. 16-21.

22. John Ziman, *The Force of Knowledge: The Scientific Dimensions of Society* (Cambridge: Cambridge University Press, 1976), p. 299.

23. V. J. Block and Gerald Dworkin, *The I.Q. Controversy: Critical Readings* (New York: Pantheon Books, 1976).

24. *Ibid.*, p. 520.

25. Cited in: Gerald Horton. "Epilogue," *Daedalus* 107 (Spring 1978), pp. 227-34.

26. Edward O. Wilson, "The Attempt to Suppress Human Behavioral Genetics," *Journal of General Education* 29 (Winter 1978), pp. 277-87.

27. Walter F. Bodmer and Luigi Luca Cavalli-Sforza. "Intelligence and Race," *Scientific American* 223 (October 1970), pp. 19-29.

28. "Two Celebrations of Free Speech," *New York Times*, June 11, 1978.

The young adult and intellectual freedom

4

(*Perhaps the most difficult area of book selection for current librarians is in the so-called young adult area. Consider the almost monthly misgivings of* School Library Journal, *the questionings of patrons, parents, and librarians alike about the increasingly frank YA novel, the self-doubts of even the most liberal of First Amendment purists about the limits of what to buy for the fifteen to twenty-one-year-old readers. The following two statements, written nearly a decade apart [the first as a talk in 1976], pretty well express my current views on this perplexing topic.*)

SOCIETAL PRESSURES AND SELECTION OF BOOKS FOR YOUNG ADULTS

Back in library school, a course in "Book Selection"—whether called just that, or, in modern parlance referred to as something like "The Parameters of Optional Media Alternatives"—is usually one of the more popular, if not likely to be "Mickey Mouse" courses. The instructor usually sets up straw-men "censors," and, almost as though they were targets with no recourse but being targets, knocks them down with the heavy artillery of John Stuart Mill, Justice William Douglas, or, maybe, even Eli Oboler to provide obviously truly logical and reasonable and demonstrably irresistible arguments. Foolish folk who dare to question the "professional"—and note that word is not only in quotes, but has some kind of magic qualities to it—those foolish folk, as I said, who would dare to question the professional librarian who has, in his or her wisdom picked a particular volume for the shelves of *your* library—well, those doubting Thomases haven't got a chance. All you have to do (so say the wise library educators and article writers and even book writers and itinerant lecturers on library matters) all you have to do is read the right books and then you can handle any censor with alacrity and aplomb—and even with ease.

There is a warning—what we, some of us who cling desperately to recollections of what was once called a liberal arts education before those dirty words were replaced by "career" and "relevant," called a *caveat*—about this matter of facing up to the censor. It was perhaps best expressed by a Victorian writer, now just beginning to get back into favor, named Lewis Carroll. Lewis Carroll wrote, in his at least semi-classic *The Hunting of the Snark*, that it is all right to hunt Snarks, but beware lest your Snark turn out to be a Boojum! You can do all kinds of things with a Snark; indeed, Carroll tells us you may "hunt it with forks and hope" and "you may charm it with smiles and soap . . ." but *do* watch out "if your Snark be a Boojum!" For then, says the poet, "you shall softly and suddenly vanish away"! This is hardly a fate that any of us, even those most likely to be members of Weight Watchers, would want to have happen.

Well, how can *you* tell if your Snark *is* a Boojum—or, to put it more directly and less poetically, whether your library's censor is or is not (a) amenable to being persuaded by the ideas of Mill or Douglas or even Oboler—or (b) even worse, going to turn out to be *you*, the librarian?

This latter contingency is really not too likely. Marjorie Fiske, studying California school and public librarians in the late 1950s, made the library world aware, if it had not already been so, of the validity of the charge that librarians, at least in the area of intellectual freedom, all too often are their own worst enemies. In 1972, Dr. Charles Busha updated the Fiske study in a different part of the country, the Middle West, via an opinion research of imposing proportions, coming to the not-too-surprising but certainly depressing conclusion that ". . . Midwestern public librarians did not hesitate to express agreement with clichés of intellectual freedom but . . .

many of them apparently did not feel strongly enough about them as professionals to assert these principles in the face of real or anticipated censorship pressures."[1]

Those of us who have been involved with the struggle for intellectual freedom in libraries during the past generation really do not need to have the evidence of either Fiske or Busha to prove to us that one of the worst instigators of censorship is the librarian. But, to give the librarian-censor the benefit of the doubt, his or hers is *not* a self-starting operation.

Earlier in this talk, I joked about the term "parameters"; now let me bring another "in" word into this discussion by introducing the term "vectors." To be highly technical, in a mathematical sense a vector means, according to my dictionary, "a complex entity representative of a directed magnitude, as of a force or velocity. It is the symbol of a definite translation from one point to another in Euclidean space." I can't think of anyone today in any profession who is not more subject to various forces or velocities of different types than a librarian of a public library or a school library or, in some ways, almost any kind of publicly supported library. These vectors or forces or velocities, whatever you want to call them, are so numerous that it might make one wonder why and how it happens that we still have librarians who have not yet succumbed to them.

Consider for a moment the gallimaufry of pressures that affect, in one way or another, every librarian whose salary comes from the public's purse. To begin with, we have the whole tradition with which I am sure you are all familiar, the undaunted fact that there is a wide discrepancy between what Americans do and what they are willing to let their taxes pay for in the form of books or other library materials. A recent study by a New York sociologist named Betty Yorburg, under the title "Sex and Society,"[2] indicates that "premarital genital sex is almost universal among young, middle-class women" in America today. Just as an example, as a recent survey of over 100,000 women subscribers to *Redbook* magazine reminds us, it was found that over nine out of ten (93 percent) of all the women who were questioned who had been married since the beginning of 1973 said in their anonymous replies that they had experienced sexual intercourse *before* marriage. Somehow one is just a little reminded of the widespread practice of bundling—

whatever that really meant in those cold bedrooms in colonial New England back in the seventeenth and eighteenth centuries—when we realize that these same women are the ones who lead the fuss about any kind of sex education of their children.

Miss Yorburg makes the point that in her judgment there is little question that the dominant faith of our society, the Protestant religion, has *not* been "successful in controlling pre-marital sexuality." Indeed, she credits something of this to what she calls "the decline of the effectiveness of the family in control of the sexual behavior of the young." The point that I would like to make is that despite a great many evidences of this decline, it doesn't mean that parents still don't try. One aspect of that effort is the existence of little groups all over the country who call themselves "concerned parents" or some such title, some affiliated with the John Birch Society and other right-wing groups and some actually home-grown, who are fighting a rearguard battle in the attempt to stem the tide of the whole battery of vectors which bear upon them. Miss Yorburg lists just a few of them. "The invention of the automobile, the growth of commercial, non-family entertainment, . . . the emergence of dating. . . ." She further adds, "The increased availability of hotels and motels helped underwrite sexual liberalism. Developments in science also encourage, although they do not instigate, greater premarital sexual freedom." And, of course, what she is talking about are the increasingly uniformly effective techniques available for birth control and the availability of rather definite means for avoiding venereal disease. She also points out that with the lesser influence of the church on the day-to-day life of the individual, and with the increasing effect of women's freedom as well as the spirit of which she calls "the fun ethic," she says we have what is undoubtedly a "sexual revolution" in our modern society. And I have not even referred to the women's liberation movement.

Now, mind you, this is just *one* set of vectors that bear on the librarian—certainly among a group of factors that influence such activities as the Kanawha County antibook activities, with which we are all familiar, which are certainly not unique to West Virginia. Most recently, as you may have heard, the school board in Levittown, Long Island, in the dead of night—hoping no one would notice, I guess—moved quite a number of titles from the school library bookshelves. These books, said one board member, "had no business being in a high school library. Our tax-payers don't have to subsidize garbage." What was this "garbage"? Well, there were two Pulitzer Prize novels, Oliver La Farge's *Laughing Boy* and Bernard Malamud's *The Fixer*, among others. These books were described as containing passages which were "vulgar, anti-Christian, anti-Semitic, or degraded women." As a *New York Times* editorial following this occurrence stated, "In fact, these books are the opposite, in tone and characterization." The real point here is that, as the *New York Times* editorial writer said, "The real target is . . . the changing world of modern social behavior and language rather than the unread volumes on library shelves." The parents, the school boards, the cowardly librarians—all are trying to cling to a world that no longer exists, and keep their children from stepping out into the world of the present, let alone the world of the future.

I would like to get back to my case against the overcautious librarian. A recent study by Judith Serebnick, commissioned by the Association of American Publishers, based on visits she made to ten medium-sized cities, and on her conversations with over 200 booksellers, librarians, and school administrators, indicated that since 1973 there has hardly been the really widespread crusade by citizens against books considered to be obscene. Former Supreme Court Justice Douglas had predicted this, but he seems to have been wrong. This is not to say that there wasn't a very concrete result to librarians from the infamous 1973 decisions. It had what the lawyers and sociologists call a "chilling effect." She found that both booksellers and librarians showed what has been described as "a greater cautiousness" in handling books with strong language and/or explicit sexual scenes, so that, just as in the 1950s when Joe McCarthyites were riding high, now comes the time when our cowardly lions, booksellers and librarians both (not all, of course, but many) are scared away from getting books which might just possibly be "controversial."

To begin with, I think that it is impossible for any self-respecting librarian to consider himself or herself a member of this profession —and perhaps if you do happen to believe so, you had better find out what the profession is all about—if you hide away the "doubtful" and "questionable" books which you have already got in the library. Furthermore, when the books are reviewed with some such caution as "not for timid souls" or "not for timid libraries," I, for one, would really see this as more an incentive to get the book than anything else. Naturally, there are many other factors to be considered, and I won't recapitulate these to you knowledgeable people. But the positive step I want to give to you is that, as you will undoubtedly have done long ago, you should remember that book selection is exactly that, book *selection*; it is certainly *not* book *denial*. If you have the money and your clientele has the interest, get the book. That is all there is to it. Certainly the book is worth getting on other criteria than simply to prove you are being brave to get it!

NOTES

1. Charles Busha. *Freedom versus Suppression and Censorship* (Littleton, Colo.: Libraries Unlimited, 1972), p. 151.
2. Betty Yorburg, "Sex and Society," *Intellect* (April 1976), pp. 509-10.

THE GRAND ILLUSION*

In 1951 a popular song had a line expressing the common plaint, "They tried to tell us we're too young." Who were "they"? "They," of course, were the ones the new generation seems to find especially annoying, the ones who are over 30, or 35, or 40. "They" are trying to tell kids that they are far too young to do what they're doing. Naturally, this leads to resentment on the part of teenagers, and in exasperation and natural reaction, they do even more of whatever it is that "they" try to tell them they are too young to do.

This problem of "the generation gap" ties in with reading and communication. Even Restif de la Bretonne, best known today as a pornographer, in his latter years waxed most eloquent on the cause and effect relationship of "bad" books and youthful delinquencies. The Durants tell us in their most recent volume, *Rosseau and Revolution*, that de la Bretonne "berated Rousseau for having unleashed the passions of the young. . . ." He charged, "It is *Emile* that has

*Reprinted from *Library Journal*, March 1968. Published by R. R. Bowker Co. (a Xerox Company). Copyright © 1968 by Xerox Corporation.

brought us this arrogant generation, stubborn and insolent and willful, which speaks loudly, and silences the elderly."[1] Today's teenage generation may not be inspired by *Emile*, but it certainly could be described by some of the same adjectives applied by de la Bretonne.

Common among the restrictions on our teenagers are those which, in the case of movies, tell them that particular movies are for those 18 and over only; or, in the case of books, tell them that they cannot buy particular paperbacks at the corner drugstore, or they cannot find them in their public libraries; if they can locate them, they may not *read* them unless they, again, are over the magic age of 18.

This matter of age is related to interest in sexual matters is often ignored in considering how best to give appropriate library services to those between 13 and 18. For many years we have known, on the basis of scientific proof, from Dr. Alfred Kinsey's famous studies and others, that adolescence, particularly for the male, is coincident with the high peak of sexual activity and interest.[2] So we have the interesting paradox that the very period in human life when the human animal is most interested and concerned with sexual activity is the period when he or she is expressly barred from reading material directly concerned with his or her greatest interests. As might be expected, this often leads to difficulties.

To clarify further, the Kinsey report, discussing the adolescent boy, says that "the peak of *capacity* occurs in the fast-growing years prior to adolescence; the peak of actual performance is the middle or later teens."[3] In other words, the typical male high school student is much more preoccupied with sex than even the college student, whom conventional wisdom accepts as the leader in this respect. Kinsey comments on "an intensification of the struggle between the boy's biologic capacity and the sanctions imposed by the older male. . . ."[4] It is about these sanctions and the *realities* of adolescent life that I am writing.

Often, the mistaken impression exists that some kind of mysterious or magic change in brainpower and self-control occurs between the last day of the 17th year of an individual and the first day of his 18th year. This is not so. People mature at different rates, and indeed, some never mature at all in the psychological or even the physical sense.

INTELLECTUAL FREEDOM FOR TEENS

Our present library rules on access to books of a presumably sexual nature for adolescents are not only outdated; the rules themselves are almost obscene in the commonly accepted sense of being "offensive to . . . decency." What could be more indecent than what Browning, in his mid-Victorian way, referred to in *The Statue and the Bust* when he said:

> "the sin I impute to each frustrate
> ghost
> Is the unlit lamp and the ungirt
> loin."

Surely our modern psychology has verified this Victorian rebel's literary attempt to single out the sin of the loin which is girt, when the human physiology calls for the opposite.

Don't misunderstand me. I am advocating neither promiscuity nor the widespread reading of obscene and/or pornographic literature by teenage boys and girls; rather, I am asking that we face up to what our own experience, knowledge, and the scientific facts of life indicate to us.

The 1967 meeting of hundreds of librarians and others interested in the topic of "Intellectual Freedom and the Teenager," sponsored by the ALA Intellectual Freedom Committee, came to several rather interesting conclusions. Among these were that if any group of library users needs protection and a "bill of rights," it is certainly the teenager in America today. A prominent lawyer, Stanley Fleishman, discussing the legal aspects of censorship, asked librarians to check into why they were restricting access to certain books. He wondered if librarians are "truly interested in complete freedom for the young, or are they interested in controlling, directing, and shaping young people in the present cultural molds."[5]

The Supreme Court of the United States, on May 15, 1967, ruled that "neither the Fourteenth Amendment nor the Bill of Rights is for adults alone." Detailed evidence indicates that despite the fact that in many states and local communities adolescents have been denied their just rights, they are still entitled to them. This is certainly another step toward indicating that these days are different from the past, and that if the majority of the Supreme Court of the United States can agree that juveniles are entitled to the safeguards of the Bill of Rights and other parts of the Constitution, surely there should be no differentiation made between laws on censorship for adults and for adolescents.

THE CASE FOR CENSORSHIP

A prominent sociologist, Ernest van den Haag, writing in *Esquire Magazine* for May, 1967, under the title *The Case for Pornography Is the Case for Censorship and Vice Versa*, has claimed that censorship on the whole is needed because "if pornography were allowed to proliferate unchecked it might influence both public and private attitudes and sensibilities, and, therefore, ultimate reactions." He says that "certainly books can follow the atmosphere so as to engender a support of abominable and criminal acts."[6] You will note that he gives no evidence to support this, but simply states that it is so. There have been many opinions to the contrary, held by equally prominent sociologists, psychologists, and other authorities, based on research and investigation.

Even if it were true that the reading of so-called "bad" books causes or contributes to socially undesirable behavior, "most believers in censorship apparently reject as too long-range or visionary the corollary that the answer to a bad book is a good one. Rather, their philosophy seems to be that the best answer to a so-called "bad" book is no book.

Let's face it. At this point, we really don't *know* for sure what the actual cause-and-effect relationship is between reading and behavior. As Bergen Evans has stated, "In the realm of sexual customs—the field in which censors are most industrious—the effect of books is very slight. Raping is a much older activity than reading, and men are rarely incited to it by the printed page."

Fortunately, something is being done about this facet of the censorship problem. At the ALA preconference I referred to, one of the major recommendations was that a truly scientific study in depth be made to ascertain the causal relationship, if any, between reading and deviant social behavior. When funds become available, it seems fairly certain that this study will be made. Furthermore, the United States Congress has passed a bill to set up a study commission on the subject. And, most important, this fall the U.S. Supreme Court issued a judgment on a New York case involving the limits of what can be published and made available for teenagers.

But whatever the results of the studies and the verdicts, they cannot really affect the most important part of dealing with teenagers as far as libraries are concerned. Librarians are prone to follow the criteria their professional groups set up, and this is probably more true of those lax in standards than of any other type.

LOOPHOLES IN SELECTION GUIDES

The leaflet entitled "Selecting Materials for School Libraries: Guidelines and Selection Sources to Insure Quality Collections," prepared by the American Association of School Librarians in 1965, states:

The individual school library collection should include all facets of the curriculum with materials which reflect different points of view on controversial subjects and which provide opportunities for pupils and teachers to range far and wide in their search for information and inspiration. . . . All materials selected for the school library, in whatever format, should meet high standards of excellence. Materials which deal with current topics should be up-to-date; those which reflect a biased point of view should make the prejudice recognizable.

Let us speculate on the possible effects of following these "guidelines." To begin with, there seems to be a pretty strong indication that school libraries must reflect whatever is in the curriculum: if there were to be no curricular matter connected with sex, surely the library would be obligated, under these guidelines, to bar materials on sex, since they would be unrelated to the particular courses taught.

Another reflection based on these guidelines might be that the injunction about the "up-to-dateness" of materials would imply a rather rigid weeding program. If one were to consider Vietnam, for example, as a "current" topic, then books and other reading materials dated before 1967 could possibly be considered out of date, and therefore not needed in the library, which certainly would hurt any historical study on this important subject.

Librarians have, to a great extent, answered the question of what to do about controversial and censorable materials. To say that "all materials . . . should meet high standards of excellence" is equivalent to saying that "God is good." What would be a *low* standard of excellence? What would be a standard of *less* than excellence? What, indeed, would be a standard? There is no indication in these guidelines to help any school librarian, or school board member, or principal, or even the people most directly concerned—the students.

Let us consult another official publication: *Standards for School Library Programs*, issued by the American Library Association in 1960. This is the latest available set of standards for this branch of the profession and it says that: "A wealth of excellent materials is available for children and young people, but there is no justification for the collections to contain materials that are mediocre in presentation of content." It also says, "Maintaining qualitative standards of selection of materials is essential. All materials are, therefore, carefully evaluated before purchase, and only materials of good quality are obtained."

This sounds very nice. But just what are these "qualitative standards"? Nothing is stated specifically; there is simply a reference to "the established criteria for the evaluation and selection of materials."

Let us try the School Library Bill of Rights. It says that:

It is the responsibility of the school library to . . . provide materials that will enrich and support the curriculum . . .; to provide materials which stimulate growth in factual knowledge, literary appreciation, esthetic values, and ethical standards . . .; to provide a background of information which will enable pupils to make intelligent judgments in their daily life; provide materials on opposing sides of controversial issues so that young citizens may develop under guidance the practice of critical reading and thinking; provide materials representative of the many religious, ethnic, and cultural groups and their contributions to our American heritage; . . . to place principle above personal opinion and reason above prejudice in selection of materials of the highest quality in order to assure a comprehensive collection appropriate for the uses of the library.

Once again, some questions are being begged or evaded here. What materials "provide growth in . . . ethical standards"? Would

Little Lord Fauntleroy be of more value than *Studs Lonigan* to a teenager living in a slum area in one of America's large cities today? How far does one go in attempting to provide "materials on opposing sides of controversial issues"? Practically everything and anything is controversial, and budgets are, after all, limited. Would ten books on religion and one book on atheism be a fair balance? Or should no books on atheism be included in a school library? How far should the school library go in including materials "representative of the many religious, ethnic, and cultural groups" which make up America? If one lives in a town which is 40 percent or 60 percent of one particular religious faith, should 40 percent or 60 percent of the books on religion in that school or public library deal with that particular faith, and should all books which are inimical to that faith be excluded?

A SOLUTION FOR THE LIBRARIAN

After these somewhat negative reflections, here is what I recommend as a simple and constructive proposal: that the librarians, responsible for selecting books, and the trustees, responsible for preparing or approving book selection policies for libraries, should not, at any time, place books in a public or school library specifically for a particular age group. Either a book should be in a library or it should not. If a teenager—a boy or girl under 18, since that is the generally accepted legal age of maturity—has a library card and requests a book which is in the library and which follows the various criteria cited above, he or she should be given that book, regardless of his or her age and no matter what the possible censorable quality of the book may be. If it is good enough to be in the library, it is good enough to be read by anyone who can read it.

The last people in the world to be censors are librarians. Once the decision has been made to add a particular book or magazine to the library, there should be no further censorship or selection that will keep it from anyone wanting it.

Finally, it is clear that trying to solve as complex a problem as the appropriate amount of intellectual freedom to which a teenager is entitled these days is somewhat like giving a pat answer to the question, "How can the U.S. get out of Vietnam with honor and with safety?" The *kind* of answer one gives to such questions as these, rather than the actual details of the answer, is what is important.

Here is a brief credo to which I hope all librarians can subscribe. The librarian should be on the side of the positive, the progressive, the one who seeks new answers rather than the one who goes along entirely with more of the same. What was earlier referred to as "the conventional wisdom" tells us that the older we are, the smarter we are. It also tells us that we must stop the young from finding out too soon what the world is really like. Librarians should disagree with both of these all-too-widely held judgments. The true librarian should be for freedom, for searching, for trying to find new and better answers to important questions, rather than relying on answers that have been given in the past. Getting down to the very basics in librarianship, librarians and library trustees are not the ones to try, and *must not* try to improve or regulate the morals of today's teenager. The family, church, and to some extent, the school (outside the library), are far better and far more appropriate institutions to see to it that American youth today becomes a mature, responsible, worthwhile, older generation. The library's function in this is to do whatever it can to make the wealth of fine books, so-called good literature, available, even if there are a few four-letter words or pictures of nudes included in the package.

NOTES

1. Will and Ariel Durant. *Rousseau and Revolution: The Story of Civilization: Part X* (Simon and Schuster, 1967), p. 919.

2. Albert C. Kinsey and others. *Sexual Behavior in the Human Male* (Sanders, 1948), p. 219

3. *Ibid.*

4. *Ibid.*, p. 222.

5. "Intellectual Freedom and the Teenager" (*ALA Bulletin*, July-August, 1967), p. 833.

6. "The Case for Pornography Is the Case for Censorship and Vice Versa" (*Esquire*, May, 1967), pp. 134-35.

7. Peter Jennison. "Freedom to Read" (*Public Affairs Pamphlet No. 344*, May, 1963), p. 17.

The etiology of censorship

5

(When Titus Lucretius Carus, some two millennia ago, told his fellow Romans that "happy is he who knows the causes of things," he was not, unfortunately, completely accurate. Sometimes it is more pleasant and relaxing neither to know nor to worry about why. The three sections of this chapter are all, in different ways, explanations of the "causes, origins, or reasons" of and for censorship. The first two are serious attempts at querying the denial of the right to inquire; the third seeks to delimit the almost delimitable term, "intellectual freedom.")

EVERYTHING YOU ALWAYS WANTED TO KNOW ABOUT CENSORSHIP*
*(BUT WERE AFRAID TO ASK), EXPLAINED**

When Dr. David Reuben of best-seller fame hit on the obviously "selling" title of his popular book about sex, the temptation to develop variations of this theme were many and have not always been resisted, as the title of this article should indicate. This portmanteau rubric does make a convenient starting place for the discussion of some (if not quite all!) facets of censorship which are usually ignored, or, at best, slighted.

**This article in a somewhat altered form has previously been published in the author's *The Fear of the World: Censorship and Sex* (Scarecrow Press, 1974).

The question of when, where, and particularly how censorship originated is one the answers to which may be fruitful for those interested in combatting it. Without really knowing why there is censorship, the fact of censorship can become so accepted that one is really just nibbling away at the edges, rather than attacking the central problem.

Going all the way back to the *Old Kingdom* of Egypt, around 3000 B.C., we find clear evidence, as the top authority in this field, James Henry Breasted, has said, "disclosing historically that man's moral ideas of the product of social conditions can form part of a social process."[1] Despite the feelings of some that morality is a transcendent set of rules which somehow arise from within the individual, there is abundant evidence through the succeeding centuries of the truth of Breasted's observation. Granted the fact, then, one of the major mechanisms for regulating the moral ideas of men has always been control over what man has thought, heard, seen, written, and read. If a government or a private group can manage to dam up the source of man's drive to find out what are really the facts of his life, then there need be no concern over any attempts to alter or even to understand the origins of the *status quo*.

Since men communicate by means of words and language, once we are past the remote predawning of the beginnings of man, it is essential that one understand the role of words in the control of men's thought. How one looks at this is, of course, dependent on how one looks at the place of the word in human life.

As far back as we can determine, and certainly attested to by the example of present-day primitive tribes, man has been afraid of the word. Father Walter J. Ong has written, "The word in its original habitat of sound . . . is not a record at all. The word is something that happens, an event in the world of sound from which the mind is unable to relate actuality to itself."[2]

In oral culture (to use Father Ong's terminology), "One can ask about something, no one can look up anything."[3] We today are in the alphabet and print stage of culture, rapidly developing into what Father Ong calls the "electronic" stage. Where we are in the varieties of communications media certainly determines a good deal of how we live.

Let us look for a moment at the way uncivilized man deals with significant words. There is, of course, no question that even in civilized society, that is, among those that believe in the Judeo-Christian faiths, Islam, or Buddhism as an example, certain ineffable names of God are not permitted to be used or are at least reserved for very special occasions and special people to say or write. If you disagree with this, and you happen to be Jewish, consider the fact that even today no Orthodox Jew will read the two Hebrew letters which spell out "Jehovah" as such, but rather looks at letters which say one thing and read off another, "Adonai." Among Christians, as a comparable phenomenon, the Catholic Holy Name Society has an aversion to blasphemy. There are many other examples of reluctance to utter certain words.

Perhaps a clearer statement of all this is simply to remind Christians of the fact that the Bible states unequivocally, "When all things began, the Word already was. The Word dwelt with God, and what God was, the Word was. The Word, then, was with God at the beginning. . . . So the Word became Flesh . . ."[4] This kind of unequivocal statement of the primacy of the word has had a very strong effect on Christian acceptance of the basic importance of what is written and what is said.

Getting back to the belief in the magical power of words among practically all men, S. J. Tambih has, looking at this anthropologically, made a most clear statement of the true significance of language: "There is a sense in which it is true to say that language is outside us, given to us as part of our cultural and historical heritage; at the same time language is within us, it moves us, and we generate it as active agents. Since words exist and are in a sense agents in themselves which establish connexions (*sic*) and relations between both man and man, and man and the world, and are capable of 'acting' upon them, they are one of the most realistic representations we have of the concept of force which is either not directly observable or is a metaphysical notion which we find necessary to use."[5]

What Ernst Cassirer has called the "phenomenon of hypostatisation" of the word—the idea that the name of a thing and its essence have a necessary and invariable relation to each other—is one of the most basic considerations behind the whole idea of censorship. Once we grant that by *referring* to sex or its manifestations, we are dealing with the actual phenomena connected with sex, we have arrived at an emotional and even metaphysical impasse which is hard to solve without simply proscribing the utterance or depiction or writing of the words involved.

Nicholas Tomalin, writing in the humorous British magazine *Punch*, stated it quite clearly: "The association of sex and privacy is a mechanical, animal thing. That is to say, it is clearly an irrational instinct built into the race for biological reasons which civilization made irrelevant aeons ago. . . . We must still have this instinct, even though the dangers no longer exist. Modesty is a result of a very primitive desire for survival. So we see an interesting progress. We start off by being afraid of anyone's being around during the act of love, because of the vulnerability of the animal even the human—to attack. Then the next thing is to give some kind of a rationalization—whether religious or 'magical'—to justify the desire for privacy. Then we get into the story of the Garden of Eden and original sin and much more complicated theories and explanations."[6]

The *Punch* theory may be somewhat facetious, but it seems to have more than a little background in reality. As Tomalin says, "Although, of course, there is no moral harm in nakedness or sexuality, it is necessary to keep them taboo in public while tacitly allowing them in semi-public and private."[7] Mr. Tomalin, of course, writing for a humorous magazine and being himself a humorist, ends his dissertation by stating, "With nakedness and frankness there is only one destination to arrive at. Beyond that there is nowhere to go. Furthermore, there is this limiting corrective, this counter-force, which will always prevent all the rats from falling off. This corrective is very sad, and ever-present. It is human ugliness."[8] He may have something there!

Anthropologists and researchers into primitive psychology have long disputed the justification for censorship, although not always in those terms. Ernest Crawley, long esteemed as one of the top early-twentieth-century authorities in the field, has stated, "Why social opinion originally resented obscenity is a difficult question of psychology." He says, "A considerable percentage of obscene matter . . . consists of natural acts and terms, and the exploitation of the organs from which they are derived, which, being made public, offended social opinion."[9] After stating the *fact* of resentment by social opinion he does not go beyond this to state *why* there is such resentment.

Perhaps we can come to at least some tentative conclusions on the reasons for social opprobrium connected with sex and descriptions of sex. The most recent writer on this general topic, Professor Harry M. Clor of the University of Chicago, writes, "Censorship cannot be confined by rational purpose because it is an inherently irrational process in which psychological complexes and desires for power combine under the guise of morality."[10] He says, further, "The censor is not a species properties of which are to be found in all members. Control of written and verbal expressions are undertaken by many different sorts of men, in many different circumstances, for many different reasons."[11] He admits that previous thinkers have felt otherwise. For example, Clor quotes Morris Ernst as saying, "Society's standards on sex and allied subjects are nothing more than a collection of fears and taboos and that the majority is all too susceptible to these fears and all too willing to acquiesce in the taboos." But when trying to give his own point of view Clor says that "censorship may be properly employed in our society to restrict such forms of sensualism as are contrary to our deepest values."[12]

Obviously, this begs the question. What is "sensualism"? What are "our deepest values"? Is it truly "our deepest values" which will permit the representation on television or on the movie screen or the stage, for example, of the most extreme forms of violence, yet restrict, or attempt to restrict, at least, those books which deal with even very ordinary sexual occurrences let alone what has been termed "abnormal" by some.

Censorship is a long-lasting operation. The Kronhausens, writing on pornography and the law, say, "There has never been any period within the Western World in the past 2000 years or so where there has been a complete absence of sexual suppression."[13] They state that one clear danger of repressing bad language is "that it tends to perpetuate censorship."[14] In fact, the concept that certain words are so bad or dangerous they cannot or must not be used is at the core of many attempts to limit the free expression not only of words, but of ideas in speech and writing. If it were recognized that the words themselves are no more than verbal symbols and cannot work magic by forcing people to commit sexual or other acts, this would go a long way toward solving the problem of censorship.

It is pretty well established that mankind has not progressed very far beyond what the Kronhausens refer to as "the period of animistic worship,"[15] so far as our nearly unquestioning acceptance of the intrinsic power of words is concerned. The Kronhausens feel that "contrary to our intentions we still lend to 'obscene' words a mysterious power by maintaining the taboo against their use, particularly in print. . . . Thus, censorship turns out to be essentially an anxiety operation on the part of society. And as long as society feels itself threatened by the use of 'obscene' words, it will continue to exert some degree of censorship on this basis alone, in literature and in speech." They continue, "If freedom of expression is a sign of a mature society, then the frivolous suppression of words and/or ideas by certain censorious groups must be recognized for what it is: the symptom of a social neurosis defending its own illness, thereby contributing to the continuance of that illness for the society as a whole."[16] They go so far as to state, "Censorship is the chief weapon of attack (for) the social repression of sexuality." As Mark Twain said, long ago, "Man is mostly and exclusively the immodest animal, for he is the only one with a soiled mind, the only one under dominion of a false shame."[17]

The power of the word has always been great. Among the ancient Hebrews, for example, there grew up, to quote Rabbi Joseph Joshua Trachtenberg, "schools of . . . mystical and esoteric exegesis which profess to discover the hidden inner significance of the Word. And it *is* more than it appears to be: not only is it the word of the Lord, it is the Lord Himself, an emanation from His being, a particle of His essence. God has revealed Himself to man, and by so doing has in a measure placed Himself within man's reach, to be aspired to as Ideal, to be prostituted as Power."[18] In the light of this feeling, it is clear that there is ample justification for the use of the words of the Bible for a specific magical purpose.

There is much reported confusion on the subject of what is obscene. The confusion, it should be fairly clear, exists because there are people who think *anything* related to sex is obscene. This dates back to the Puritan ethic, and to the ideas of the early Christian fathers. Sex equals something bad; so writing about sex is demonstrably bad. Writing about sex and using dirty words to do it is by far the worst thing one can do, even worse than what many people would consider to be much more significant problems.

Senate Majority Leader Mike Mansfield recently stated, "The growth of pornography in the United States is the number one pollution problem. The people want something done to curb it." There is, of course, a simple way to remove pornography as a problem. This is to say that it is not having any bad effect, and therefore there should be no laws attempting to censor anything at all, that is, *no* censorship, so far as sexual discussion or language is concerned.

British philosopher John Wilson has said, "Plenty of writers can be found to say that sex is a matter of Christian morality, or a matter of taking 'adult' attitudes, or a matter of mutual perceptivity and awareness, or something of the kind; but few to say they can take all sorts of legitimate forms, including just good fun." In fact, he says, "Anyone who claims that sex should be, for the most part, just a matter of physical enjoyment would immediately be accused of insensitivity, immorality, incapacity for deep relationships, and practically every other crime."[19] And, although he wrote this several years ago, the situation in this regard has certainly not changed.

There is no question that there are some actual dangers to sex. John Wilson says, "It is reasonable for a girl to dislike rape, and if she doesn't side with her rapist, her sex is a real danger in this sense. But many of the rules, and the whole desire to have rules at any cost and in any form, reflect our own nebulous fear of these dangers, our fear of sex itself. Hence we insist on providing sex with the metaphysical, that is, with a set of principles not based on empirical fact to which we can always refer our problems."[20] The whole point in all this is that much of what we do we do not for *reasons* but because of *circumstance*. Franz Boas wrote a whole book to come to the conclusion that "the origin of custom of primitive man

must not be looked for in rational processes."[21] And the further
one looks into the reasons for the fear of words throughout history,
as expressed in censorship, the more one must come to similar conclusions.

The old folk dictum, expressed in the children's phrase, "Sticks
and stones may break my bones, but words can never hurt me," is,
unfortunately, not widely accepted once one is beyond childhood in
age, if not in philosophy. Leaving aside even the laws on libel and
slander, the laws against obscenity and pornography are quite
clearly there to carry out the idea that words can indeed hurt one.
And this is nothing new in the history of civilization. "To Western
Europe the peoples in the Mediterranean, accustomed for thirty
centuries to an alphabet, the written word is something of a magical
charm," says Paul Radin. "In the beginning," he continues, "was
the Word, i.e., the *written word.* In its manifold repercussions this
worship of the written word finally included the unwritten word,
extended itself until it ended in the deification of thought. Thus the
word and thought became a thing in themselves, living in real enti-
ties, instead of retaining their old function of merely giving validity
to certain reality."[22]

For Paul Radin, the Lévy-Bruhl notion of primitive mind as
being different from ours is definitely unproven. He sees and main-
tains that the minds are alike, but that modern civilization has
simply added the written word, which he feels makes the fundamental, lasting, absolutely colossal difference between the way
primitive man acted and the way civilized man has acted and is
acting.

On this whole topic the anthropologist Bronislaw Malinowski
suggests, "The principle that the development of speech in humanity" in essence repeats "the development of speech within the life
history of the individual."[23] In other words, he is describing a sort
of an "ontogony recapitulates phylogeny" of language. According
to him, "The child actually exercises a quasi-magical influence over
his surroundings. He utters a word and what he needs is done for
him by his adult entourage. . . . The mastery over reality, both
technical and social, grow side by side with the knowledge of how
to use words." Malinowski reminds us that "familiarity with the

name of a thing is the direct outcome of familiarity with how to use this thing." So, "The belief that to know the name of the thing is to get a hold of it is empirically true." He says, "There is a very real basis to human belief in the mystic and magic power of words . . . verbal communication from the earliest infantile dependence of the child and his parents and the developed use of full citizenship, scientific speech, and words of command and leadership, is a correlate of this. The knowledge of right words, appropriate phrases, or highly developed forms of speech, gives man a power over and above his own limited field of personal action."[24] But this power of words, this cooperative use of speech, is and must be correlated with the conviction the spoken word is absolutely sacred. He says, "The fact also that words add to the power of man, over and above the strictly pragmatic effects of this, must be correlated with the belief that words have a mystical influence."[25]

Perhaps the most commonly accepted origin for censorship is simply that there are bad things and good things, and someone has to be the one to decide. If in the tribe it was the *shaman*, the medicine man, or possibly the chief, in civilized society it must be the Law, backed up by those stalwart cooperating institutions, the Church and the School.

This is, perhaps, an over-simplification. We might get further on this track if we look at the different ways that different kinds of people look at sex, which is really what we are talking about in all this.

There are now and always have been those whom John Wilson characterizes as "authoritarian, strict, puritanical, or moralistic." These are people, says Wilson, "who 'want to keep sex in its place' by hard and fast rules, possibly derived from religion, and they are in favor of taboos on sexual language and behavior." Naturally, on the other side there are those people whom most of us would call, as Wilson does, "the liberals or progressives." This group, he says, "are in favor of a more permissive attitude toward sex, at least so far as law and convention are concerned; they want to bring sex out into the open and teach people to incorporate it into their lives in a mature and meaningful way."[26] For this group, certainly, with a far different point of view than the first group, Wilson says, "Sex is important but not shameful: It may even appear as something beautiful or of potentially spiritual significance."

This has been but a very brief and almost superficial examination of what is admittedly not quite "everything" you really want to know about censorship. Actually, if the author were in the Immanuel Kant title-creating tradition, like Father Ong, this article might well have been headed "A Preliminary Prolegomenon to an Introduction to the Future Study of Censorship." Any considered attempt to inquire into the causes of the censorship of sex writings, the reasons for the fear of the word, must take into account a multiplicity of possible causes and reasons and explanations: (1) anthropological ethnological, (2) psychological, (3) philosophical, (4) linguistic, (5) historical, (6) legal, (7) social, (8) moral-ethical, (9) theological-religious, (10) mythological-symbolic.

And that's really only a beginning. . . .1

NOTES

1. James Henry Breasted. *The Dawn of Conscience* (New York: Charles Scribner's Sons, 1933), pp. 122-23.

2. Walter J. Ong. *Presence of the Word: Some Prolegomena for Cultural and Religious History* (New York: Simon and Schuster, 1970), p. 22.

3. *Ibid.*, p. 23.

4. *The New English Bible* (Oxford University Press, 1961), p. 15.

5. S. J. Tambih. "The Magical Power of Words," *Man* (NS., vol. 3, no. 2, June 2, 1968), p. 184.

6. Nicholas Tomalin. "Monday I Touched Her on the Ankle . . ." *Punch* (June 11, 1969), p. 855.

7. *Ibid.*

8. *Ibid.*

9. James Hastings, ed. "Obscenity," *Encyclopedia of Religion and Ethics*, vol. IX (Scribner's, 1951), p. 441.

10. Harry M. Clor. *Obscenity and Public Morality: Censorship in a Liberal Society* (University of Chicago Press, 1969), p. 49.

11. *Ibid.*, p. 117.

12. *Ibid.*, p. 185.

13. Eberhard and Phyllis Kronhausen. *Pornography and the Law: The Psychology of Erotic Realism and Pornography* (Ballantine Books, 1959), p. 26.

14. *Ibid.*, pp. 141-42.
15. *Ibid.*, p. 142.
16. *Ibid.*, p. 143.
17. *Ibid.*, p. 155.
18. Joseph Trachtenberg. *Jewish Magic and Superstition: A Study in Folk Religion* (Philadelphia: Marion Books and Jewish Publications Society, 1961), p. 104.
19. John Wilson. *Logic and Sexual Morality* (Baltimore: Penguin Books, 1965), p. 59.
20. *Ibid.*, pp. 67-68.
21. Franz Boas. *The Mind of Primitive Man* (New York: Macmillan, 1938), p. 236.
22. Paul Radin. *Primitive Man as a Philosopher* (New York: Appleton, 1920), p. 59.
23. Bronislaw Malinowski. *Coral Gardens and Their Magic* (New York: American Book Company, 1935) vol. 2, p. 232.
24. *Ibid.*, p. 233.
25. *Ibid.*, 235.
26. Wilson, p. 58.

"JUST LIKE THE CHILD IN THE FAMILY":
PATERNALISTIC MORALITY AND CENSORSHIP*

Just before the 1972 presidential election, Richard Nixon, in an interview with a reporter from the *Washington Star-News*, said, "The average American is just like the child in the family."[1] In accord with this view, in March 1973 he submitted, as part of a projected massive revision of the U.S. Criminal Code, a decided "toughening" of the legal definition of obscenity. Under the Nixon view, obscene material would be defined as explicit detailing of sexual intercourse, violence involving sado-masochistic sex, and/or explicit, close-up views of human genitalia. Such materials would be banned if it made up a major portion of a published work, if it pandered to prurient interests. (This legislation proposed by the

*Reprinted from *Library Journal*, September 1, 1973. Published by R. R. Bowker Co. (a Xerox Company). Copyright © 1973 by Xerox Corporation.

Executive is, by an interesting coincidence, very much like the most recent Supreme Court decisions on obscenity, particularly as this relates to the localization of contemporary standards and the denial of the significance of social importance.) Those convicted of the proposed statutes could spend up to three years in jail.[2]

As the June 21 Nixon Court decisions on obscenity should have made abundantly clear, what we are discussing is not an academic question. It is a reality of current political life, and it is a problem that we must face up to, whatever our private beliefs, since public decisions will be made for us on this matter. Long ago Edmund Burke told us—and who can really deny him?—that "nothing universal can rationally be affirmed of any moral or any political subject."[3] What we discuss here is basically a moral-political question, and what we conclude—if we do, by some miracle, come to any agreed upon conclusions—certainly will not be inscribed on marble tablets to stand as a guide for all time to come.

British legal philosopher Morris Ginsberg gives these distinctions between public and private morality: public morality is "the working code to which people are normally expected to conform." Private morality he defines as "the morality accepted by the individual conscience, which may differ from the public morality in approving acts conventionally condemned and condemning others conventionally approved."[4]

But perhaps this is really a distinction without a real difference, if we examine closely private versus public morality, or, to put it another way, the morality of the individual versus the morality of society. Certainly it has recently become quite an accepted point today that morals and laws are not identical; if they were, we would have a theocracy, and not a democracy.

Going back some seven centuries, St. Thomas Aquinas wrote, "Private Sin is different from public crime, and only the latter lies in the province of man-made law." And, less than a century ago, John Stuart Mill declared, after a long, carefully worked out argument, that "the only purpose for which power can be rightfully exercised over any member of a civilized community, against his will, is to prevent harm to others."[5]

PROTECTING THE PUBLIC

Public morality, it seems to me, has already been defined by many critical theorists in the common usage of the words "the public interest." This was more or less started by Jeremy Bentham and has been perpetuated in political thought ever since his day. For "the public interest" let us accept a definition which was framed by Dr. Wayne Leys some 21 years ago, in the course of dealing with the topic of "ethics for policy decisions" in a book by that name.[6] Leys' definition was that " 'in the public interest' is that fraction of human wants that can be pulled out of the depths of inarticulate wishfulness and objectified into a basis for agreement in common action." Leys equates the public interest with such terms as "in natural acts, natural law, public interest of the common good, public morality, ideals of justice and right." He says that they all may be a creative effort to answer the question, "How must I modify my actions so that it is worthy of acceptance by others?" There is certainly nothing absolutely permanent or even binding about the "public interest"; it is not, one may hope, as Supreme Court Justice Oliver Wendell Holmes, Jr., once described it, "a brooding omniscience in the sky."

But if we are seeking what is in the public interest in relation to the freedom to read, let us remember that we have had, within this generation, whole societies in which the public interest was equated with complete intolerance. Under the Fascist governments of Mussolini and Hitler, there is no question that all unorthodox and disapproved ideas were suppressed. There was the feeling that the popular intelligence was just not great enough to recognize the truth, and that the populace as a whole was much too selfish—or stupid—to be dependable, either morally or politically.

The purpose of totalitarian censorship, as Dean Leys pointed out, was "to protect national and secular interests: jobs, security from foreign aggression, and the comforts and necessities of this life." Unfortunately, it does not sound too far away from some of our present national concerns and problems to note that one of the basic reasons commonly given for imposition of censorship by the Fascists was this very presumed "necessity" of insuring "national security."

We must face the fact that where there is a complete dichotomy between the way Americans act, so far as sexual behavior is concerned, and how they want others to act—so far as control over so-called obscene and pornographic materials are concerned—the paradox is not something that can be settled, really, on a rational basis. If an individual or group are controlled by traditional taboos, they will not accept any rational arguments, because they are appealing to faith, not to reason. There is certainly no question, based on any fair study of history and anthropology, that morals based on taboos do change in the long view, but neither logic nor factual evidence will serve to convince those who do not wish to be convinced that their taboo regulated moralities should be changed.

In Idaho today, for example, it is illegal to disseminate (and I suppose that pun *is* intentional) information about birth control devices. The statistics for the last few years, however, have indicated that Idaho has one of the highest percentages of unmarried mothers in the country! When the Idaho legislature had a chance earlier this year to rectify their former "Blue Law," in fear and trembling of their political destinies, the legislature refused to cancel the old law. But, just the same, there are advertisements for birth control devices in every Idaho drugstore and in many of the national magazines of general circulation they sell, and no one does a thing to stop them from circulating.

So we have a complete dichotomy, as I said, between theory and practice. As Dean Leys said years ago, "The most persistent disagreements regarding sex conduct do not spring from conflicts of economic interest, but depend upon diverse family and religious traditions."[7]

No one says that removing laws against obscenity would imply any moral approval or condoning of what is in the published books. What is important is to face up to the need for other ways of dealing with the kinds of problems of which the widespread reading of obscene and pornographic materials are simply symptoms. We have to realize that, even though we may agree that the first business of society is its own protection and to make sure that it will continue, that law which aims at the good of *society*, and not, in the long run, at the good of the *individual*, cannot be anything but a bad law. If the whole principle of moral action is that it is free action, then this must mean some freedom granted to make even wrong moral choices, and to carry them out.

What society is worth preserving if it does not recognize that the only really valuable thing there is on Earth is a human being, a single, living creature? That society which negates this principle is really a society against itself. It is surely not the highest possible good to set up some code which is for the continuance of a society which in itself may be bad. I hope we can all agree that the highest possible good is what is good for the individual.

Also, certainly there is very little in law which is absolutely permanent; the same thing cannot possibly in every age be regarded in the same way. So the law has to be related to those standards in life which change, not necessarily giving way to every possible impulse which changes around at popular will, but taking into consideration the purposes of society, the purposes of the individual, and whatever we can accept as basic human values.

PATERNALISM

A legal philosopher, Gerald Dworkin, has brought up an important concept in this connection—paternalism. Writing in *Morality and the Law* (Richard A. Wasserstrom, ed., Wadsworth, 1971), he defines the concept of paternalism as "the interference with a person's liberty of action justified by reasons referring exclusively to the welfare, good, happiness, needs, interests, or values of the person being coerced."

Dworkin argues that where we do not either advance the best interests of the individual by compulsion, or where the attempt to do so involves evils which outweigh the good which is achieved, we certainly are dealing with paternalism. He says that "in all cases of paternalistic legislation there must be a heavy and clear burden of proof placed on the authorities to demonstrate the exact nature of the harmful effects (or beneficial consequences) to be avoided (or achieved) and the probability of their occurrence." He concludes that "if there is an alternative way of accomplishing the desired end without restricting liberty although it may involve great expense, inconvenience, etc., the society must adopt it." With this conclusion I heartily agree.

You will undoubtedly hear that the reading of so-called pornographic or obscene words and episodes is far from being victimless. You will probably be told that the years of unbiased social and scientific research on this issue by the Presidential Commission on Obscenity and Pornography were devoted to poor research, unscientific and biased. Indeed, you may even be told that the testimony of policemen and local states' attorneys is far more acceptable than social science research. The late J. Edgar Hoover will perhaps once more be cited as a sort of final authority on this highly debatable question.

But I don't think we can settle in one day the matter of whether reading pornography does indeed lead, directly or indirectly, to other crimes—particularly sex crimes—to sexual permissiveness (which may be or may not be a crime), even to the ultimate—if not, indeed, almost immediate—decline and fall of our civilization. I would rather stick to the main point of this discussion: the obvious gulf between what the people of America claim as their moral principles and their actual way of living, between public and private morality. After all, this is something that is fairly demonstrable, if not obvious, to any unprejudiced observer.

America has a long tradition of the "holier than thou." The statistics on bastardy in Puritan New England certainly are in decided contrast to the pervasive, censorious public morality of the Puritan Church and schools and town meetings. It is hardly a secret that the censor, throughout the ages, is himself one with some suppressed impulses which he often wishes others to suppress also.

THE CHARACTER OF CENSORSHIP

Another way of looking at this problem of the relationship of public and private morality is to see just how it happens that public moralizers wish to punish private morality. In his book *Moral Indignation and Middle Class Psychology: a Sociological Study* (Schocken, 1964), the distinguished Danish sociologist, Svend Renulf, has offered an hypothesis that "moral indignation (which is the emotion behind the disinterested tendency to inflict punishment) is a kind of disguised envy. . . ." He gives a great deal of evidence to indicate that this "moral indignation" is especially

strong in the social class which he defines as "the 'small bour-
geoisie' " or the "lower middle class." He says that actually there is
pretty good evidence to indicate that this "disinterested tendency to
inflict punishment" hardly exists at all in most communities where
the lower middle class is of not too much significance. Indeed, he
gives ample evidence that "the tendency in question tends to dis-
appear in the middle class, as soon as it has acquired a certain standard of wealth and prestige." One of the most clear-cut examples
of this "moral indignation" is that certainly Calvinism has
throughout its existence been characterized by what he describes as
"an unusually strong desire to see other people punished for their
morality." Renulf states specifically that the Comstock campaign
against pornography was "the expression of petty, bourgeois
protest movements against the rising power and immorality of the
millionaire class." It is interesting to note that there is ample evidence, as Renulf says, that "the Puritans as a group . . . were characterized by a strong disposition to indulge in a number of those
kinds of sin which they indignantly denounced in others." This has
been confirmed by a great many case studies, and I will not belabor
this point. After all, there has to be *some* particular motive behind
the censor to justify the holier than thou attitude he always assumes.
Renulf did a great deal of study to indicate that the following is
true: "The Puritans believed that men must be made to suffer, and
that God actually inflicts suffering upon men in a number of circumstances where we should think any kind of punishment unjusti-
fiable: when men fail to be sufficiently censorious against one
another, when they are happy and self-confident, when they have
sinned only under compulsion or temptation from God, or even
sometimes when they cannot be blamed for anything at all. This
acceptance of every possible pretext for the infliction of punishment makes it natural to suspect that the Puritans in reality took a
delight in human suffering for its own sake, quite apart from the
question of whether there was any sin to be atoned for or not."
This is beginning to sound like the very "sado-masochistic abuse"
that the President of the United States claims as something we
ought to punish.

It is really not possible to talk very long about the relationships
between public and private morality, especially as related to the
freedom to read, without at least referring once more to Jeremy

Bentham. In his "Indirect Legislation" Bentham has given a classic statement against censorship. He stresses that a censor must be someone who is "that rare genius, that superior intelligence, that mortal, accessible to all truths, and inaccessible to any passion, to whom can be intrusted this supreme dictatorship over all the productions of the human mind."[8] He further states that:

... the evil which results from a censorship ... is impossible to measure ... because it is impossible to tell where it ends. It is nothing less than the danger of stopping the whole progress of the human mind in all its paths. Every new and important truth must of necessity have many enemies, for the single reason that it is new and important. Is it to be presumed that the censor will belong to that class, infinitely the smaller, which elevates itself above established prejudice? And though he should have that uncommon strength of mind, will he have the courage to endanger himself on account of discoveries of which he will not share the glory? There is but one sure course for him to take; to proscribe everything which rises above common ideas, to draw his pen through everything elevated. He risks nothing by prohibition, but everything by permission. In doubtful cases, it will not be he that suffers; it will be Truth.

In the event that the human mind had depended upon the good will of those in authority, where should we be today? Religion, legislation, morals, the physical sciences, all would be in darkness. But it is not necessary to dwell upon so common an argument. The true censorship is that of an enlightened public, which discountenances false and dangerous opinions, and useful discoveries.

Supreme Court Justice Oliver Wendell Holmes, Jr. once said that the 14th Amendment did not put into force Herbert Spencer's *Social Statics*. It is equally true that we cannot freeze Anthony Comstock's mid-Victorian ideas or St. Augustine's early medieval opinions into laws on sexual morality for all times. This is a free country; let's not permit the censor, or the censorial group, or the law-evading prosecutor to turn America into Calvinist Geneva of the 15th Century, or Puritan Massachusetts of the 17th Century, or even Cincinnati of 1973!

The lip-licking glee with which the general public follow newspaper stories involving sexual misbehavior—particularly, of course, if the great, near-great, or the notorious are involved—is well known to all of us. Certainly the soap-opera-loving housewives

who have complained of being deprived of their daily portion of
other people's sexual troubles and triumphs by the Senate Watergate hearing would have numbered far less if the Watergate scandals
had somehow been intertwined with sexual peccadilloes, as well as
political misfeasance and malfeasance.

LAW AND MORALITY

Let us turn to the distinction between law and morality. Surely
we can all agree that there are moral matters with which the law in a
democracy such as ours does not and should not concern
itself—which faith we each follow, for example. And equally we
can all agree that there are legal matters which, except in the most
convoluted and attenuated sense, do not concern morality. As an
example of this, is it more moral to require that traffic keep to the
right side of the road, as in most of the world, or to the left, as in
Great Britain? Granted, the word "sinister" means "left" in Latin,
but I really can see nothing either sinister or sinful in left-handed
laws. So laws and morals are—should be—considered as separate
institutions.

But a law can present a moral problem. For example, is it moral
to put our fellow man to death? Isn't the imposition of capital
punishment a moral problem for any society? And, to drop a long
way down in significance, isn't a law which prevents the individual
from exercising his God-given freedom of choice among alternatives—such as a law, *any* law, against the distribution and sale of a
particular book or magazine—a violation of moral laws of vastly
more significance than the prevention of the supposed causal relationship between reading about rape and committing it?

Let's have a look at this problem from another viewpoint—that
of practicality. Surely there is no reasonable, experienced adult
who will not agree that the greatest sexual stimulation, for most
normal people, comes from contact, from touching the other
person, not from reading about it or looking at pictures. Carried to
ultimate absurdity, then, to avoid so-called sexual arousal which
might lead to sexual crimes, no two people of opposite sexes should
ever touch each other unless they intend to marry each other, and—
since homosexual relationships, even between consenting adults,
are crimes in all but eight states—not even two persons of the same

sex should ever touch each other. But, you will say, this is a ridiculous argument; in dealing with normal individuals, a touch or a
viewing will not invariably cause sexual misbehavior. In my judgment, granting this, it is just as ridiculous to argue that reading a
so-called "dirty" book will invariably have immoral results.

About 50 years ago a pioneering sociologist questioned a large
number of adolescent girls as to what caused them to have any
symptoms of sexual arousal. The almost unanimous answer—as
you may have guessed!—was "Men." The super-moralist, the
ultra-censor always seems to overlook the fundamental desires of
mankind; it is as impossible to alter these as it is to reschedule the
precession of the equinoxes.

Now, to the discussion of how librarians can, have been, and
should be affected by the one possible victimless crime which
obviously can directly affect them—the distribution of pornography. Remember, please, it is no crime, victimless or not, to *print*
pornography. The First Amendment and the Supreme Court decision in the Pentagon Papers case, among other precedents, speak
against prior restraint. As I said earlier, it is no crime to possess
pornography within the confines of one's own home.

But a great many state laws, including one that our own Freedom
to Read Foundation and a group of censor-fighting California
librarians have been battling against for over a year—the California
"Harmful Matter" statute—put librarians in real danger of
becoming criminals if they are found guilty of distributing what
some court defines as obscene and/or pornographic reading and
viewing materials. So, as I said earlier, we are not talking of an
academic or a philosophical problem, but of an actual one that
deserves our earnest consideration and early resolution.

The librarian is, ideally considered, the chief modern promulgator
of knowledge; there is just too much to know and learn for any one
man or even any group of men to be able to serve as conveyors of
knowledge to the unknowing, the unlearned. Professors, unfortunately, are just that—persons who *claim* to know. The burden of
storing and arranging and making available what there was and is
to know is carried by the librarian. No computer or set of linked
computers, no other of the fantastic array of modern machines and
technologies can match the trained librarian in accomplishing the
essential tasks of knowledge accumulator and relayer.

Granted that fact, what should restrain the librarian in the exercise of his important responsibilities and duties? What the laws limit him to doing, of course. But beyond that, what? The local vigilante group, whether organized on a local or state or national basis? The complaint of a single unhappy patron? The censorious impulses which very well may exist within his or her own mind? The desire to please everyone, to be popular? The fact that a great many choices of book selection or manner of availability will be relatively unknown to or unconsidered by anyone besides the librarian himself?

Perhaps the best general reply to these alternatives—not by any means all hypothetical—is that the self-respecting librarian must live by both public morality (as covered in laws and attitudes) and by his own private morality, his morality as a professional—his morality, finally, as a librarian.

Look up at the sky some night. That planet that looks reddish from Earth, we all know, is Mars. It is unique among the planets in our heliocentric universe; it has two moons. These moons have been named Phobos and Deimos—Fear and Panic—and they are the constant companions of Mars, the God of War. Surely we have enough Fear and Panic with the nuclear Sword of Damocles hanging over all of us. Do we really have to add to our already overloaded stress factors, for individuals and for nations, with needless hysterical fear and panic? Perhaps we should realize that Phobos and Deimos *are* satellites of death and destruction, and let us leave Fear and Panic where they belong—closely associated with death-dealing Mars, and not with life-bringing Eros.

NOTES

1. *Facts on File, 1973*, Vol. 32, No. 1672, November 12-18, 1972, p. 910.
2. *Ibid.* Vol. 33, No. 1691, March 25-31, 1974, p. 251.
3. Weldon, T.D. *States and Morals.* London: John Murray, 1946, p. 1.
4. Ginsberg, Morris. *On Justice in Society.* Cornell Univ. Pr., 1962, p. 232.
5. Kiester, Edwin, Jr. *Crimes with No Victims.* Alliance for a Safe New York, 1972, p. 2.

6. Leys, Wayne A. R. *Ethics for Policy Decisions: The Art of Asking Deliberative Questions.* Prentice-Hall, 1952.
7. *Ibid.*, p. 219.
8. Mack, Mary Peter, ed. *A Bentham Reader.* Pegasus, 1969, p. 176.

THE PARAMETERS OF INTELLECTUAL FREEDOM: TOWARD DEFINITION AND EXEMPLIFICATION

Parameters, loosely defined, are boundaries, limits. More accurately defined, a parameter is "a variable or an arbitrary constant appearing in a mathematical expression, each value of which restricts or determines the specific form of the expression." At least, so my *American Heritage Dictionary* tells me.

And I like that tighter, that seemingly more restrictive but actually more open, much more usable way of thinking about the topic we are discussing at this colloquium. If we think of a type of quadratic equation, where the unknowns are partly known, "on the shore dimly seen," and then one in which the results are clearly conjectural, then we do get a better picture of the nebulous outlines of the domain of intellectual freedom than we might with such a word as "boundaries" or "limits."

But enough of logomachy; what is important is what is within, rather than without. In thinking about intellectual freedom, it is important to be sure that all of those thinking about it mean the same thing. Don't confound the term with academic freedom, a much more restrictive and, these days, somewhat embroiled term. Intellectual freedom, very simply defined, is just that: the freedom of the mind, not the freedom of the librarian to do or say or write something. It is certainly *not*, as I have heard it described, the librarian's version of academic freedom.

We who work in the academic library must, of course, have the same comparable rights and privileges as our fellow academicians in the classroom, and *academic* freedom—the right to freedom in research and in the publication of results of that research, the right to freedom of discussion in the classroom in dealing with subjects on which the teacher had acknowledged expertise, and the same rights to speak or write off campus as any other American citizen—is of course our right, too. But we librarians have a particular interest in a broader area than freedoms of speech and press, best subsumed under the rubric of *intellectual* freedom. Like all freedoms, this is not a right to be considered lightly. With rights come obligations, responsibilities, and duties.

When that grand old man of Pacific Northwest academic librarianship, William Hugh Carlson, delivered his dictum on intellectual freedom (and he was writing just after the news of the assassination of John F. Kennedy had reached his ears), he said, speaking of extremist hate-writings, that "we . . . can only hope that the wise, good, and strong words . . . will literally drown out the evil words. This is the only effective antidote for the national 'cancer of the psyche'. . . ."[1] You will note that Carlson recognizes the primary obligation of the intellectually free, which is not only to believe in, but to *practice* intellectual freedom. As Carlson says, ". . . all librarians are a part of and party to this never ending struggle . . . this eternal warring by and for the human mind. . . ."[2]

Let us return to the more general, less directly library-linked aspects of intellectual freedom. It is a well-known phenomenon in psychology to see what is known as an "ambiguous figure" or "reverse perspective." Many of you have probably seen a well-known drawing of a white vase whose outline is created by two human profiles in solid black. Without any conscious effort the picture will appear to be a white vase—the center of the picture (called the "figure"); or without any more deliberate effort to shift one's view, suddenly the two black profiles, the so-called "ground," are definitely what one is viewing. In seeing one possible picture, the other is excluded, and it never seems possible to see both the "figure" and the "ground" simultaneously.

Look at intellectual freedom how one will, it does seem to have this kind of double or simultaneous set of appearances. Most librarians can only with the utmost difficulty, if at all, see the negative aspects of the operation of intellectual freedom in our civilization. But an audience of members of the John Birch Society or of followers of Herbert Marcuse would almost as certainly see *only* the negative, civilization-destroying aspects of what looks all good to liberals. And, we should be aware, there are increasingly large numbers of intellectuals who consider themselves "moderates" or neoconservatives who, like the New Left and the Old Right, find censorship a positive good, and intellectual freedom, as usually defined, a very dangerous concept indeed.

Probably today's outstanding spokesman for this neoconservative point of view is Professor Robert Nisbet, holder of the prestigious Albert Schweitzer Chair in the Humanities at Columbia University. As a sociologist and historian of social thought, his views have considerable impact on American intellectual freedom. What does he say about it? Like a modern male Cassandra, he claims, in his 1975 volume, *Twilight of Authority*, that "what we are . . . witnessing . . . is rising opposition to the central values of the political community as we have known them for the better part of the past two centuries: freedom, rights, due process, privacy, and welfare."[3] He thinks this is good, because, to quote him again, "The proliferation of civil rights in the areas of speech, press, theatre, and the arts generally is attended by license and anarchy, in the judgement of many, rather than the hoped-for liberation of the creative mind and the sense of intellectual buoyancy that liberty carries with it." Leaving aside for your consideration these obvious contradictions between a call for liberation at the same time that anarchy and license are decried, note particularly that Nisbet—and others of his ilk—are preoccupied with the form rather than the content of liberty or freedom or intellectual freedom. As one might expect, he cites Edmund Burke as his prime authority, that same Burke who once said, "Men are qualified for civil liberty in exact proportion to their disposition to put moral chains upon their own appetites." This is rather obviously antithetical to every belief held by men who *really* consider themselves free. This talk of chains— even "moral" ones—smacks very much of the Inquisition and John Calvin.

And, of course, Nisbet and his fellow true believers can see no usufructs from intellectual freedom other than moral degradation —the disaster-laden, sin-packed, civilization-threatening results of letting people think and write and view and speak for themselves. This goes back a long way in history, perhaps best expressed by Dante in the well-known line from the *Paradiso, "E'n la sua volontade é nostra pace,"*[4] that is to say, "In His will is our peace."

This was certainly quite satisfactory for the thirteenth and fourteenth centuries; a long line of dissenters have in great measure
altered modern man's views of life and living from that level. John
Locke and John Milton and de Tocqueville and John Stuart Mill
and Thomas Jefferson and a great many others of that sort have
not, I hope, lived and written in vain!

But wherever did all of this begin? Surely intellectual freedom
has flourished somewhere, sometime, and proven its value, or we
wouldn't be talking about it today. And, of course, it has—and
most significantly in the almost unique environs of Athens, Greece,
in the Age of Pericles, well over two millennia ago. This was the first
time in history when liberty and equality were given full political
status.

There is no way of discussing intellectual freedom in ancient
Greece without facing up to the fact that a very great proportion of
the residents of Athens were not citizens but slaves; most authorities
estimate that nearly 50 percent of the 225,000 residents of that city
in the fifth century B.C. were actually slaves and had none of the
rights of which we now boast. To look at it another way, however,
many thousands of people, for the first time in history, *did* have a
chance to say their say in Periclean Greece. When Aristophanes felt
like satirizing the politicos of his time, even the religion of his time,
he somehow *did* get away with it. He wasn't immediately punished,
although he certainly suffered some personal difficulties. But does
the course of true creativeness ever run smooth?

There are, it is generally accepted, three types of freedom: the
freedom which a national state has from being dominated by other
states, the liberty of any citizen of a state *as* a political citizen, and,
perhaps most important to most persons, the actual independence
of the individual, under which certainly must be highlighted the
freedom of the artist and/or politician to express himself. In discussing Periclean Greece Ehrenberger distinguishes between political and individual freedom, freedom *within* the state, and freedom
from the state![5] Certainly, as indicated earlier, Athenian liberty
was based on the freedom of the Athenian citizen to think, speak,
to discuss whatever he wanted to, *as* he wanted to.

The importance of what happened in the free part of Greece is,
to some extent, made evident by the contrast with what happened

in that portion which did *not* have *political* freedom, even for its non-slave citizens—Sparta. As Ehrenberger says, "The fact that there can be no true freedom in an authoritarian state was proved by Sparta and is confirmed by modern instances."[6] Whether democracy can really exist without intellectual freedom is very doubtful indeed. A free society must include free minds, for, by every historical and logical evidence we know, without the freedom to think, to speak, to dissent, there can be no truly free social community. The freedom of the individual is concomitant with the freedom of the society.

In all of our societies today, democratic or otherwise, there is clearly a trend to what has been most commonly generalized as the "welfare state." Big Daddy watches out for us all, and, as Ehrenberger says, ". . . The omnipotence of the state, even though clad in the trappings of democracy, seems to be fully established. It is therefore all the more important that the freedom of the individual should preserve that proud power to have for the sake of truth, against the state and its all too human representatives, its thundering *J'accuse.*"[7]

The librarian has various roles to play in dealing with intellectual freedom. He or she (and I shall conserve time and energy by referring to "he," meaning both sexes, from now on) must, obviously, be a staunch defender of intellectual freedom. He must go beyond the perhaps comparatively passive posture of simply defending it, but most actively promulgate it. In the process of so doing, he should be able to clearly define what is meant by intellectual freedom and also who its opponents are, whether they are simply ideological or active. First, it is obviously not enough in this regard simply to be an *opponent* of the opponents of intellectual freedom —that is to say, in general, the censors. The librarian must also be a supporter of its friends. This last is perhaps the most difficult role of all.

When your library is under attack, self-preservation, if nothing else, will normally force you into being a defender of the intellectual freedom of your institution. But when it is *not* your institution that is directly involved—indeed, when your institution is not even indirectly involved—how likely are you to put your neck out to call to the attention of the censor that you are actively his enemy for sure? It is the librarian who is willing to take that extra step, to commit himself to that risk, who is perhaps the only one who can really say he is a true exponent of intellectual freedom.

Putting it another way, those cases which affect political freedom—the instance of the individual or the board member or the group who wishes to eliminate all books on, say, communism or in favor of abortion, or anything along these general lines of doctrines involved in the political, social, and economic affairs of our country and other countries—will not be very hard to justify, whether to yourself or to others. But it is the defense of the obviously trivial, even, by most considerations, the *worthless* under any reasonable standards of taste—*that* is the book or periodical that takes a lot of courage to defend.

When the Freedom to Read Foundation a few years ago agreed to put its money where its mouth is and donate $500 to the legal expenses of Harry Reems, it was *really* being a "Freedom to Read" foundation, perhaps more so than ever in its past. If you are not already aware of it, Mr. Reems is known world-wide as the individual who was the "hero" of such diverse and yet similar motion picture films as *Deep Throat* and *The Devil in Miss Jones*. Mr. Reems, in fact, played the character of the Devil in the latter film.

His problem was that he was picked as a test case by the District Attorney in Memphis, Tennessee, and, sad to relate, the federal case was won by the prosecutor. Mr. Reems's case was put on appeal, and the legal fees for appeal were more even than those in the original jurisdiction. What the Freedom to Read Foundation was doing in getting involved in this case was to assert that the term "Freedom to Read" is actually a rubric under which we are covering *all* of man's right to say, read, speak, publish, show on film and filmstrip, or by any other medium what he wants to, without interference by government. Mr. Reems was singled out, despite the fact that he had no money invested in the firm which produces the films and was paid only a more or less nominal fee for his work. Yet he was the one under indictment. The chilling effect of this kind of endeavor, if Reems—or someone like him—finally is found guilty under a Supreme Court decision (and it is very likely it will ultimately come to that), will be extreme. Obviously, it can affect the librarian whose library is the site of the showing of a particular film as much as it can affect the actors in the film. To put it on a rather different level, it is as if the Nuremburg cases were trials of the *rank and file* involved in the crimes against mankind which were committed during the Hitler years. So the Anglo-American system of legal jurisprudence does not carry things to the extreme; there is a so-called law of agency which has its limits. In the Memphis case and others like it, one sees attempts by the government to see how far they can go. It is up to us as librarians to do everything we can to say, "Hold! Stop! You've reached your limit!"

Here is another event which is pertinent to this discussion. On August 30, 1976, the United States Court of Appeals for the Sixth Circuit (the Middle West) ruled, in the case of *Minarcini et al.* v. *Strongsville City School District*, that no school board can act as a censor board. In fact, the decision said some rather vital things that have not previously, to my knowledge, appeared in any court decisions on a federal level. Here are some examples:

... It would be consistent with the First Amendment (although not required by it) for every library in America to contain enough books so that every citizen in the community could find at least some which he or she regarded as objectionable in either subject matter, expression, or idea. [p. 9, ftn. 1]
... A library is a mighty resource in the free marketplace of ideas. ... It is specially dedicated to broad dissemination of ideas. It is a forum for silent speech. [p. 10]

The *New York Times* said of this decision that it ". . . should place school boards [and, may I add, library boards of all types] in every section of the country on notice that it is not their function or right to remove books from school library shelves which, for some reason, displease them."[8] And every adherent of the freedom to read should rejoice at this latest addition to the comparatively sparse legal defenses librarians have in recent judicial decisions.

What *is* the appropriate role of the librarian vis-á-vis intellectual freedom? Is he or she a defender, a promulgator, a clarifier, an aggressive opponent of its foes or strong supporter of its friends? Is the librarian to seek out occasions to demonstrate his championship of the cause, to sound a clarion call for the freedoms of expression and communication and viewing and listening and reading? Is he to be a Don Quixote, flailing away at windmills, or a Sir Galahad vaunting his purity of liberal thought on these matters, or a Joan of Arc, prepared to be a willing sacrifice in the cause of freedom?

Any of these roles and activities sounds like a lifetime task, and no one librarian can even pretend to assume (or, preferably, even *want* to assume) all of these various guises. But somewhere, sometime, in each of our careers, we *must* come down from our ivory towers, out from behind the rows of stacks, perhaps blinking and befuddled by the shining light of immediacy, but ready to "fight the unbeatable foe." And we can have no better fighting equipment than a thorough knowledge of the history and the reasons for the defense of the freedom of the mind, and equally full knowledge of the dark purposes and deleterious activities which make up the history of censorship through the ages.

I am well aware that intellectual freedom is an ideal. I might even go so far as to say that complete intellectual freedom is an *impossible* ideal. Let me make this concrete by instancing the librarian who uses his position to make "his" library (perhaps better described as the taxpayer's library!) contain those books favoring only his own personal predilections and opinions. Should a librarian remove all the books in the library he administers that use "chairman" instead of "chairperson," or remove one of Joseph Conrad's novels because it was so prejudicially entitled *The Nigger of the "Narcissus"?* The tendency of librarians to get on bandwagons these days is very well known to all, I am sure. Rather than fall for the latest panacea, I think we need to help those publishers who are beginning to feel the chilling effect of the propagandists who want books to be published which only carry their own viewpoints, particularly on such difficult matters as ethnic and so-called sexist matters.

George Santayana once described a fanatic as one who redoubles his efforts after he has forgotten his aims. I hope this and all future generations of librarians will never be even thought of as fanatics on intellectual freedom; perhaps the Santayana statement should be revised to something like this: A believer in intellectual freedom is one who redoubles his efforts, always *remembering* his aims.

These aims are, to be once more rhetorical about it, high and holy ones. They are an integral part of a long and honorable Anglo-

American, even classical, tradition which librarians, of all workers in the vineyards of the intellect, are most uniquely obligated and qualified to preserve and capable of preserving. I never have been quite sure whether "love conquers all," but I have also never had a single moment's doubt that "The Truth is mighty and shall prevail." Or perhaps even better, as George Washington rewrote this statement, in his book of maxims, "Truth will ultimately prevail where there is pains taken to bring it to light"!

NOTES

1. William Hugh Carlson, *In a Good and Awful Time: Essays from the Librarian's Desk on Twentieth Century Man and His Books* (Corvallis: Oregon State University Press, 1967), p. 67.

2. *Ibid.*, p. 66.

3. Robert Nisbet, *Twilight of Authority* (New York: Oxford University Press, 1975), p. 5.

4. Dante Aligheri. *The Divine Comedy*; *Paradiso*; *Canto III* (Princeton, N.J.: Princeton University Press, 1975), pp. 32-33.

5. Victor Ehrenberger. *Man, State, and Deity: Essays in Ancient History* (New York: Harper & Row, 1974), pp. 24-25.

6. *Ibid.*, p. 31.

7. *Ibid.*, p. 32.

8. "No Midnight Librarians," *New York Times*, September 2, 1976.

Public relations and fighting censorship

6 ―――――――――――――――――――――――――

(The sad truth is that the free exercise of intellectual freedom is not usually a reward which comes to the complaisant librarian who doesn't work for it. This chapter includes two views of the problem, with suggested practical solutions. None of them will work, of course, in every instance, but they should help in most situations, assuming that preventative, rather than remedial, measures are the best way to deal with threatened dangers.)

PUBLIC RELATIONS AND INTELLECTUAL FREEDOM

At first blush, the title of this paper may seem either ridiculous or obvious. If any self-respecting librarian who believes in and practices (as well as talking and attending meetings and conferences about) intellectual freedom *doesn't* have good public relations, that librarian most certainly doesn't have the opportunity to use intellectual freedom either. And the intimate, synergistic relationship between public relations and intellectual freedom *should* be so obvious that it is hardly worth discussing.

Or *is* it so obvious? Do librarians have at least *part* of their library's public relation programs (and I'm presuming each of you has one in your library, acknowledged and labelled so, or at least, operating *pro forma*) devoted to making clear to the staff and patrons and administration and board and fund providers and anyone else where your library stands on intellectual freedom? Or is posting the Library Bill of Rights on the door of your locked case sufficient?

But public relations for intellectual freedom is more—*much* more—than even *telling* your patrons your intellectual freedom ideals and ideas. It is, really, what any kind of public relations is: "the planned effort to influence opinion through acceptable performance and two-way communication."[1] This definition, as written by Scott Cutlip and Allen Carter some years ago, seems to me to sum up in precise language exactly what we librarians who believe in intellectual freedom must do to convince our patrons, our bosses, and our friends of the importance, the vital necessity, of our libraries being more than mere repositories of what will be tolerated.

Note the elements of the Cutlip-Carter definition. There must be *effort.* It must be *planned.* It must try to *influence* opinion. Its techniques involve *both* ". . . acceptable performance and two-way communication." And it is the *performance* that so often is forgotten by all of us at various times.

The Freedom to Read statement and the Library Bill of Rights both have very definite public relations implications; indeed they both call for what are unquestionably public relations activities by librarians and library trustees. For example, the Freedom to Read statement says, "It is the responsibility of publishers and librarians, as guardians of the people's freedom to read, to combat encroachments upon that freedom by individuals or groups seeking to impose their own standards or tastes upon the community at large." Obviously this refers to *performance,* to *being* something, not to just lip-service. And although no one likes to go out of his or her way to risk a job or a good annual budget or even public disfavor, it is exactly when the extra-legal censors are in question—whether in the local newspaper or TV or radio station or even the local "porno" shop—that the librarian needs to be heard. If we say we are for the Freedom to Read, we must also be for the clarifying sentence that appears with it, to the effect that "freedom is no freedom if it is accorded only to the accepted and the inoffensive." So—speak up or shut up! You can't expect the communications community in your community or state to back you when you need help, if you hide in your ivory tower when one of them needs help. Remember that the definition of public relations refers to *two*-way communication.

The Library Bill of Rights also has its public relations clauses. It says, quite explicitly, "censorship should be challenged by librarians," and "librarians should cooperate with all persons and groups censored concerned with resisting abridgment of free expression and free access to ideas." In other words, the librarian who advocates the freedom to read cannot wait for a censorship problem to hit his or her library before doing something about censorship. By word and deed, by precept and example, the self-respecting, liberty-loving librarian must fight the censor—not only when the comfortable refuge of a supportive board of trustees or school board or academic administration is there, but in the hurly-burly of *another* man's fight.

There really *is* no censorship fight that is someone else's. If you have done your basic day-to-day public relations job well by establishing your place in your community—whether that community is the public or school or academic library's community—you will be listened to; your voice will count. And, just from pure self-interest, it might pay off in the long run.

Actually, it is the library that is responsible for what is (or is not) accomplished by the individual librarian seeking to influence opinion on intellectual freedom. The library, as I'm sure you're aware, is not what *you* say it is, or what published *literature* about it says it is; your library is what its *patrons* say it is. If your patrons see it as a place which features "silence" signs and fingertips at the lips of all its staff, "shushing" its users and somehow trying to convert itself into a modern-day museum, then, in essence, that's what the library really *is*. If the library features books and non-book-materials on every possible phase of human life, controversial or not, and its staff works at creating an easy, friendly, quieted-but-not-silenced atmosphere, then, there's a fair chance that's the way the general public (whatever *that* is!) will see it.

Some years ago a perceptive pamphlet,[2] written by Miriam McNally, stated that library public relations included: (1) the library's resources and their organization (the sum total of the library's image to some); (2) the way a library cooperates with other libraries to meet its community's needs; (3) the role that reading and books play—or should play—in citizen life, in the way of "... diffusion of information, education, culture, personal enrichment, and sense of social values . . ."[3]; (4) local library activities, such as programs, exhibits, or displays; (5) how the library is supported financially and what its patrons know about such support, and finally, (6) the place of the library considered in relation to librarianship in American life.

And Mrs. McNally concludes that all of this multiple-aspected view of a library is focused "in the example of how a local librarian, and local trustees, both envision and perform their jobs."

And this brings us back to the prime requirement of good public relations for the librarian trying to promote intellectual freedom and the freedom to read. No spoken shibboleths, no well-framed statements, no image without substance back of it is going to convince your patrons either of the high importance of intellectual freedom or of your devotion to that ideal as much as your own willingness to go out on the proverbial limb for it. If it's *really* that important, it's *really* worth the risk you take and the concern you show.

In this connection, let me tell you a little story that comes out of a trip I took a few weeks ago to another state library association's intellectual freedom workshop. One of the speakers on a panel there, the head of a public library in one of that state's larger cities, told us, most frankly, of the choice he had made in a dilemma involving the freedom to read. When he was asked to speak on a local TV program, after a city-wide issue had arisen concerning reputed pornography being sold in a local bookstore, he refused to participate, he told us, rather than jeopardize his next year's library budget, which was coming up about that time for city council discussion. Much comment came from the audience—"pro" and "con"—after his recital; I made just one statement, or rather I asked a question: "What is a man profited, if he should gain the whole world, and lose his own soul?"

I'm sure some of you here—as at that other workshop—will feel this was an uncalled-for or at least exaggerated reaction. But that *is* the way I felt and still feel about it, and I hope the way most (if not all) librarians will feel about it. It's very easy to avoid and side-step and shilly-shally; it's very hard finally to face up to a library crisis; if and when one comes, if one has followed a lifetime pattern of avoidance and equivocation. The hesitation waltz—one step forward and two steps back—may be fine for a ballroom, but it's deadly for achieving any favorable results in the real world where libraries must, necessarily, co-exist.

Now, after these sundry exhortations on how to behave in general as freedom-loving librarians, let me suggest a few very specific, hopefully practical, and direct ways to help get the kind of intellectual climate all of us would like to have in our respective communities *before* an intellectual freedom or censorship crisis actually arises.

One obvious way to help toward this goal is to be on good terms with your campus or school or town newspaper, and whatever other mass media are available and likely to cooperate. One of the best ways to do this is to carry out the *non*-freedom-to-read-centered portion of your library public relations program in full cooperation with the media. Keep your town paper's editor or library news reporter fully aware of the more or less routine matters which come up about your library; then, when you have a real newsy piece of news about attempted censorship, the lines of communication are already open and available to you—whether in print or on the air.

In line with this, take full advantage of appropriate national or state news which deals with the freedom to read, and express your local feelings about it so that it makes a good story with *local* interest. For example, when on September 30 the Association of American Publishers announced that it endorsed the major recommendations of the 1970 Commission on Obscenity and Pornography, calling for the repeal of all federal, state, and local legislation that prohibits the sale, exhibition, or distribution of sexually explicit materials to consenting adults, did you, *the* authority on the freedom to read in your community, have anything to say—publicly, that is—on their recommendations? Indeed, were you even aware of *the fact* of the AAP's new policy?

This brings up a facet of the public relations dilemma which is often either overlooked or at least not mentioned. Do you make a *real* effort to keep in touch with what's going on in relation to the freedom to read? A very high proportion of the news on this front comes quite neatly packaged in each issue of the bimonthly *ALA Newsletter on Intellectual Freedom*, along with an almost complete and quite up-to-date bibliography of current writings on intellectual freedom. Keep up with this one publication, and you'll probably be better informed on the never-ending battle for the freedom to read than the vast majority of even your own professional colleagues.

Also, I would hope that you note discussions of freedom to read matters in such publications as *Library Journal, Wilson Library Bulletin, American Libraries*, the *PNLA Quarterly*, and your state's library bulletin. Or, even better, get involved yourself. The last word on any phase or feature of intellectual freedom is far from being spoken or written. If you have, based on your personal experience or research, something new and constructive and pertinent to contribute to the continuing dialogue on these important matters, don't hesitate to do so. A good part of public relations is certainly involved in saying your say when you do have something worthwhile to contribute.

During World War II a well-known publisher and writer of the day, Ralph Ingersoll, wrote a best-selling book entitled *The Battle Is the Pay-Off*. And, I suppose, despite its sanguinary implications, that is the *key* to public relations. It is the *battle*, the *encounter* that will tell you whether your efforts at public relations have *really* paid off.

Whether you deliver a dozen impassioned speeches on TV and radio and before public forums, or write a model jeremiad on the subject of censorship for your widely-read local newspaper, or present a really stunning display on the deleterious effects of book-banning, you still have to be able to deal with the actual censorship situation when and if it develops. And then, certainly, *The Battle Is the Pay-Off*.

Another way to look at the relationship of public relations and intellectual freedom is by using as a background a pamphlet I found in our library's file entitled *Your Image is Showing: A Manual for Personal Public Relations.*[4] Actually, it was not intended for use by librarians, but let me hold in abeyance the revelation of the particular profession or calling for which it *was* written.

This "manual" gives seven slogans or mottoes which the writer says will result in a better image for an individual; this just might help you in your quest for a better library image. Here are the suggestions in this "manual":

1. Determine Your Public Relations Goal.
2. Classify Your Publics.
3. Put Your Best Foot Forward.
4. Practice Good Citizenship.
5. Sharpen Your Communications Skills.
6. Keep in Touch.
7. Sound Off!

Now that you've heard them, when I tell you that these rules and the manual from which they are quoted was intended for life insurance salesmen, I'm sure at least some of you won't be surprised. The pertinacity and personal magnetism of the typical "insurance man" are well known to all of us. But why shouldn't the librarian break his more or less "Casper Milquetoast" image and be just as assertive and charismatic?

We are dealing—in discussing intellectual freedom—with the bread and butter of librarianship, or, to change the figure, its life blood. If we can't sell the importance of intellectual freedom for all at *least* as well as the life insurance salesman sells his policies, we *deserve* to be forgotten, neglected, overlooked, and stepped on.

If public relations is really "the planned effort to influence opinion through acceptable performance and two-way communication," then the public relations of intellectual freedom must include *all* of these elements to be successful. Plan and make an effort to influence opinion your way, perform acceptably, and be sure there's communication of your point-of-view to your publics, and that you *hear* what they have to say on the topic.

It's a never-ending problem and, at best, there's always going to be only a partical solution to it. The censor will never give in permanently and completely. You might not achieve all you want to achieve if you follow along some of the paths I have set for you today, but, to quote my favorite philosopher on really significant matters, Jerry Lewis, "It wouldn't hoit!"

NOTES

1. Scott M. Cutlip and Allen H. Carter. *Effective Public Relations* (Englewood Cliffs, N.J.: Prentice-Hall, 1964, Third edition), p. 3.
2. *The Library Image: a Manual of Library Interpretation* (Helena, Montana: Montana State Library Extension Commission, 1960).
3. *Ibid.*, p. 15.
4. John Thompson. *Your Image is Showing: a Manual for Personal Public Relations* (Indianapolis, Indiana: The Research & Review Service of America, 1948).

THE PURPOSE OF A LIBRARIAN

The title for this talk seems almost too simple for discussion. We *all*, of course, know *exactly* what a librarian's for. A librarian's purpose is to administer or work in a library; what could be more obvious?

But let's consider the question a little more philosophically—in the sense, that is, of wanting to know "why" as well as "how." Instead of *what* is a librarian, let's ask: *why* is a librarian? A librarian is to guard books; a librarian is to decide for the library's patrons which books they should read; a librarian is to look into his or her own prejudices, mind-set, *gestalt*—you name it—and then run the library to suit those predispositions.

Well—perhaps I have gone too far. Let's try again. A librarian, then, is the one who acts for society in allocating provided financial and personnel resources and building space to provide society with the heritage of wisdom accumulated through all our yesterdays. There, that sounds better. But who tells the librarian what *is* the proper way to "act for society"? The librarian's superiors, of course . . . his or her supervisors, managers, executives—ultimately, the school board or city council or board of regents, depending on which type of library we are discussing. And who tells the superiors? The voters or the appointing authority. Who tells the voters?

Maybe that's the place to start. The purpose of a librarian is to please the voters or other top authority. The more a librarian pleases his or her ultimate bosses, the better is the librarian. What could be a more accurate guide to a librarian's quality, his or her exemplification of high professional standing, than how the librarian fulfills that God-given purpose . . .

Now, now, let's wait a minute. I've *never* heard of a lawyer who said his purpose was to do anything but win a case for his client, or a doctor who ever said he or she had anything to brag about except saving a patient's life or recovering his or her full health. If we presume a librarian is a professional, then his or her analogous purpose must be to serve his or her patron . . . *not* his or her boss.

Let's go with that awhile.

May I here interject a couple of authorities on the subject? A leading nineteenth-century librarian, Fredrich Adolph Ebert, wrote a classic study in 1820, entitled *The Training of the Librarian.*[1] In considering the librarian as book-selector, Ebert said something that seems very apropos to the question of defining the librarian's purpose. Ebert said, "He must, while not oblivious to the phenomena of his time, never incline to servile one-sidedness nor obscure his judgment by yielding to tendencies and prejudices which are local and contemporary." Ebert said further that the librarian who followed this rule would certainly be classed as one "who desires to work for posterity . . . (and stand above his contemporaries)."

José Ortega y Gasset, Spain's leading twentieth-century philosopher, told an International Congress of Bibliographers and Librarians, assembled in Paris in 1934, that the mission of the librarian is to be what he called the ". . . master of the raging book."[2] Without going into all the nuances and philosophical considerations of Ortega y Gasset's remarkable essay, let me briefly explain what he meant by that challenging phrase. To be "the master of the raging book," according to Ortega y Gasset, is to look at the book as what he calls a "living function" of society. He decries the "torrential abundance" of books as likely, without proper organization, bibliographical control, selection, to hurt, rather than to help, readers. He also points out the paradoxical fact that at the same time there is an excess of books, there are also not *enough* books—that is, books which the author describes as filling "lacunae in previous research." Finally, Ortega y Gasset redefines the mission of the librarian of the future as follows: "Imagine the librarian of the future as a filter interposed between man and the torment of books."

Which is the librarian, then? What Ebert over a century ago described as an unprejudiced individual who works for posterity, what Ortega y Gasset termed "the master of the raging book," or, perhaps, something else again? The librarian is only human, all-too-human; he or she can no more be a paragon of all the virtues than should he or she become the rather machine-like automaton which our current slavish subservience to OCLC-DIALOG-BALLOTS-and-Company would make him or her.

The librarian's purpose, as I see it, today and always, is basically to do everything possible to ensure a free flow of information and recreation and even enlightenment to his or her library's users. The librarian, in short, is an opener of blocked pathways in the maze of knowledge, a blazer of trails in the encompassing dark forest of ignorance, a leader in keeping the human mind free.

Up until now I have been talking about theory, not practice. Let me be more specific now, and talk about *solutions* to these problems as I see them. There is never a permanent solution to the always-ready censor; we would be kidding ourselves if we thought there was. However, there are some things that people who are concerned with this particular civil liberty can do.

In the first place, they must realize that there is nothing wrong with people criticizing what is in the library, whether it is a public library or school library or whatever. Under the First Amendment, of course, people have the right to criticize. But they ought to meet at least two criteria in criticizing. In the first place, they should have respect for fundamental liberties, both in the kind of education that they look for and the kind of library they want and in the methods that are used to try to bring about this kind of education or this kind of library. Secondly, there should always be adherence to procedures which have already been established which are calculated to safeguard teachers, administrators, librarians, and public schools and library boards from what usually turns out to be most arbitrary interference. Any attempts to influence what people read and what students are taught are only legitimate if the ways of doing this are calculated to protect the liberties of all concerned and not to interfere with the basic professional responsibilities of teachers, librarians, and duly constituted boards and staffs.

Again, let me say that there is no question that our system is always in need of constant criticism and evaluation, but librarians have a primary responsibility, which is to carry on their work, free from the meddler, the dictator. That right must and should be respected. Or, putting it another way, professional procedure is the right of professionals to determine. Once that is given up then you might as well forget about calling yourselves professionals. If the fundamental basis of free discussion is undermined or when methods that try to shut off free discussion are used, so that if you want to defend a book, you are told you can't do it, then clearly that is about as un-American as you can get.

Very commonly, the criticism of the schools comes from ultra-conservative sources, which claim that they want fundamental Americanism and that only *their* books can produce the philosophy they want. Such criticisms come in all sorts of guises, and usually, to give them credit, are very well-intentioned. We must always remember, however, that, as Samuel Johnson said in his dictionary when he defined the word "Patriotism," "Patriotism is the last refuge of a scoundrel." It *has* been known for people to wrap themselves in the flag for their own advantage. I will simply mention the name of Richard Nixon and let it rest there.

The extremists on both sides of the American spectrum of political thought have tried to make sure the books and periodicals that they want are *in* libraries and the books they don't want are *out* of libraries. It is just as bad on the Communist side, on the Ultra-Left, as it is on the Ultra-Conservative, the at least proto-Fascist. Somewhere in the middle most of us reside. To attack a book as helping promulgate Communism, as I have heard, because it is an autobiography of a well-known Communist, seems pretty ridiculous to me. And to say that Americans should not read such books is even more ridiculous. How can you defeat your enemy if you don't know what he is saying?

The complaints we have all heard that a book is obscene and undermines sexual morality simply because the book goes beyond the standards that the censorious individuals had when they were 40 years younger seem rather naive. What we see and hear these days in all the media, indeed what is actually going on in our contemporary society, is, of course, not what the 1940s approved.

Some people have said that librarians had better be sure that they are dealing with American authors, to avoid getting un-American sentiments into people's minds. Surely, no matter how chauvinistic and ultra-patriotic we may be, we have to admit that there *are* a few authors from Europe and Asia and elsewhere who have written a few things which deserve reading in American classrooms or in an American library.

Well, let me try to be very specific on the "how to fight censorship" matter. The suggestions to follow are based on some recommendations made by the American Civil Liberties Union some years ago. In the first place, when there is a censorious attack on a school or library or individuals connected with them which is really serious, then start with organizing a citizens' committee. Get together five or six representative community leaders, to make sure that all sides have a chance to be fairly heard and that the democratic rights of teachers, librarian, and the community as a whole are respected. Second, ask for public hearings by the local board of education or the local library board, at which all sides that want to be heard may be heard. Sometimes a special general public meeting may be desirable, and then whichever board is involved should certainly be included. Third, make sure the time and place and purpose of these meetings is publicized well in advance, and that there is an announced order of business, and, very important, make sure that minutes are kept of these meetings and are available for examination. Fourth, ask the accusers for specifically stated charges, in writing, with proof. It isn't enough to say, "I don't like this book," or "I don't think my child should read it," or something of that sort. Fifth, guard against over-long meetings, for the obvious reason that, as we all know, decisions may be taken by small groups after everybody else is tired out and has long ago left the premises. Sixth, try to obtain as full coverage as possible by the local media . . . radio, television, newspapers . . . and help them to get the facts. Seventh, seek help from your local community—the usual sources in Utah would be people at the nearest college or university (even in Provo!) and the State Education Association, the Utah Library Association Intellectual Freedom Committee, American Civil Liberties Union Affiliates, National Council of Teachers of Social Studies, and the American Library Association, particularly the American Library Association's Office for Intellectual Freedom, which is devoted to dealing with this kind of matter. Finally, get in touch with the State Board of Education and take appeals to it from the local board when it seems proper to do so. Or, get in touch with the State Librarian if it is a public library which is affected.

The best way to deal with complaints about books, periodicals, newspapers, tapes, records, films, or whatever, is that you have a definite book selection policy showing how and why you select books, a policy already available in writing, one which has been approved by your local board. Make this policy known to local media and to community groups . . . repeatedly, if necessary. Secondly, you should establish a clearly defined method for handling complaints. The first thing you have to do is to be sure the complaint is filed in writing and the plaintiff properly identified before the complaint is considered. Anonymous gripers can gripe all they want. Third, as I suggested before, set up a committee of teachers or library personnel to review all complaints, confer with plaintiffs, make appropriate recommendations to administrative authorities. Fourth, if the plaintiff remains adamant and refuses to accept the committee's decision, then take your case to the media and try to get outside-the-library community groups to support you.

As a continuing proposition, there should always be going on a campaign to establish the importance of the freedom to read in a community. I'm sure you all would have a lot of ideas about how to achieve this. One suggestion is as simple as this: Encourage people to read. The more people read, the more likely they are to want the *freedom* to read whatever they want to read. And that starts in the family, rather than in the school or the library itself.

In conclusion, let me suggest that, as the ACLU says, "American schools and libraries, which stand in the Western tradition of the free mind, have a primary obligation not to allow themselves to be turned into propaganda forums. The widest possible range of instruction and reading is the birthright of all Americans, and all have a stake in preserving and extending the opportunities for the development of the inquiring mind. Emotionalism, fanatical one-sidedness and the hysteria of crisis are not conducive to this. . . . The schools and librarians can only fulfill their tasks in an atmosphere which is free from such fear, hysteria, and suspicion."

And, remember that the purpose of a librarian is to *be* a librarian, not to be a timid, pussyfooting, crowd-pleasing, namby-pamby individual who dances to the censor's tune. The librarian, as I quoted Ortega y Gasset earlier as saying, must be the "master of the raging book," *not* its servant.

NOTES

1. Fredrich Adolph Ebert. *The Training of the Librarian* (Woodstock, Vt.: Elm Tree Press, 1916, trans. ed.).

2. José Ortega y Gasset. *The Mission of the Librarian* (Boston: G. K. Hall, 1961), p. 19.

The censorship battle in a conservative state

7

(The past two decades in Idaho have been a microcosm of the same years nationwide so far as fighting censorship is concerned. In university classes, newspaper articles and editorials, Idaho Library Association magazine articles, and ILA conference meetings I have spoken and written to the point where the media in Idaho seems to contact me more or less automatically when any censorship brouhahas come up. This chapter could, I'm sure, be repeated in almost all fifty states; Idaho's chief claim to uniqueness, in this respect, would seem to be that it spawns independent, ultraconservative, obscenity-and-curriculum-baiting groups as frequently and as numerously as its native Snake River salmon.)

IDAHO SCHOOL LIBRARIANS AND SALINGER'S *THE CATCHER IN THE RYE*: A CANDID REPORT

Last summer some 69 Idaho school librarians, active and prospective, attended a workshop at Idaho State University dealing with book selection and attendant problems. At the end of the 10-day workshop a written examination was given, including the following questions: "Your school board of education sends you a written memorandum requiring you to remove all copies of Salinger's *The Catcher in the Rye* from your school library immediately.

What steps do you take concerning this? You are the school librarian, and supposedly in charge of book selection." This article summarizes their replies as probably indicative of general opinion held by the school librarians of Idaho on a matter of importance to all librarians—the censorship of books of unquestioned literary merit.[1]

Only 16 of the 69 said they would remove the book immediately from the shelves of their library, upon the school board's request. Most of these gave as justification, as one woman stated, that "Since I was hired by the school board of education, I would have to do as was asked." Two simply said they would remove the book at once, and then, substantially, leave it at that, without making any particular effort to get it back on the shelf. One said that "I would call it to the attention of my school principal, and then I would remove all copies, disposing of them as the principal suggested. I would put this in writing, with his signature okaying my action." The other, without clarifying the reasons behind her statement, said "In our library I would do as they asked. In others I would read the book, then go before the board and ask for their reasons for this memorandum. As they were given, I would try to justify my choice of the book and how I thought it would fit with the collection as a whole. If they still held to their request, I would remove the book."

Rather unexpectedly, a few among this group of "removers" said they would, in one way or another, see to it that the book did get back on the open shelf. As one of these put it, most candidly, "if the trouble couldn't be settled, if they still insisted, and if I hadn't seen their way of thinking, I would probably have the books on the back shelf for awhile and then quietly put them back on the proper shelf." Another in this group wrote ". . . not wishing to create a huge hassle, I would perhaps place the 'Catcher' away until the heat was off. People soon forget, and sometime the book will not be scorned." Another, even more frankly, said, "Since I am the school librarian and well-read and informed—as most of the board of educators are not—I'd see that the book got back on the shelf." Still another most confidently announced, "I will convince them of my feelings and firmly, but quietly, win my point, to get the book back."

Perhaps the most judicious reply from this group who would immediately remove the book from circulation, upon the board's request, was this one:

"I would comply. The school board is my employer and I am sure this is the politic first step.

However, I would defend my integrity as the person responsible for book selection by presenting evidence that my choice was justified. The book has favorable reviews and many recommendations. It is read widely by teenagers, it is widely available from other sources. It is not pornographic; realistic, but certainly not obscene.

I would ask the Board's reasons for their action. I would enlist the support of the English teachers, provided they are also English *readers*, and of school patrons whose judgment would be respected by board members. I would ask the Board members to read the book for themselves. They might not be able to identify themselves in the book, but with their wide experience with teachers they could recognize Holden's English teacher immediately!

I would hope that after all three procedures, and with closer acquaintance with the book, the board would allow me to return it to the shelves. I believe my school board would. We can usually talk things out."

Of the 69 respondents, 33 would ask to meet with the school board to discuss the board request. Thirty would ask for written statements of complaint, either from the school board or directly from the parent or group who or which had complained to the school board, and eight librarians would ask who had complained.

Assuming there was a written library book selection policy, 22 would use this as their basis for defending retention of *The Catcher in the Rye*. Twelve would bring the local press in (some only as a last resort). Seven would consult the American Library Association for advice, one the Idaho Library Association, and two the Idaho State Board of Education.

Eleven thought that the librarian should read or re-read the book before coming to its defense, and nine would expect one or more members of the school board to have read the book before any meeting between the librarian and the board. Ten would act only through the principal or superintendent, not directly with the board.

In general, the examination answers seem to indicate a laudable courage and strength among Idaho school librarians, even though this was only a hypothetical exercise. Assuming similar action would actually be taken in case of a real censorship attempt, it looks as though Idaho school librarians are pretty well prepared for any possible attacks on the freedom to read.

Perhaps the general attitude of the "typical" (if such there be) Idaho school librarian might best be summarized by quoting one more reply in full. This individual wrote:

"First, I would read the book (I haven't). Then I would go to my principal and superintendent. I would give them my reasons for ordering it. (Right now I can't think of a very good reason for having it in the Blank Junior High School Library.) There are so many more books I can think of that we need more, as we do not have a very adequate library. I must have a good reason, though. I hope it is listed in the aids to book selection.

I would ask for the school board's reasons for wanting it removed from the shelf. If it happened to be poor literary value, and the critics would bear this out, and I, after reading it, felt it was—I'd remove it from the shelf, because I'd not feel it an informational book. If it were censored by the school board because it is unfair to minority groups, or because it was definitely unkind or unjust to religious groups, and I felt they had a point, I'd remove it from the shelf. If it were censored on account of sex, and the junior high students were not old enough to discriminate between good and bad in literature, and it was having a bad influence, I'd remove it.

Now, if none of these were the reasons, I'd have to be convinced before I'd take it off the shelf."

To summarize, Idaho school librarians, if this group is a valid sampling, are neither headline-seeking zealots nor self-effacing, timid librarians; they know how to combat censorship and are prepared to do so, in a professional and constructive and tactful and cooperative way. And the suggestions above offer good advice as to possible procedures for those not previously so informed and so prepared.

NOTE

1. None of those taking the exam knew they would be quoted, and therefore no names of individual librarians or references to particular libraries are included.

IDAHO LIBRARIES AND INTELLECTUAL FREEDOM

Through the years Idaho libraries on all levels—public, school, or academic—have been relatively free from outside interference with the selection of the books they have been buying and circulating. Only a very few cases of censorship have been important enough to reach the public prints of Idaho; only one reference to any attempt to force an Idaho librarian into buying particular books is to be found, in my knowledge, in library literature. A featured article[1] in the *ALA Bulletin* revealed that in September, 1961, the following event occurred in our state:

Typical of the efforts being made to compel public libraries to provide more conservative publications on their shelves and to counteract what some believe are leanings toward liberal and leftist publications is the approach made last September to the city librarian of Boise, Idaho, by a "special committee of the Anti-Communist Study Center" in Boise, concerning the library's book selection policy. A letter from the committee, accompanying a packet of anti-Communist tracts, said, "Charges that the public has been subjected to a measure of (thought control) over a long period of time are giving concern to many people. We believe the enclosed material, if read and analyzed, may help produce some answers, and may be a basis from which you can approach the problem of assuring the public a well-balanced selection in reading material.

This is rather a new departure in pressures on librarians, intended to tell us what to *put in*, as well as to *exclude* from libraries we are charged with supervising. Of course, it is no secret that, in Idaho, as elsewhere, some public libraries have been greatly influenced by itemized recommendations as well as broad policies on book selection from their boards of trustees, that some school librarians have had their recommended book choices affected by what principals or superintendents or school boards tell them, and even that some academic librarians may have found their book or magazine selections decided for them, to a limited extent, by administrators or off-campus pressures. No one says that posting the Library Bill of Rights on a library wall automatically brings with it complete adherence to its principles.

The results of Marjorie Fiske's study[2] of California public and school libraries are not likely to be found inapplicable to Idaho libraries. Undoubtedly we too have our share of timid librarians, who avoid any possibility of controversy about books by the very direct method of just not buying any books—especially fiction— which they have reason to believe might be dubbed "controversial." We too have our share of the ultra-cautious who follow the course of least resistance by treating isolated cases of individual or small group objection as justification for not buying volumes dealing with matters of public concern lest there be any possibility of stirring up community controversy.

This is not said to deprecate unrealistically the very genuine problems all librarians face in this era of swiftly changing mores and morals, of volatile issues which do affect all of us and need judicious consideration. Most of us here can remember when such authors as John O'Hara and James T. Farrell were considered as "sensational"; beside the writers of *Candy* and *Naked Lunch* they look like Frances Hodgson Burnett and Kate Douglas Wiggins, respectively.

How many books do you now have in your library which say that America should turn Communist or Socialist? How many books do you now have in your library which say that the cause of the segregationist is right and just? How many books in your library say that the Viet Cong deserved to control Viet Nam? If you live in North Idaho, what material concerning the question of silver coinage do you have—pro and con? If you live in Central Idaho, what material does your library have on the right wing and left wing of American opinion? If you live in Southeastern Idaho, what material does your library have on the Bonneville Power Administration or on Federal controls for wheat farming or potato growing?

None of these, I assure you, are to be considered as rhetorical questions. Rather, they are to remind you that the Library Bill of Rights, given lip service by most librarians, says, unequivocally, "There should be the fullest practicable provision of material presenting all points of view concerning the problems and issues of our times, international, national, and local." It also says that "censorship of books, urged or practiced by volunteer arbiters of morals or political opinions or by organizations that would establish a coercive concept of Americanism, must be challenged by librarians in maintenance of their responsibilty to provide public information and enlightenment through the printed word."

Because the Idaho Library Association, as a group, has never
found it necessary to do so, the ILA has never had an Intellectual
Freedom Committee. The president of ILA, this year, appointed
me as a sort of one-man Intellectual Freedom Committee for Idaho.
She was aware of my strong interest in such matters, as evidenced
by many publications in library periodicals during the years and
some activity in ALA national conventions on such matters,
intended particularly to insure that ALA as an organization does
not practice segregation.

Representing the Idaho Library Association, I was invited by
Dean Martha Boaz, this year's chairman of the ALA Intellectual
Freedom Committee, to be one of a comparatively small group
(about 60) of librarians, journalists, lawyers, and other interested
individuals from all over the United States to attend a conference
on intellectual freedom held in Washington, D.C. in January of
this year. The two major purposes of this conference were to get the
current issues of intellectual freedom out in the open and discussed
by people of various disciplines and to see, concretely, what the
American Library Association could do, with and for its membership, to help librarians who got into censorship legal trouble or who
were even threatened with loss of their livelihoods over censorship
questions.

We met for two lively full days and one evening, January 23-24,
1965, with sessions alternating between talks by experts on topic
one and group meetings on topic two. Among those who spoke to
us were Dr. Boaz; Archie McNeal, the most recent intellectual freedom chairman and Librarian of the University of Miami; Dan
Lacy, Managing Director of the American Book Publishers
Council; Professor William C. Kvaraceus, Director of Youth
Studies, Tufts University; Dr. Theodore Gill, formerly editor of the
Christian Century and a noted Presbyterian clergyman; and others
equally capable and thought-provoking. The activities of the conference will be recounted in detail in the June, 1965 issue of the
ALA Bulletin, I understand, so I shall not attempt to give more
than its flavor in today's brief report.

To begin with—and most surprisingly, to me—there was not one
voice raised in disagreement with the general tenor of the conference, to the effect that all censorship was bad. I had half hoped that

someone from the Council on Decent Literature or from one of the ultra-rightist groups might be invited, but such was not the case.

Instead, we heard from the lips of a liberal clergyman, a liberal lawyer, a liberal sociologist, and many liberal librarians that we must have "total faith in the free market place of ideas" (to quote from one of the speakers, Wesley McCune, Director of Group Research, an anti-right-wing outfit in Washington, D.C.), Dr. Gill gave us a new definition of obscenity—namely, anything that "has degradation of persons" as its object. He plumped for a "new ethics," in which love is the *only* absolute, and in which sex is no longer, to quote him, "heavy and dark."

Noted Washington anti-censorship lawyer Edward DeGrazia, fresh from his Supreme Court triumph for Henry Miller's books, discussed at length what I referred to earlier, what he called the *worst* kind of censorship—namely, self-censorship by the responsible librarian. He stated unequivocally that "unless librarians overcome *their own* shortcomings on censorship, then legal help against *outside* censorship will be useless."

DeGrazia's most salient point, I thought, was that librarians, and only librarians, can and should decide what books can stand openly displayed on their shelves. He urged librarians—if such there be who lack it—to *develop* the will to defend the freedom of reading. Any professional librarian, he stressed, is better qualified to do this and is more likely to have the will to do this, than "volunteer" book-selectors.

His last vital point was that as the laws of obscenity and pornography now stand interpreted by the Supreme Court of the United States, anything with, to quote the recent decision, "the slightest social importance" is legal. According to DeGrazia, "under present laws, no book selected by a librarian can be constitutionally held obscene." This is because the very *act* of selection by a librarian gives the book social importance, he claimed.

Out of the group discussions came an agreement to ask the ALA to tax every ALA member $2.00 per year to support a $50,000 per year legal office, manned with capable lawyers, able to serve at least in an advisory capacity whenever a librarian is threatened by lawsuits over censorship. DeGrazia had earlier said that the newest drive by constitutional lawyers will be to clarify so-called "in rem" cases, which means *books*, rather than *people*, may be sued in the future. This proposal is in process of discussion by the ALA Executive Board.

Incidentally, another proposal, for a so-called "network" of lawyers willing to serve in censorship cases involving librarians throughout the United States, is still in the working stages, also. I found several prominent lawyers throughout Idaho who have agreed in writing to do so, if and when called upon. Of course, they will still require a fee—and maybe ALA can help in this, too, if the $2.00 tax proposal is approved.

At any rate, I found the conference most fruitful and worthwhile. I believe it will serve as a benchmark from which further progress toward winning the librarian's perpetual battle for intellectual freedom may someday be won. I feel sure, speaking personally, that I must have contributed *something* to the conference, since last month I was asked to serve a 2-year term as one of 11 members of the ALA Intellectual Freedom Committee.

To get back to our mutual direct concern, Idaho libraries and reading in Idaho, we can safely—but certainly not smugly or finally —say that we are blessed with little if any outside censorship problems at the moment. If and when any such come up, I beseech any of you who do get involved to let me know immediately. Just possibly, in both my statewide and national capacities, I might be able to be of assistance to you in what will, at the time, probably look like an impossible dilemma.

The librarian, traditionally, has been a leader in seeing to it that all that is available in print is also as available as possible to his patrons. We librarians in Idaho must maintain and strengthen this proud tradition and fight for the Library Bill of Rights, remembering DeGrazia's sad reminder which points out that all too often the librarian has been his own worst enemy.

Instead of following the three F's of Failure—Fear, Futility, and Frustration—let us uphold the three C's of Conquest—Courage, Choice, and Confidence. Remember, no one can do the job of book-selection so well as the librarian. If he *doesn't* do it, someone else—very likely less capable, less understanding, and certainly much more likely to be less dedicated to the cause of Truth for all— will do it for him!

NOTES

1. Everett T. Moore. "Why Do the Rightists Rage?" *ALA Bulletin* (January, 1962), pp. 26-31.
2. Marjorie Fiske. *Book Selection and Censorship: a Study of School and Public Libraries in California* (Berkeley: Univ. of California Press, 1959).

PORNOGRAPHY IN MODERN AMERICA

Just a few years ago, the only way a curious Pocatellan could see erotic films in the city was at a so-called "stag" movie, in secret, with the viewer usually feeling some trepidation lest the place of viewing be raided by the police and the curious one exposed to public shame, at the very least.

But the times have definitely changed. Regular movie-houses in Pocatello have been showing "R" and "X" rated films (including quite explicit sex scenes and language) for several years. Now Pocatello has attracted a so-called "adult theater"—located in the middle of the city's downtown, to which anyone over 18 may go, if he or she can afford the price charged.

When and how did this change happen? Is Pocatello suddenly likely to become a modern version of Sodom and Gomorrah? Will the rate of sex crimes go up here in direct relation to the popularity of the "adult theater"? What is the legal-historical background of the U.S. pornography problem—if it really is a problem?

There are those who feel that Idaho and the rest of the nation are in real danger if pornography, particularly in film form, is readily available. Last fall Charles H. Keating, Jr., executive director of the Cincinnati, Ohio-based organization, Citizens for Decent Literature, sent out thousands of letters to residents of this state (and of others), calling on them to contribute to the CDL cause because, to quote Keating, ". . . in Idaho Falls, Pocatello, Boise, and other Idaho cities there are theaters that show movies of men and women having sexual intercourse."

In each letter was enclosed a pair of pre-printed postcards, which each agreeing recipient was supposed to send to the Governor and the Attorney General of Idaho. The cards addressed to Governor Andrus said (in part), "I would like for you to crack down hard on the smut peddlers who are flooding our state with pornography. There are laws on the books to stop this filth. Please write to me and tell me what you are doing to halt this flow of obscenity." The pre-printed card addressed to Attorney General Park said (in part): "Please advise me on the efforts your office is making to prosecute the peddlers of obscene movies and books. Police records show that this filth is connected with sex crimes." (On this last statement, see below.) In a letter to the writer of this article in October of 1971 Attorney General Park said (in part): ". . . this office has better and more important things to accomplish than to assume a censor's role. The free speech guarantees in the U.S. Constitution have been jealously protected by the courts, especially where prior restraint of printed material is threatened."

Governor Andrus replied to the several hundred Idahoans who sent him postcards pre-printed in Cincinnati that ". . . I, too, share your concern and want to report to you that smut peddlers are being prosecuted to the fullest extent of the law. As you know, the first duty of the local prosecuting attorney is to enforce the laws of the state. . . ." He went on, ". . . if you know of specific violations you may contact your local prosecuting attorney and swear out a complaint."

Perhaps the best way to get a perspective on this is by way of a brief historical review. The first American law concerned with pornography and obscenity was one put into effect in 1711 in the Colony of Massachusetts. This law said, "Evil communication, wicked, profane, impure, filthy and obscene songs, composures, writings or prints do corrupt the mind and are incentives to all manners of impieties and debaucheries . . ." The law, obviously particularly concerned with protection of the prevailing religious faith of colonial Massachusetts, explicitly prohibited ". . . the composing, writing, printing or publishing of any filthy, obscene, or profane song, pamphlet, libel or mock sermon, in imitation of preaching, or any other part of divine worship." It was 110 years before anyone was prosecuted under this statute: in 1821 the first American publisher of *Fanny Hill* was tried and convicted.

Actually the very first obscenity case to have happened in the U.S. took place in Pennsylvania in 1815. A private showing for profit of a picture of a man and a woman in what was described as an "indecent posture" was ruled to be a common-law (rather than statutory) offense, as a violation of public decency. The first federal obscenity statute (1842) prohibited importing "indecent and obscene prints, paintings, lithographs, engravings, and transparencies." It was just over 100 years ago (1865) that Congress passed the first U.S. law to prohibit sending obscene materials by mail.

Anthony Comstock and his New York Society for the Suppression of Vice became a nationally powerful group with passage of the so-called "Comstock Act" in 1873, a law which barred from the mail "every obscene, lewd, lascivious, or filthy book, pamphlet, picture, paper, letter, writing, print, or other publication of an indecent character." Using this law (which also specifically dealt with the dissemination of information about birth control), Comstock and his successors (such as Boston's John S. Sumner and Cincinnati's Charles Keating) have managed to ban (at least for a while) poetry by Walt Whitman, sculpture and painting by leading American and European artists, and such movies as "The Lovers" and several Ingmar Bergman films.

It was "The Lovers" which resulted in the first real breakthrough for what today are called "X-rated" movies. It is no longer legal to have prior restraint of films; no one can legally stop any film from being shown publicly at least once, no matter what it shows. Back in 1915 the U.S. Supreme Court, in the case of *Mutual Film Corporation* v. *Ohio Industrial Commission*, held that movies were not under the protection of the First Amendment, and were "purely business undertakings offered for profit." But in 1952, in *Burstyn, Inc.* v. *Wilson*, the court held just the opposite opinion, and stated that the film, "The Miracle," could not be banned as sacrilegious because the basic American principles of freedom of speech and of the press DID apply to motion pictures. Then, in 1964, by a 6-3 vote, the Supreme Court ruled that "The Lovers," which included an explicit if brief scene, was not obscene.

Out of this case came the now famous Brennan opinion, which has affected federal, state, and local rulings on obscenity and pornography ever since. Supreme Court Justice Brennan stated that ". . . material dealing with sex in a manner that advocates ideas . . . or that has literary or scientific or artistic value or any other form of social importance, may not be branded as obscenity and denied the constitutional protection. Nor may the constitutional status of the material be made to turn on a 'weighing' of its social importance against its prurient appeal, for a work cannot be proscribed unless it is 'utterly' without social importance." He also said that ". . . the constitutional status of an alleged obscene work must be determined on the basis of a national standard. It is, after all, a national Constitution we are expounding."

This latter statement is probably the single feature of the recent Supreme Court decisions about obscenity and pornography which most bothers those people who feel deep concern about the subject as a local problem. Why, they ask, shouldn't a local community's standards, the standards of Pocatello, Idaho, for example—not those considered "national"—affect what may be shown or sold or read hereabouts? Anti-censorship proponents point out that standards for race relations, for example, would certainly be quite different in Mississippi or Idaho. In many places films or books dealing with various important and presumably controversial social problems such as race relations, drug abuse, homosexuality, or smoking tobacco might be considered contrary to various local standards; should these films or books be censored?

As Federal District Judge Curtis Bok said in 1949, in *Commonwealth* v. *Gordon*, "It is no longer possible that free speech (or press) be guaranteed federally and denied locally. . . . If speech is to be free anywhere, it must be free everywhere. . . . Unless a restriction on free speech be of national validity, it can no longer have any local validity whatever. Some danger to us all must appear before any of us can be muzzled."

Probably it is fear of bad effects which bother most who differ with the justice or the legality or, more likely, the morality of reading and viewing materials which include nudity, explicit language, and/or descriptions or depictions of sex activities. Is it really true that reading or viewing such leads to illegal behavior? Or to immoral behavior (since law and morals are not by any means identical in a non-theocratic society such as the United States)?

There have been numerous studies of this—most recently and authoritatively by the Commission on Obscenity and Pornography (whose 1970 report, based on several years of the most scientific research ever conducted on matters related to obscenity and pornography, was rejected by both President Nixon and the U.S. Senate before either had even read it!). Since the original report appeared, nearly two years ago, nine of the ten technical reports on which the Commission's conclusions were based have been issued. Among other findings which are contrary to the so-called "conventional wisdom" is the following statement (in volume VII, *Erotica and Anti-Social Behavior*): ". . . analyses of United States crime and illegitimacy rates do not support the thesis of a causal connection between the availability of erotica and either sex crimes or illegitimacy."

Anyone interested in the factors and reasoning behind this conclusion (obviously contrary to the claims of the Citizens for Decent Literature and of others who favor censorship) should read pages 311-323 of this book. It is only fair, however, to report that the investigators do say, ". . . because of limitations in the data and in the inferences which can be validly drawn from them, the data cannot, however, be said absolutely to disprove such a connection." But, then, what is "absolute" proof of any human-related activities?

The above discussion has, of course, only hit a few of the high spots of a very complex problem, which will not be resolved in the minds of men or in judicial or legislative councils for a long time to come. The writer's own views were perhaps voiced best by famed Hollywood film director John Huston, who recently said, "Those sexy films are repetitive and dull. And from dullness they will die."

If so-called pornographic films are really boring rather than morally subversive, perhaps they do not justify all the fuss about their present popularity and reputed influence. They may be worth only our passing, minor concern, as a faddish phenomenon of our times.

OBSCENITY AND PORNOGRAPHY: THE LEGAL QUESTION

The Constitution of the State of Idaho, dated 1889 but going into effect on Idaho's admission as a state in 1890, says (Article I, Section 9): "Every person may freely speak, write and publish on all subjects, being responsible for the abuse of that liberty." The first codified laws of the state (Penal Code of the State of Idaho 1901) clarified what "abuse" meant:

Section 4718. Indecent Exposures, Exhibitions, and Pictures: Every person who wilfully and lewdly either:

1. Exposes his person, or the private parts thereof, in any public place, or in any place where there are present other persons to be offended or annoyed thereby; or,

2. Procures, counsels, or assists any person to so expose himself, or to take part in any model artist exhibition, or to make any other exhibition of himself to public view, or to the view of any number of persons, such as is offensive to decency, or is adapted to excite to vicious or lewd thoughts or acts; or,

3. Writes, composes, stereotypes, prints, publishes, sells, distributes, keeps for sale, or exhibits any obscene or indecent writing, paper, or book, or designs, copies, draws, engraves, paints, or otherwise makes any obscene or indecent figure; or,

4. Writes, composes, or publishes any notice or advertisement of any such writing, paper, book, pictures, print, or figure; or,

5. Sings any lewd or obscene song, ballad, or other words, in any public place, or in any place where there are persons present to be annoyed thereby, is guilty of a misdemeanor.

Nothing affected or changed these laws until 1971—a period of 70 years—when the Idaho legislature, as part of a complete revision of the Idaho Penal Code, omitted entirely ALL laws affecting obscenity involving consenting adults. From January 1, 1972 through March 31, 1972 Idaho joined several other states in having NO laws whatsoever in effect regulating "obscenity," "pornography," or "indecency" in print, picture, or film, for adults. When the 1971 Code revision was revived by the 1972 Legislature, the 1901 laws (as detailed above) went back into effect. (Please note that NO fantastic invasion of Idaho by lust-crazed readers or viewers, no numerically noticeable increase in sex crimes was noted by our law enforcers or anyone else during the January-March 1972 "open season" for reading and viewing.)

The 1973 Idaho Legislature passed a highly-detailed, brand-new law in line with model laws as passed in many other states, which included, among other notable provisions, sections which (a) took away from all Idaho cities and counties the power to adopt or enforce ordinances relating to obscenity, (b) excepted employees of schools, colleges, universities, museums, or public libraries or non-owners of motion picture theaters from the act's provisions, and (c) admitted evidence in obscenity cases relating to "contemporary community standards of appeal to prurient interest or of customary limits of candor in the description or representation of nudity, sex, or excretion, or which bears upon the question of redeeming social value. . . ."

Unfortunately for the good intentions of this new law, which brought Idaho state law up-to-date with U.S. Supreme Court decisions from 1957-72, a series of five decisions made by the U.S. Supreme Court on June 21, 1973 invalidated much of the new Idaho law ten days before it went into effect. The June 21 decisions set the following new national standards for obscenity: whether the average person, applying contemporary community standards, would find that the work, taken as a whole, appeals to the prurient interest; whether the work depicts or describes, in a patently offensive way, sexual conduct specifically defined by the applicable state law; and whether the work, taken as a whole, lacks serious literary, artistic, political or scientific value.

Clearly, the 1973 Idaho law, especially in its terminology referring to ". . . utterly without redeeming social value," is not in line with the latest Supreme Court decisions. Also, since even the "clarifying" 1973 decisions are considered by leading constitutional lawyers (including four of the nine Supreme Court justices themselves, in strong dissenting opinions) to be vague, confusing, and contradictory, there are now two significant cases under consideration by the Supreme Court which may well set up new and different rules (cases involving the movie "Carnal Knowledge" and an illustrated edition of the 1970 report of the National Commission on Obscenity and Pornography).

Some of this state's political leaders have stated that the Idaho laws on obscenity can be made to fit the 1973 Supreme Court majority decisions by removing only a single word—"utterly"— from the present law. This really does not seem possible. During 1973-74, 38 state legislatures (of the 44 states in regular legislative session) considered over 150 new or revised obscenity statutes. As of May 1st, 12 states had declared their present state obscenity law constitutional, nine had decided their law unconstitutional; 10 passed revised laws. Among the issues raised in current state obscenity legislation, these seem to be the most prominent: lack of mandatory prior civil proceedings for judicial determination of the obscenity of questioned material; clarification of what "community" standards mean—statewide, county, or what; meaning of the "value" test—especially since religious values were NOT included in the Supreme Court decision; clear definitions of prohibited conduct; and what is meant by "public display"—can minors be prohibited from even entering a bookstore or a library which contains items that MIGHT be questioned or prohibited?

Before the Idaho Legislature in 1975 decides on a viable, modern, constitutional law concerning obscenity as it affects adults, it might be a good idea for it to reflect at some length upon the following statement by Chief Justice Burger, delivered as part of the majority decision given in one of the five June 21, 1973 cases (*Paris Adult Theatre I* v. *Slaton*): "States are told by some that they must await a 'laissez faire' market solution to the obscenity-pornography problem, paradoxically 'by people who have never otherwise had a kind word to say for laissez-faire,' particularly in solving urban, commercial, and environmental population problems. . . ."

"The States, of course, may follow such a 'laissez faire' policy and drop all controls on commercialized obscenity, if that is what they prefer, just as they can ignore consumer protection in the market place, but nothing in the Constitution compels the States to do so with regard to matters falling within state jurisdiction."

"It is asserted, however, that standards for evaluating state commercial regulations are inapposite in the present context, as state regulation of access by consenting adults to obscene material violates the constitutionally protected right to privacy enjoyed by the petitioners' customers" (The adult theater's customers, in this case—ed.).

This is also what the 1970 majority report of the Commission on Obscenity and Pornography recommended, in stating that "federal, state, and local legislation prohibiting the sale, exhibition, or distribution of sexual materials to consenting adults should be repealed." The report said that if all such laws were repealed, then it would be left up to what should always be the determinant in our free society—the individual's conscience—as to what he or she reads or views.

I agree with the dissent by Supreme Court Justice William Douglas in one of the June 21 cases (*U.S.* v. *12 200-Ft. Reels of Film*):

Most of the items that come this way denounced as "obscene" are in my view trash. I would find few, if any, that had by my standards any redeeming social value. But what may be trash to me may be prized by others. Moreover, by what right under the Constitution do five of us have to impose our set of values on the literature of the day? There is danger in that course, the danger of bending the popular mind to new norms of conformity. There is, of course, also danger in tolerance, for tolerance often leads to robust or even ribald productions. Yet that is part of the risk of the First Amendment.

Irving Brant summed the matter up: "Blessed with a form of government that requires universal liberty of thought and expression, blessed with a social and economic system built on that same foundation, the American people have created the danger they fear by denying to themselves the liberties they cherish."

(Dianna Hull, 1975 ILA President, addressed a letter to me, to inquire about procedures in offering support and counsel to Idaho librarians when censorship incidents occur and to ask if the Intellectual Freedom Committee, as presently organized, was adequate to deal with such difficulties. The correspondence went on to ask two specific questions: "(1) Are we always aware of censorship disputes within Idaho and (2) what are our specific procedures for handling such difficulties?" The paragraphs which follow were excerpted from my return letter of July 9th, 1975.)

THOUGHTS CONCERNING CENSORSHIP DISPUTES

Dear Dianna:

In the many years I have been chairman of the ILA Intellectual Freedom Committee, I have found very little except apathy and, in some cases, actual fear in the minds and actions of most Idaho librarians and trustees when intellectual freedom matters come up. Who is on the Intellectual Freedom Committee really does not seem to matter as much, or to be as important, as what the membership as a whole is willing to do. As chairman, I can only take action when I know there is a problem—and a 3 or 4 person committee, without a clipping service, can't possibly keep me fully informed of what's going on in the entire state. I only heard about the St. Maries' case through the *Newsletter on Intellectual Freedom*, published in Chicago! By then it was all over, and there was nothing I could do about it. I certainly would have done the usual—written or phoned, asked what the situation was, and offered constructive advice. I have done this many times in the past. But when I'm not told there is an intellectual freedom situation, what can I do?

Now—in direct response to your specific questions:

1. No, we are *far* from being "always" aware of Idaho censorship disputes. As President maybe you can exhort the members to act as individual 1-person information sources on such matters, stressing that the most useful thing in these matters is if they would let me know immediately when and if help is needed. Oddly enough (maybe not so oddly) it is the librarians who are directly involved who usually try to keep intellectual freedom problems to themselves and *do not* keep me informed.

2. Our specific procedures in the committee vary with the type of problem:

   a) Very minor (no book selection policy in library; "authority" demands right to add or throw out book or periodical): I usually recommend using the incident to *ask* for board approval of ALA-recommended types of book selection policies.

   b) Minor (the library *has* policies; patron or authority asks for the censorship of a particular publication): I usually recommend that the matter be handled by the Board, since it is their policy. This usually works a good deal better than putting the onus of responsibility on the librarian himself or herself.

   c) Major (librarian threatened with dismissal): I usually write a letter to the chairman of the Board and ask for their side of it. If I find that it looks as if they have really violated their own policy, then I point out the Library Bill of Rights and the possibility of censure by the ALA, and so on if they continue in this path. It has worked in the past, and, I would guess, normally would work out in the future.

All this might seem to indicate to you that I've been operating as a one-man committee. This is not really true; whenever matters come up that do not require immediate action, I always consult with whomever is on the Committee and get their advice and approval by members of the Committee, and, in many cases, they have handled minor and very minor situations on their own.

I hope all the above will clarify some matters; they have clarified some matters in my own mind, and, I hope, for you.

THE FIRST AMENDMENT: THE GROWING AFFRONTS ON FREE SPEECH

Flushed with our local/national victory in protecting the individual's and the corporation's rights against governmental invasion,[1] just maybe we can now begin considering how affairs are going on the "freedom of speech" front. The First Amendment has long been considered first, not only in sequence among the Bill of Rights of our Constitution, but also first in the sense of both primacy and basic importance.

Unless we continue the never-ending fight to keep our right to speak out freely, surely our other rights are in fundamental danger. What use is it, for example, to preserve what many hereabouts see as a fundamental right—to bear arms—if we cannot publicly argue for it? What is the value, anyhow, of the First Amendment if we claim to know, respect, and abide by it—and then violate it, or try to, every chance we get?

There are many indications that the First Amendment is in trouble. For example, as recently as April 26th, Supreme Court Justice William Rehnquist—one of the four Nixon appointees—in a dissent on *First National Bank of Boston* v. *Bellotti*, referred to his belief in the "limited application of the First Amendment to the States." He had indicated previously that he is just about the most conservative jurist sitting on today's court, certainly as far as the First Amendment is concerned, and that he would—if he could—permit the individual states to suppress *all* dissenting speech. So far, he seems to be only one of nine in this group. But he *is* one-ninth!

IDAHO CASES

There have been several cases in Idaho recently which involve the endangering of the First Amendment. By now, most Idahoans are familiar with the case of the censorship of Ken Kesey's *One Flew Over the Cuckoo's Nest*, whereby the Fremont School District Board is now involved in a law suit based on its refusal to permit an English instructor to offer this very well-known modern novel as *optional* reading (the book is listed in the national guide to book selection for high school books—the *Senior High School Library Catalog*). We, of course, don't know how that case will come out, but the Idaho Library Association, at its recent conference in Sun Valley, voted to back the censorship fight with $100 of its money. This is a precedent in the Association's history.

A few weeks ago there was an attempt being made by individuals, and even by members of the school board in a nearby school district, to bar Senator Frank Church from speaking at the graduation exercises, even though the student body had voted overwhelmingly to invite him. Fortunately, wiser and calmer heads prevailed; and even though one of the school board members said that Senator Church's attitude on the Panama Canal indicated that he was not in agreement with the voters of that area, somebody managed to convince the board to table the matter. It is to be hoped it was on the basis that this is still a free country, and the First Amendment is still in force to help make it so.

THE NATIONAL LEVEL

On a national level, Senate Bill S. 1437, now under consideration by the U.S. Senate, has several provisions which would definitely erode the full and free functioning of the Bill of Rights. The proposed bill prohibits peaceful picketing on the grounds of a courthouse while the court is in session, if the picketing is intended to protest the judicial proceeding or decision. And it prohibits publishers from disseminating so-called "obscene" material, which, although lawful under the jurisdiction where it is published, may be considered obscene under the community standards of the place where distributed. This would be true even if the materials were not being sold for profit. Obviously, this would affect library transactions—such as interlibrary loans—because it would inhibit the nationwide and statewide distribution of items which might possibly be considered obscene somewhere, some time. Without the very useful practice of interlibrary loans, states such as Idaho, which are already hurting in respect to the availability of reading materials, would be sorely affected for purposes of reading and research.

As another indicator of how widespread the attacks on the First Amendment have become, the American Library Association's *Newsletter on Intellectual Freedom* has, through the last decade, verified that a great many books have been barred from school libraries or school reading lists throughout the United States. These titles range from quite trivial works to outstanding, generally accepted classics, from dictionaries to science fiction. Most of them were censored because—although they were meant to be read by students considered old enough to vote or go to war or be married —they included one or more four-letter words, or they expressed points of view with which some few parents or school board members differed.

Incidentally, the ALA itself recently succumbed to the prevalent censorship plague. Its executive board last November voted to stop distributing a pro-free speech documentary film "The Speaker," produced by the ALA earlier last year. Some of the board's more ultra-sensitive members claimed the movie was "racist" because it dealt with the right of even racist speakers to have their public say in America. As chronicled on CBS "60 Minutes" several weeks ago, the ALA Council last January voted, by a large majority, to reverse the executive board's decision. So, though "The Speaker" is once more on sale, censorship by librarians *does* occur—and "The Speaker" incident is not the only example. Public and school librarians—motivated in the most cases by the chilling influence of censorship-minded groups and individuals—have themselves practiced censorship throughout the country

THE MAIN ISSUE

But leaving all this aside, the most important issue involving the First Amendment is clearly our attitude toward it. When a case comes up which involves both the freedom to assemble and the freedom to speak—such as the distribution of anti-Semitic pamphlets in Pocatello or the marching Nazi-clad, so-called "American Nazis" in Skokie, Illinois—if we *really* believe in the First Amendment, I think we have no choice. We have to buy the bitter with the better, and accept what former Supreme Court Justice William O. Douglas once referred to as the "freedom for the things we hate."

It is very easy to be in favor of free speech when it is not controversial. It is certainly a difficult proposition when it hits us where we live. I, for one, despite whatever prejudices I may have, think that I have no prejudices against the rights of all Americans under the First Amendment. If someone is going to be denied the right to read or the right to speak or the right to do all the things which those who are against the First Amendment—particularly involving freedom of speech—advocate, I think we stand to lose much more than we gain as soon as we support censorship by our silence.

Dissent is, of course, the only way we progress. If we accepted everything that was said without argument, we would still believe that the sun goes around the earth and that the earth is flat. The Establishment is never going to try to change; that is *why* it is the Establishment. It is the minority who ultimately always become the the majority, on practically every issue. Without the right of minority groups and individuals to speak out and to write what they have to say publicly, by whatever legitimate means possible, we are not only violating the First Amendment, it seems to me we are violating our own basic human rights.

Senator Church said it very well, recently, when he gave a high-school address which some had tried to stop: "Since you are not horses, don't wear blinders." If we wish to exploit to the fullest our human abilities and human rights, at the very minimum let us say what we have to say and write what we have to write, and then take whatever reasonable consequences may ensue. But don't try to stop progress by insisting that somebody, somewhere, is saying what you disagree with and should have no right to say it or write it.

NOTE

1. The reference is to a Pocatello businessman's victory over OSHA in a U.S. Supreme Court decision in 1978.

IDAHO'S PORNOGRAPHY AMBIVALENCE

Since 1901 there has been a law against obscenity in Idaho. The state's very first comprehensive law code (which excluded a great many matters later considered criminal) took care to guard the morals of the rip-roaring, wide-open Idaho of that era. It was not until 1973 that a "modern" anti-obscenity law was passed. Unfortunately, it was not quite modern enough.

Although the new Idaho law was passed in April 1973, the June 21, 1973 decisions of the U.S. Supreme Court made the 1973 Idaho law obsolete before it officially went into effect on July 1. During its first two years of life, there were only a total of three prosecutions: one in Pocatello and one in Idaho Falls in 1974, plus one in Caldwell in 1975. The Pocatello case (involving the city's only "adult" bookstore-movie theater, The Gallery) resulted in a jury verdict of "not guilty." The Idaho Falls case (concerning the showing of *Last Tango in Paris*) came up with a hung jury and a dropping of prosecution. The Caldwell case (concerning showing of *Deep Throat* and sale and showing of other purportedly obscene items) also resulted in victory for the defendants.

To focus more specifically within this broad landscape, let's take up these cases in a little more detail. The Gallery began business in August 1972, in a little store on Pocatello's Main Street, near the center of the city's downtown business district. Its owner, an Arizona-based firm that owns other such store-theaters in the West, managed to make a pretty fair amount of money out of selling "adult" books and showing "adult" movies. Its lease expired 30 April 1975, and was not renewed by the owner of the building where it was located. That owner was a member of the Pocatello City Council and a local merchant, who obviously did not feel the Gallery's presence near his own place of business helped either his business or his political standing.

What are the figures in The Gallery's popularity? According to a recent Associated Press story, "about 16,000 persons have become members of the private club which entitled you to watch a double-feature skin flick." In a city of 50,000 or so, within a thirty-two-month period, this would indicate a profitable, popular enterprise. Since The Gallery required a "membership card," at a cost of $1, plus $4 for one's first movie-viewing, and a $4 rate for further attendance, there was clearly a rather high percentage of Southeastern Idaho's over-eighteen population who found pornography worth paying for.

Almost a year after a six-person jury—men and women of various faiths and ages, but all local citizens—unanimously indicated Pocatello's local, contemporary standards, in accordance with both the 1973 state law and the 1973 U.S. Supreme Court decision standards, the prosecutor of Bannock County made an appeal to the Idaho courts to redefine "obscenity" for the benefit of the city, the county, and the state. The Caldwell case, according to the current Idaho Attorney General, Wayne Kidwell, was instituted for the same ultimate reason—a hope that somehow, somewhere in the Idaho system of justice an understandable, modern definition of the obscene could be found that would, hopefully, result in victories for the legal censors.

But even the U.S. Supreme Court has admitted, in their June 1974 *Carnal Knowledge* decision, that only they can really define this elusive term. That decision, in essence, stated that only a majority of the highest court in America could make a determination as to whether a *particular* movie or book or magazine or pamphlet was or was not "dirty" enough not to fall under the First Amendment's broad cloak of protection for American freedom of speech and press. And there is no doubt that those citizens or corporations with sufficient funds to carry such cases up through the U.S. system of courts will continue to do so.

In 1975 the Idaho legislature passed a new law which somewhat modified the useless 1973 statute, especially aiming to be compatible with recent U.S. Supreme Court decisions on the topic. A 1975 *Idaho State Journal* (Pocatello) editorial summarized the ultimate solution to the so-called pornography problem in Idaho, and the nation, in a brief paragraph. The editorial concluded: "The best legal way to put pornographers out of business is still economic. If people do not spend their money for such material, the doors of the business will sooner or later close."

Perhaps Representative Steve Symms (1st District, Idaho) in his February 27, 1975 testimony before the crime subcommittee of the House Judiciary Committee, best stated the present writer's point of view on censorship, when he said, "Gun prohibitionists and liquor prohibitionists both reach their conclusions by convoluted logic and human behavior: The Prohibition period should have taught us that this kind of reasoning is nonsense, that deviant behavior is primarily a function of human free will." Of course, to be fair to Representative Symms, he *was* talking about "the desire to ban firearms as a solution to crime." But what's wrong with accepting a combination of his basic theory and the *Journal*'s? Free will and free enterprise will, in the long run, satisfy the obvious ambivalence of the Idahoan who wants to be free himself, but also to try to keep the other fellow's "badness" under control.

Editorials and letters on intellectual freedom

8

*(A miscellany of letters, including one sent to but never pub-
lished by* Wilson Library Bulletin, *and editorials, all of which
may add up to what clever Ron Norman of Kearney, Nebraska, memorably described [in Morte d'Arthur terminology] as
"Sir Eli . . . sallying forth from . . . Academe . . . to protect
the holy cause of intellectual freedom." But at least I avoided
one of the more gruesome quarters of Dante's Inferno by not
staying neutral. Incidentally, it is a pleasure to include* the
entire Norman-Oboler colloquy in print; it was fun—even if
somewhat stuffily ended by "Sir Eli.")*

EDITORIALS

THREE AND FOUR LETTER WORDS [for *PNLA Quarterly*]

The acronym "ACLU" may become as familiar to librarians as
ALA, PNLA, and LC, if the recently announced policy statement
by the American Civil Liberties Union dealing with censorship of
allegedly obscene material becomes widely accepted. The June 18,
1962 issue of *Publishers' Weekly* states that the American Civil
Liberties Union, "having considered a three-year review of the issue

*With Ron Norman's personal approval, of course.

of censorship of allegedly obscene material," claims that "limitations of expression on the grounds of obscenity are unconstitutional."

The ACLU states that "prosecutions invoked under anti-obscenity laws . . . should be based on clear proof that the material would cause in a normal adult behavior which has validly been made criminal by statute."

This is certainly a revolutionary view of obscenity, censorship, and the law. If the ACLU idea prevails, practically no reading material could be proven obscene. They admit this, stating that "because of the special need in a free society to guard against the stifling affect of censorship, no ban should be placed on allegedly obscene material, even though such material may be intensely disliked by many persons."

The recent decision of the U.S. Supreme Court permitting mail distribution of magazines which print male nude photographs is one sign that the ACLU "policy statement" may be along the lines of the current Supreme Court thinking. Also, no less a reputable publisher than E. P. Dutton has announced that this year it will publish, in both hardbound and paperbound editions (Everyman!), the erotic classic of India, the Kama Sutra of Vatsyayana. Henry Miller may yet seem to be at the Elsie Dinsmore level!

We may be at the threshold of a brand-new era in openness of expression, where "sex" and "book," put together, may be the accepted vogue, rather than the embattled exception. And librarians will be, along with booksellers, on the firing line—or should that be "on the target-line"?—as usual.

ALL OR NOTHING AT ALL [for *Newsletter on Intellectual Freedom*]

Sometimes the over-conscientious librarian who feels his professional obligations heavily is faced with a dilemma that seems beyond rational solution. This all-too-common quandary is what to do when faced with the issue of just how far the librarian's individual relationship to the obligations imposed by the Freedom to Read really goes.

Read over the Freedom to Read statement, and you'll find it urges "publishers and librarians, as guardians of the people's freedom to read, to contest encroachments upon that freedom by individuals or groups seeking to impose their own standards or tastes upon the community at large." Does this mean that every time a patently pornographic or obscene item is sold in a local store, and a "decency group," or even a single individual, prevails upon the local prosecuting attorney to do something about it, and the proprietor is then arrested, that Mr. Local Librarian, as one of the "guardians of the people's freedom to read," must become directly involved in the case?

It is not, usually, very easy to determine where concern for the freedom to read ends and protection of other filth starts. The two-dollar one-shot magazine with deliberately pornographic photographs seems to carry a good deal of material that is not *too* different from the casually nude or near-nude advertisements to be seen in many major national magazines, particularly of the fashion type. Should the "guardian" librarian start writing letters to the editor or even become an *amicus curiae* in a particular case that seems pretty remote from the local library?

Within the space of this brief editorial statement, there is hardly an opportunity to go very deeply into the issues involved. Every librarian who feels deeply about the question of intellectual freedom should be prepared, however, to justify either his activity or his lack of it in a particular situation. In other words, know *why* you do or don't do what you're doing or not doing!

There are all too many librarians who seem to be looking for trouble constantly these days, and there are about as many or probably more who are going out of their way to avoid it. What with the growing concern for the social responsibility of the librarian, as evidenced by the newly approved ALA Round Table, this might well be a good time for earnest ratiocination on the very moot question—am I my brother's keeper? We all know in what circumstances the question was asked in Biblical days; perhaps it is not being too far-fetched to say that this has become more than an academic question, and is beginning to become a problem for almost every practicing librarian. If you, as a librarian, do *not* act as a "guardian of the people's freedom to read," then who will?

And is that freedom absolute, or restricted? It would be very interesting to see some answers to these obviously intentionally provocative questions.

VIEWPOINT: THE CASE AGAINST "LIBERAL" CENSORSHIP
[for *Newsletter on Intellectual Freedom*]

The Henry Luce Professor of Urban Values at New York University, Irving Kristol, was rather less than urbane in his strictures against pornography and obscenity—or what he defines as such—in his March 23, 1971 article, "Pornography, Obscenity, and the Case for Censorship," which first appeared in the *New York Times* magazine and was recently reprinted in two issues of this *Newsletter* (September and November, 1971). He has exhumed a great many of the tired old pro-censorship arguments, but added a new dimension; he has coined a new phrase, "liberal censorship," which, despite all protestations to the contrary, is clearly a contradiction in terms.

Indeed, his whole essay is on the hyperbolic, exaggerated level illustrated by his undocumented statement that ". . . pornography . . . is inherently and purposefully subversive of civilization and its institutions." He is even more specific and direct in this: ". . . if you care for the quality of life in our American democracy, then you have to be for censorship." Blithely, he sells creative art down the river: "There are . . . some few works of art that are in the special category of the comic-ironic 'bawdy' (Boccaccio, Rabelais). It is such works of art that are likely to suffer at the hands of the censor. *That is the price* [my italics] one has to be prepared to pay for censorship—even liberal censorship." Snick-snack! Off with Boccaccio's head! Snip-snip! Eliminate Rabelais! And Joyce and Swift and Henry Miller and—but Kristol, contrary to all factual evidence, says, "If you look at the history of American or English literature, there is precious little damage you can point to as a consequence of the censorship that prevailed throughout most of that history."

Let alone the gross inexactitude of this dogmatic opinion, Kristol really ought to do a little study of the hundreds of years and thousands of literary creations between the writing of *Beowulf* and the first English legal censorship, that of Edmund Curll's *Venus in the Cloister*, in 1727. During those centuries after centuries, "most" of the history of English literature occurred. The quoted statement is only one of many examples of Kristollian *obiter dicta* which have a nice, ringing sound—but are actually quite hollow of solid fact, when closely examined.

It is really almost incredible that he would seriously make such a statement as "very few works of literature—of real literary merit, I mean—ever were suppressed; and those that were, were not suppressed for long." The long, long list in Anne Haight's well-known *Banned Books* is a simple answer to the first claim; and it is certainly a specious, unsound argument to say that "those that were, were not suppressed for long." *Any* length of time is contrary to the fundamental tenets of freedom of speech and expression in which, presumably, "liberal" Kristol believes.

Incidentally, near the end of his article, he admits that "We had censorship of pornography and obscenity for 150 years," which in simple mathematical process would indicate that censorship began in 1821. This is a most interesting date, just about 93 years after it historically began! Kristol, as I said, needs at least a capsule course in the facts of the story of censorship.

If Kristol's facts were right, one might be willing to consider the logic of his argumentation, which, on the whole, is rather persuasive. But if "liberal" censorship has to be based on misinformation and exaggeration, then it is no more worth the consideration of reasonable men and women than *il*liberal censorship.

Admittedly, this brief reply to Kristol is itself a polemic, rather than in a reasonable vein. The reader is referred to my forthcoming book for a lengthy, historically based, positive set of facts and arguments concerning the merits and demerits of censorship of writings about sex. Suffice it here, in a necessarily limited space, to say that Kristol has clearly failed to consider the most basic of all issues in the censorship/non-censorship dispute.

In a long perspective, the fear of the word is really the fear of the human. Like reverse Terences, those who censor and favor censorship are really saying, "I am human, but everything human is alien to me." Men and women are men and women *because* of their sexual drives, and denial of this fact by even a never-ending line of censors—liberal *or* illiberal!—will not eliminate maleness and femaleness and the male-female relationship. The censor will never outlast biology.

POST JULY 4TH THOUGHTS: A VIEW OF AMERICAN PATRIOTISM
[for the *Idaho State Journal*, Pocatello]

Several weeks ago ENJOY printed a lengthy, thoughtful, provocative statement on American patriotism written by a distinguished historian and scholar, Dr. Merrill D. Beal, professor emeritus of history at Idaho State University. The topic of patriotism is, of course, of interest and importance to all Americans, and what follows is a view of another position and an attempt by a non-historian to state some opinions on this vital matter—opinions which, to some extent, differ with those of his colleague and friend.

The emphasis in Dr. Beal's article was on the need for unity. My feeling is that America needs to erect as its standard Carl Schurz's 1872 rewording of Stephen Decatur's famous toast. Contrast "Our country! In her intercourse with foreign nations may she always be in the right; but our country, right or wrong," with Schurz's speech in Congress, wherein he said, "Our country, right or wrong. When right, to be kept right; when wrong, to be put right." Blind allegiance and unquestioning reverence are NOT the attributes of free men or free societies.

The arrogant and unthinking bumper sticker, seen occasionally hereabouts, "America: Love It or Leave It," is not truly a patriotic statement. Love of country means, if it means anything, love of the TRUTH about a country; if a national leadership's policies cause widespread national distaste, the cure is not to run away from facing up to that leadership and those policies. It is to stay, and, by constitutional and lawful means, strive to reform that leadership and/or its policies, in order to get the nation back on the right road.

I agree wholeheartedly with the statement in the article that this nation needs ". . . an intelligent, whole-souled devotion," but I cannot see that "whole-souled devotion" must mean antagonism to reasonable, reasoned dissent. If I disagree with you, am I thereby less patriotic than you, simply because I am in disagreement? Love of country does not mean complete acceptance and agreement with all that is going on in that country.

It was quite interesting to me to note that, despite the headline over Dr. Beal's page-long article, the word "patriotism" is, actually and curiously, not used in the article itself. There is a reference to "representative patriots who made and preserved the nation." Among those named as such are Sam Adams, Patrick Henry, Washington, John Marshall, Madison, Franklin, Jefferson, Brigham Young, John Taylor, Tom Paine, Lincoln, Wilson, and Franklin D. Roosevelt.

America's patriots certainly include a more "representative" group than this; they include (among many, many others who might be named) such men and women as Martin Luther King, Supreme Court Justices Oliver Wendell Holmes, Brandeis, and Douglas, Eugene V. Debs, Horace Greeley, Victoria Woodhull, John P. Altgeld, Henry David Thoreau, Medgar Evers, Ralph Nader, Dr. Benjamin Spock, and U.S. Senators William E. Borah and Frank Church. All of these great Americans, and many others, have disagreed, or are now actively disagreeing, with the supposed sentiments of "our country"—or, at least with what in each of their respective eras was or is considered majority (generally accepted) opinion. But they are or were definitely patriots, every one of them, citizens who loved their country and showed their love by trying to improve it.

On June 29, 1971, Daniel Ellsberg, the self-confessed distributor of the "top secret" Pentagon Papers on Vietnam, surrendered to federal authorities. In an interview he gave at that time, Ellsberg described what he did as "an act of patriotism." Many of those named in the preceding paragraph also ran afoul of the law (or, in the case of the Supreme Court Justices who were named, almost always disagreed with the majority of the Court). Is Ellsberg a patriot or a scoundrel, an American who helped his country or, as General Maxwell Taylor recently described him on television, "another Benedict Arnold"?

The arguments on both sides of this question are very similar to the arguments in past years about such people as Debs, King, Altgeld, and other crisis-figures. But, leaving the arguments about individuals aside, who is the example of the greater patriot—the one who accepts without argument or free discussion or dissent whatever his leaders tell him is so, or the man who seeks for the truth, no matter where it takes him?

Justice Holmes stated this very cogently in his famous 1919 dissent, in the case of *Abrams* v. *United States*, when he said: "I think we should be eternally vigilant against attempts to check the expression of opinions that we loathe and believe to be fraught with death, unless they so imminently threaten immediate interference with the lawful and pressing purposes of the law that an immediate check is required to save the country."

We have set up a unique and totally American Bill of Rights as part of our U.S. Constitution. These rights and their protection are surely an essential part of American patriotism. When the Supreme Court recently voted by a majority of six to three against "prior restraint" on newspaper publication of anything at all (whether legal or illegal), they were defending one of the most basic of these rights, the freedom of the press. The newspaper, of course, must take the consequences and responsibilities for whatever it prints— but clearly, as long as the Supreme Court keeps to its present feelings, which is likely to be for a long time, no matter who is on the Court, loss of press freedom is impossible in a nation not frightened into hysteria.

As far back as 1798, the Sedition Laws, strongly supported by John Adams and Alexander Hamilton, were passed in an effort to bar "disrespect" to the President, Congress, and various other government agencies and functionaries. These laws were voided very soon, and Thomas Jefferson, the next president after Adams, not only released every critic of the government who was then in jail, but even remitted the fines of those who had been forced to pay such fines under these infamous laws.

So, Gerald W. Johnson has written in his *This American People* (in a chapter entitled, "Free Speech Is for Bold People"), ". . . both by action of the people at the ballot box and by formal admission of the government itself, it is established that freedom of speech, especially as regards criticism of the government, cannot be abridged by act of Congress." Johnson also said, ". . . how free we can afford to be depends upon how scared we are. If we are not scared at all, we can be as free as the Declaration of Independence asserted we should be. If we are somewhat scared, but nevertheless resolute—as the men who signed the Declaration were—we can still be free beyond anything possible in a nation frightened into hysteria.''

Ideas like this go back a lot further than 1776. Plato, in his dialogue entitled "Meno," quotes Socrates as saying, ". . . we shall be better and braver and less helpless if we think that we ought to inquire, than we should have been if we indulged in the idle fancy that there was no knowing and no use in seeking to know what we do not know;—that is a theme upon which I am ready to fight, in word and deed, to the utmost of my power." And, as we all know, those words were much more than fancy rhetoric in Socrates' case; he gave his life for the cause of truth. There, I say, is the true patriot, the man who is willing to face up to public disapprobation, even to greater sacrifice than that, if need be, for love of country, as well as love of the truth.

I agree wholeheartedly with Dr. Beal that ". . . a truly great, good society can only be developed by a sensible, virtuous people." Perhaps where we differ is in our rating of the relative importance of some of the virtues. Self-discipline, in my opinion, is not the top virtue which led to America's greatness, nor will it enable our country to remain great if it ever does get top emphasis. To me, the greatest American virtue is honesty, and as long as we have a government which lies to its people—even to its elected representatives —we are in deep trouble indeed.

Let Americans know what is going on, what truly are the problems, foreign and domestic, which are confronting our country, and the genius of America will solve them. Those who contribute the most to this goal are, have been, and always will be our greatest patriots.

"THE OLD MAN ON THE HILL" [for *Newsletter on Intellectual Freedom*]

It was not quite a small town—too small to be known without atlas reference but too big to ignore. It had a fire department and a water department and a police department and a public library. It had a school system. In each school was a collection of books called a "library"—and each library had a "librarian"—a book-keeper— an order-maintainer, a room-minder.

And one day I spoke in that town to a meeting of educators—teachers and librarians—and asked the wrong question: "Do you have any censorship problems?" And the young woman who was in charge of the school library in that town said, rather plaintively, "Well, yes—I've had to take *The Catcher in the Rye* off my open shelves and into my closet." "Why?" I asked. "Because there's an old man on the hill who says it's a bad book." Was he someone in a position of authority over her? No. Was he on the school board—or even a past member? No. Was he a town leader? Well, sort of. Politician? Banker? Lawyer? No, none of these . . . but everyone in town knew about the old man on the hill. And because he had told her he didn't like the book, she had hidden it away? Yes . . . it just wasn't worth the hassle.

How many intellectual freedom committees in how many states take for granted that the Library Bill of Rights, once promulgated —via state library association periodical or "intellectual freedom kit," or by whatever means—automatically becomes part of the practices of those who have received it? Or how many give lip-service to its principles, voiced at a state conference, as equalling reality?

My point is, of course, an old one, but, unfortunately, one that seems to have to be made over and over. Librarians—even professionally trained ones—are human, all too human. We react to pressures; and public opinion (even if epitomized in "the old man on the hill") is much more often what we heed than the bare bones of rhetoric, lacking meaningfulness unless they are fleshed out by our actually doing what we say we do.

Have you an "old man on the hill"? Then dig your library's copy of *The Catcher in the Rye* out of its hiding place, and put it where it belongs—*on the open shelf.* And be damned to the Censor!

THE PROGRESSIVE H-BOMB ARTICLE AND LIBRARIANS *

All too often, these days, the call, even from those who in the 1960s were considered "library radicals," is for caution and practicality. The demand for caution is more or less a "don't touch the

*This was intended as a *Library Journal* editorial, but was never published.

fragile objects on sale" kind of demand. The call for practicality seems to center on the Freedom to Read Foundation, the ALA Office for Intellectual Freedom, and the ALA Intellectual Freedom Committee. *If only*, the critics say, they would be "practical" and not go a-whoring after such recondite issues as the freedom of the press or the freedom of the pornographer. . . . What is needed, one gathers, is a delicately balanced sort of approach to First Amendment controversies which makes sure in advance that all relevant court decisions will be completely favorable to the cause of intellectual freedom and, furthermore, that such decisions will be completely pertinent to libraries.

This is something like a counsel of perfection. In dealing with human, all-too-human, interests and with judges who put on their pants or panties one leg at a time just like the rest of us, to expect ideal legal situations that will produce Gladstone-perfect decisions is, of course, to expect cloud-cuckoo-land on terra firma. All of this brings me to the stated topic of this effusion.

What possible connection could there be between the recent heavy-handed federal attack on the about-to-be-published article in the May *Progressive*, the one that was going to be titled, "The H-Bomb Secret: How We Got It, Why We're Telling It," and intellectual freedom for libraries? It really is almost obvious. Libraries circulate magazines; *The Progressive* is a magazine; the U.S. Federal Judge in Milwaukee, who on March 26, 1979, issued a preliminary injunction as requested by the government to prevent *The Progressive* from printing and distributing what it wanted to print and distribute, was preventing the magazine from printing what it wanted to print. So *The Progressive* was censored in the worst possible way for the integrity of American intellectual freedom—that is, by governmental prior restraint. Thus, the patrons of America's libraries (at least those whose libraries subscribe to *The Progressive*) were denied the right to read what they wanted to read.

Let me present this issue in another way: if *The Progressive* must have its articles preread and precensored by the federal government, why shouldn't the federal government—and perhaps state and local governments as well—begin precensoring the local, or national, newspapers as well? And books? And nonprint materials?

The American library has grown and flourished in an atmosphere of general intellectual freedom, certainly to a very great extent in matters involving politics. The federal government's arguments that the publishing of the article in question would "irreparably impair the national security of the United States, and prove a grave threat to the peace and security of the world," as stated in an affidavit by Secretary of State Vance, seems hysterical, to say the least, when compared with affidavits to the contrary by various scientists, who state that the disclosures made in the Morland article will *not* "significantly influence the national security."

But leave the issue of national security aside; what about the argument that if *The Progressive* proceeds to appeal and eventually reach the Supreme Court on this matter, then it could possibly result in an official secrets policy, if not law, for the United States such as this country has never had in the past? Even with the very conservative Burger Court, I believe this is a risk worth taking. If *not* taken, then governmental prior restraint has, by default, become an accepted practice which cannot but have dire consequences for the freedom to read and for the libraries of America.

LETTERS

EDITOR, *COMMENTARY*:

From the unnecessarily cute title to the gratuitously sexual and tasteless references to "hardware, or perhaps software" (in connection with the North Carolina study on the effects of erotica on male college students) to the quite illogical conclusion, the Packer Report on the Report not only is inadequate to its subject but is a real disservice to the cause of intellectual freedom.

A number of facts are misstated (some admittedly trivial, but still of importance in setting the general tone of the article):

1) Only someone without a sense of humor could possibly recognize *The Obscenity Report* (Stein and Day) to be anything but a satirically-intended hoax. It is full of completely and obviously faked charts, statistics, and quotations. . . .

2) ". . . the Government Printing Office printed just enough copies of the whole Report and the various dissents for the officials immediately involved. . . ." So says Mr. Packer. The fact is that the Government Printing Office had enough copies of the whole Report, including the various dissents, to send them to the several hundred Government Depository Libraries throughout the United States early in December (1970), and copies were then and are now readily available from the Government Printing Office. . . .

3) The Senate rejected the Commission Report on October 13, 1970, *thirteen* days after the COP Report was issued—not on October 17, *seventeen* days later, as Mr. Packer states.

4) The Commission expenditures came to approximately $1.8 million, which is considerably more than the "hundreds of thousands" mentioned by Mr. Packer as the cost of the Commission. . . .

The single most obviously "self-inflicted hotfoot"—to quote Mr. Packer's quote—in his Report on the Report is his admission of a "bias that research is the opiate of the behavioral scientists." Really, Mr. Packer, this *is* 1971, and there is just too much clearly valuable and appropriate research by behavioral science on record to dismiss this study and its research so highhandedly or to depreciate *all* such research.

As a long-practicing academic librarian and a former long-time member of the American Library Association's Intellectual Freedom Committee, who is at present completing a book on the origins of censorship, may I attest to the fact that I find the Report of the Commission on Obscenity and Pornography a pioneering, useful, and significant publication which, although like any manmade production, is far from perfect, still deserves a less biased and captious critique than the one presented in Mr. Packer's article.

EDITOR, *LIBRARY JOURNAL:*

Berninghausen's polemic is, as usual with polemics, well-intentioned, vigorous, and, to some extent, acceptable to most people to whom it is directed. But, as is also usual with polemics, it carries a good deal of excessive over-kill rhetoric, some irrelevant jabs, and is in part a labored attempt to make what seemed to me some rather obvious points, points which hardly needed to be made.

Let me dispose of a few minor cavils I have against this statement, before I come to the more positive part of my reaction. Surely the paragraphs concerning his feelings about the library press are hardly either relevant to the main topic of his discussion nor, in some respects, justified. I will certainly accept Berninghausen's *expertise* on matters of intellectual freedom, but I do not think he is up to date on how magazine articles should be written and how news reporting should be done. This is an entirely different topic, and, in my opinion, his animadversions on *LJ*, *WLB*, and *AL* vitiate some of the strength of his very important critique.

Also, I am a little perplexed by his idea that it is something new for American librarians to consider the possibility of social responsibility as being *their* responsibility. Surely the library profession showed its deep concern with social responsibility during both World War I and World War II, as well as in the rather odd period in American history between the beginning of World War II in 1939 and our actual entrance into it in 1941, which at that time was called the "emergency" period. Anyone looking back at the library literature of this period will find there was almost universal agreement that *only one side* of the matter of cooperation with the government should be shown, and it would be a little difficult to find anything but advocacy on the part of the library press and also of the library profession during those years.

The dissenting group which lasted for a couple of years after its beginnings in 1939, called the Progressive Librarians Council, had very little effect on American librarianship, but still was sort of a precursor of SRRT of today. I make this point only to indicate that there was a direct attempt to discard the principle of intellectual freedom for librarians almost immediately after it had gotten started, and that the present "social responsibility" movement of the 1970s may itself by only a temporary phenomenon, as the Progressive Librarians were.

Now, to what seems to be the chief thrust of the Berninghausen article, and my reaction to it: There need not really be, in my opinion, a knock-down-drag-'em-out fight between the proponents of social responsibility and the proponents of the Library Bill of Rights. Surely those who believe in the Library Bill of Rights *also* believe in librarians who are not completely insulated from the world as it really is. And, just as surely, those interested in social responsibility *must* believe very strongly in the Library Bill of Rights. At least, most of them do. Also, I don't see quite the point of Berninghausen's citation of the *attempted* change in ALA's point of view on intellectual freedom, because, as he says himself, this attempt *failed.* If all of the odd ideas that did *not* succeed in ALA history were given as much attention as this one, we would be enveloped in unnecessary internal turmoil from now on.

I, for one, am in perfect agreement with Berninghausen that the ideas in the Library Bill of Rights should be our fundamental charter, as professional librarians. I cannot see how these rights can be denied or diluted (and I speak as one of a subcommittee of the Intellectual Freedom Committee back in 1967 which did the actual revision of the Library Bill of Rights to which his article refers) without extreme danger to our profession and, possibly, even our country as we know it. Perhaps the matter could be clarified if we were to see ourselves basically as communicators, rather than opinion leaders. Every profession is having its problems with definition. Not every doctor is a Dr. Spock, or, equally, a Dr. DeBakey; among lawyers one finds about as many would-be William Kunstlers these days as one does Justice Burgers. It is even becoming increasingly difficult for the college professor to stay in his ivory tower—and there is certainly division between the academic community as to the appropriate role of the professor in the social milieu.

Librarianship—a sort of Johnny-come-lately to the professional fold—is a long way from having a clearly defined place in the scheme of things cultural. Back in 1940 a library school student named Ruth A. Ogilvie, at Simmons College, said some things ("Keeper of the Keys," *Wilson Library Bulletin*, May, 1940, pp. 640-41) which may be useful in this whole discussion:

Librarians have a great influence within their grasp. To them falls the work of holding forth bases on which people can found their beliefs. No longer are members of the profession mere collectors and distributors of books; they are agents in a most vital task. The recent turn of events carries even more responsibility for them. If rational thought is necessary in ordinary times, how much more important is it then that the public should be taught in times of stress to guard against mass hysteria!

Ogilvie also said that "if the library abandons its position of tolerance and starts to suppress the literature that does not fit in with
stereotyped ideas, where is it to draw the line?" Then she said
something that seems most important of all in this connection:
". . . librarians must be on the alert for homegrown suppression,
take care that in manning their outer bulwarks against the onslaught
of alien untruths that they are not undermined from within."

The kind of librarian who would buy "social responsibility" as
his *sole* guide in book selection would surely be practicing "home-
grown suppression." The single most important point in the Berninghausen article, in my judgment, is his statement that "it is
unethical for a librarian in a publicly supported library to suppress
statements he does not like, or to exclude expressions of ideas that
are objectionable to any religious, political or other organization to
which he belongs."

The day ALA becomes an advocacy organization, pure and
simple, it will lose more than the Obolers and the Berninghausens
from its membership; it will also lose its reason for existence.

EDITOR, *LIBRARY JOURNAL:*

It is always interesting to hear from the conservative Catholic
point of view on censorship. Williams and Pearce of Rosary
College did a pretty good job of using "faulty terminology," *un*
"systematic expression," and "factual error" in their article. It
was really too bad their position was "founded on untenable principles," flew "in the face of social and legal reality," and "is impossible to implement."

But all that is not so important as what they said. To answer it
fully would require a book (but I've already written it: Eric Moon
and the Scarecrow Press will publish it next spring, under the title,
The Fear of the Word: Censorship and Sex). To answer their article
at medium length would require at least an article (but maybe
"'Just Like the Child in the Family': Paternalistic Morality and
Censorship" did that, to some extent). So I'll stifle the urge to
answer in kind the name-calling they used ("transcendent liberal
among fools" and similar expressions) and conclude with this little
limerick (*verbum sap*):

Pearce and Williams are pundits who say,
"We must think in a relative way;
Since the freedoms we prize
Are not fit for the wise,
Who should censor and censor all day!''

EDITOR, *LIBRARY JOURNAL:*

In nearly 35 years of being part of the honorable profession of librarianship, I cannot remember any more pernicious—indeed, vicious—an attack on one of the basic elements of our profession than the article by Leo N. Flanagan mis-titled as "Defending the Indefensible: the Limits of Intellectual Freedom" (*LJ*, October 15, 1975, pp. 1887-91). It *should* have been titled "Running Up the White Flag: the Limits of Cowardice."

Alexis de Tocqueville, writing about the prospects of American democracy as he saw them in 1840, wrote: "I trace amongst our contemporaries two contrary notions which are equally injurious. One set of men can perceive nothing in the principle of equality but the anarchial tendencies which it engenders: they dread their own free agency—they fear themselves. Other thinkers, less numerous but more enlightened, take a different view: beside that track which starts from the principle of equality to terminate in anarchy, they have at last discovered the road which seems to lead men to inevitable servitude. They shape their souls beforehand to this necessary condition; and, despairing of remaining free, they already do obeisance in their hearts to the master who is soon to appear. The former abandons freedom, because they think it dangerous; the latter, because they hold it to be impossible."

Flanagan, in various ways, seems to hold *both* opinions. Since Mr. Flanagan cites "heaven" as his authority for the fallibility of "human decision and action," let me use heaven as my own authority, via Robert Browning's well-known call for daring and idealism, "A man's reach should exceed his grasp / Or what's a heaven for?"

In a brief letter, the errors of fact and informed judgment, explicit and implicit, in Flanagan's farrago of fear cannot be detailed. But there are, I know, many spokesmen for courageous, unlimited professional librarianship who can reply seriatim, if *LJ* will provide the forum. Surely a man who uses flagrant mis-statements of John Stuart Mill's point of view on the freedom of expression and uses those well-known authorities on the subject, Patrick Williams and J. J. Pearce, as a contemporary "proof" of his own opinions should be answered. I find Flanagan's article full of impracticality, over-simplifications, legal difficulties, anti-intellectualism, and want of professionalism. By some coincidence, these are exactly his charges against the Introduction to the *Intellectual Freedom Manual*!

The fear of freedom would ill become an ALA *Intellectual Freedom Manual*; I fervently hope the *Office for Intellectual Freedom Manual* will not do as freedom-fearing Flanagan suggests. There is no question that the Introduction to the *Manual* is imperfect—but at least it is not pusillanimous.

EDITOR, *INTELLECT:*

The May-June, 1976 issue of INTELLECT included an article by Dr. Victor B. Cline, entitled "The Scientists vs. Pornography: an Untold Story," which is neither the telling of a story that has not yet been told (see, for example, the *Journal of Social Issues* [v. 29, no. 3, 1973], which devotes an entire issue to "Pornography: Attitudes, Use, and Effects"; there are other reports on the Commission studies, and reports of more recent research on the purported causal relationship between exposure to pornography and deviant or criminal action), nor does it tell the story of the Commission research accurately, fully, or fairly.

There are so many ways in which the article is in error that perhaps a *seriatim* list might be easiest to check:

1. It is true that the Davis-Braucht study included a statement that "one finds that exposure to pornography is the strongest predictor of sexual deviance among the early-age-of-exposure subjects. . . ." But after giving some further research data, in the very next paragraph they say, "In the case of sexual deviance, there is, then, a plausible case for the contribution of exposure to pornography to deviant behavior but also a *plausible case for the use of pornography simply being part of the routine social practices of some deviant and adolescent subgroups.*" (Italics added for emphasis.)

2. It is true that the Davis-Braucht study "found a positive relationship between sexual deviance and exposure to pornography at all ages of exposure levels." But the rest of that paragraph says, "We have also found a positive relationship between peer pressures for sexual activity and both exposure to pornography and sexual deviance. Because we do not have age-of-commission data for the more deviant and sexual behavior *we cannot pin down casual* hypotheses.*" (Italics added for emphasis—E.M.O.)

3. Davis and Braucht comment on the relationship between early-age-of-exposure to pornography and various "deviant" sexual behaviors (on p. 207, the next page to the one cited by Cline) that "these data are hardly conclusive in their support of a causal connection between exposure to pornography and engaging in a variety of early heterosexual and 'deviant' sexual behaviors, yet they are not inconsistent with such an interpretation." Can this kind of conclusion be used as proof of causal connection?

4. *All* the Davis-Braucht conclusions are very tentative and *non*-definite; yet Dr. Cline says, ". . . the possibility of causation is highly suggested." Highly? Judge for yourself from the above quotations.

5. The Goldstein-Kant research (and, incidentally, Cline quotes from their 1973 book on the topic, *not* from the original report to the Commission, which is what he is supposed to be criticizing) is misrepresented by use, in Cline's attack, only of data resulting from a "peak adolescent exposure to pornography." In discussing *normal* exposure to erotica, the Goldstein-Kant study states that ". . . a reasonable exposure to erotica, particularly during adolescence, reflects a high degree of sexual interest and practice."[1] This hardly sounds like a *causal* relationship; if anything, it is a normal concomitant.

6. As for Dr. Cline's arithmetical-algebraical "proof" of the "danger" of having pornography cause even a single adolescent or adult to develop "some manner of antisocial deviancy," it is simply too ridiculous to try to refute. By his muddled reasoning, it would be equally true that if exposure to pornography *helped* one person into normal sexual behavior, and "this person yearly influenced only one other individual who, in turn, affected only one another, in 20 years, 1,048,575 . . ." healthy, *non*-disturbed people could be the result!

---

*Typographical error for "causal"—E.M.O.

[1] Michael J. Goldstein and Howard S. Kant, with John L. Hartman, *Pornography and Sexual Deviance* (Berkeley: University of California Press, 1973), p. 70.

As for the reputedly "unreported" studies by Commission-financed researchers, they simply don't exist. Every single study *was* at least alluded to in the Commission on Obscenity and Pornography's report. The full studies are readily available from the Government Printing Office, or in the hundreds of depository libraries throughout the United States.

I find Dr. Cline's article, in sum, as ". . . highly unethical, irresponsible, and contrary to most canons of the scientific community" as his article found the Obscenity Commission's report. There was no data hidden, none suppressed in the report.

I recommend that any interested INTELLECT reader read the report for himself, and see who is correct in these diametrically opposite expressions of views.

EDITOR, *LIBRARY JOURNAL:*

The Williams-Pearce duo has produced ("Censorship Redefined," *LJ*, July, 1976, pp. 1494-96) a masterpiece of *reductio ad absurdum*, an old technique in argumentation which is very effective as a rhetorical device, but hardly of much practical value. Using their kind of logic, one would never, for example, go on a diet, because various pettifogging distinctions and redefinitions of the Williams-Pearce type would oppose gormandizing and fasting, and anything in between would be unacceptable because it would not be "pure."

Despite the fact that their article is an obvious satire, several of their offhand *obiter dicta* need some comment. It is neither true that "censorship controversies rarely consist of more than accusations and denials" nor that "they go nowhere." Censorship controversies *do* result in reading or viewing either being circumscribed or denied or permitted, and the end result is *never* "nowhere."

Once again, as I said in my *LJ* letter (November 15, 1973, p. 3324) about their "Common Sense and Censorship" (*LJ*, September 1, 1973, pp. 2399-2400) these critics of intellectual freedom have expressed the conservative Catholic point of view, but this time they gave gone completely Aquinian. The thirteenth century was a great time for scholastic arguments about how many angels could dance on the point of a pin; 1976 is a little late for such. And it would be an utter waste of thought and time to spend "a mil-

lennium of controversy" on the niggling points tongue-in-cheeked
by Mr. Williams and Ms. Pearce; maybe a Bicentennial minute?

EDITOR, *LIBRARY JOURNAL:*

I am thoroughly dismayed by some of the quoted remarks from
not one but several librarians at the 1976 Pittsburgh Conference on
Resource Sharing in Libraries (*LJ*, November 15, 1976, p. 2336-38),
statements which went so far as to intimate that it was the responsibility of librarians to stop so-called "unnecessary literature," that
"most stuff published today . . . is pure crap." If this isn't precensorship, then I don't know it when I see it. Surely the librarian's
responsibility is selection, *not* to tell the publisher what to publish
and the author what to write. Upon what food do these fanatics
feed that they are grown so utterly irresponsible? If such advice as
theirs is heeded, then truly librarianship has lost its real *raison
d'être*!

EDITOR, *WILSON LIBRARY BULLETIN* [never published by *WLB*]:

Peter Marshall's "Case Against Information Power" (in your
November 1976 issue) is a very weak one, indeed. It is entirely logical, but, unfortunately for its success at persuasiveness, is based on
a very, very weak major premise. Just why *should* "the library
profession admit that it has a responsibility to the spiritual well-
being of its clientele"? Somehow Mr. Marshall has confounded the
library (presumably, the *public* library) with a church or synagogue.

No reasonable librarian can question that "the librarian must
have the intelligence and maturity necessary for discriminating
judgment." I only wish Mr. Marshall had exhibited these qualities
in his own essay; instead, he took the space afforded him as an
opportunity to indicate all of his various prejudices—such as those
against integration, social welfare, and (most important of all for
librarianship) intellectual freedom.

For Mr. Marshall's information, intellectual freedom is not in
opposition to decency (the greatest of Marshall's virtues). By his
definition of decency, the only books which would be available in

libraries would be those which suited his ultraconservative set of values. Intellectual freedom, far from being value-free, as he keeps saying, is in support of one of the very greatest of traditional values. Or does Mr. Marshall disagree with the quite traditional view that "Ye shall know the Truth, and the Truth shall make you free"?

Finally, what evidence can Mr. Marshall give that "universities [have] abandoned moral education"? Many recent studies seem to indicate quite the opposite. For example, Douglas H. Heath's *Growing Up in College: Liberal Education and Maturity* (Josey-Bass, 1968) found that "the college powerfully effected a reformation of the consciences of its students. They became more liberal, less tied to conventional ritual and rite." I'm sure Mr. Marshall's set of value judgments would call these results "immoral" and "indecent." Others would differ. America academia is not of a single pattern; surely Brigham Young University and the Jewish Theological Seminary might well produce the kinds of value judgment which Marshall seeks. But it is quite jejune to make such easy and indefensible generalizations about the moral effects of the university as did Mr. Marshall. There just is not a roaring vacuum into which the librarian must rush to redeem the failing moral values of college students. This is all too simplistic a cure for the many ills of our society.

Mr. Marshall and I agree that society needs improvement; we differ on "what" and "how."

EDITOR, *WILSON LIBRARY BULLETIN:*

Clara Jones has certainly added to our knowledge of Constitutional theory and practice in her "Reflections on *The Speaker*" (*WLB*, September, 1977). Since *she* does not believe "the subject of the inferiority of black people is . . . an open question," then it, perforce, becomes (for her) a "spurious subject," and, as such (she says), "is not entitled to open discussion." As a member of a minority group which has endured persecution and prejudicial discussions for thousands of years, I understand her feelings. But I cannot understand her reasoning about the First Amendment, or, indeed, about *The Speaker.*

The Speaker is not racist, except in the sense of U.N. Ambassador Andrew Young's recent public statement that Abraham Lincoln was racist. In that sense, I suppose, Clara Jones is, then, racist; so is Eli Oboler, and indeed, so is everyone! We *all* have feelings about superiority/inferiority—and the *facts* are not easily ascertainable. But denying the right to *discuss* these facts and feelings and opinions is certainly contrary to any reasonable understanding of the First Amendment or of the Library Bill of Rights.

To carry her reasoning one logical step further, the *Wilson Library Bulletin* had no right to carry her article; after all, it did discuss (albeit negatively) this "spurious subject" and *non*-"open question" of racial inferiority. With this kind of Lewis Carroll logic, we will end up with intellectual freedom for no one to discuss *anything*.

THE NORMAN-OBOLER-JOUST

EDITOR, *LIBRARY JOURNAL* [from Ron Norman, Director, Kearney Public Library, Kearney, Nebraska]:

Once upon a time in Libraryland, there lived a noble and valiant knight named Sir Eli. It was his mission (perhaps divinely ordained) to protect the holy cause of intellectual freedom—the most sacred cause in all of Libraryland. On occasion, he would sally forth from his redoubt of Academe, located in the rarified and crisp air that was the blessing of that northern sector of Libraryland where he resided, for at times from the lower regions of Libraryland rumblings would reach him which would indicate that the precepts of intellectual freedom were being questioned.

Now on a recent occasion word reached him that a craven miscreant named Flanagan had written a tract "Defending the Indefensible: The Limits of Intellectual Freedom." "Foul Flanagan," he cried, "Pusillanimous, perfidious, pernicious Flanagan! Oh, what a farrago of fear! Vile, freedom-fearing Flanagan! Verily, his tract should have been called 'Running Up the White Flag: The Limits of Cowardice.' Although there are undoubtedly many in the land like myself—couragious, professional—who are waiting in line to test him in combat, I cannot, may, I dare not renounce my mission. Is it not true that a man's reach should exceed his grasp / or what's a heaven for?''

So ever impatient to enter the fray, Sir Eli sallied forth from the walls of Academe—a bludgeon in one hand and a hacking sword in the other. With his bludgeon he smashed at a Flanagan impracticality, then with his hacking sword he chopped away at an oversimplification. Warming to his task, wielding both weapons simultaneously, he rapidly dispatched Flanagan's legal difficulties and anti-intellectualism. Finally, drawing a dagger from his belt, he administered the *coup de grace*—so much for want of professionalism.

Never willing to wait for the acclamation of the crowd which would surely be his because of his quick and decisive victory over Flanagan, he turned back to the heights of his beloved Academe. Later, one small child was found who was willing to testify (under oath if necessary) that Sir Eli's last words as he strode away were, "Withhold nothing from the shelves. Seriatim! Rest in peace, knowing that I shall return whenever I am needed."

EDITOR, *LIBRARY JOURNAL* [from Ron Norman, Director, Kearney Public Library, Kearney, Nebraska]:

Once more the hills and dales of Libraryland reverberate with the sound of combat for the noble and valiant Knight Sir Eli has sallied forth again from the heights of his beloved Academe (*LJ*, November 1, 1976, p. 2203). Having dispatched "Foul Flanagan" in his last adventure, he now has engaged not one but two miscreants, the ignoble Williams-Pearce duo, who had conspired to create "a masterpiece of reductio ad absurdum."

As he left his beloved Academe, he had assured the crowd which had gathered to see him off, "Experto credite for facile princips and operose nihil agunt," and upon encountering the deadly duo he had rushed them with the cry, "Proh pudor! Me judice! O santus simplicitas! Fiat justitia, ruat caelum!"

Now, locked in fierce battle, first one combatant then another could be heard to exclaim, "Argumentum ad hominem" (Sir Eli), to which came the responses, "Arcades ambo," and "Can you not take anything cum grano salis?" "Ad rem," Sir Eli retorted.

"Never let it be said of me that (as I have said on January 1, 197__ and which I said before this date on August 15, 196__ and which I first said on April 1, 195__) nemo me impune lacessit. I dispatch you currente calamo."

Then there was silence.

Slowly, as the dust of battle settled, the erect figure of Sir Eli took sharper form, and he quietly uttered these words, "Salvo pudore . . . tenax propositi . . . what I have done is mirabile dictu . . . satis verborum."

In nuce—finis coronat opus.

EDITOR, *LIBRARY JOURNAL* [from E.M.O.]:

In a January 15th letter to *LJ* (p. 139), Ron Norman continued his own version of the *Morte d'Arthur*. Let me remind him—and anyone else interested—that, according to Tennyson's version, the code for Knights of the Round Table included these goals: "To ride abroad redressing human wrongs / To speak no slander, no, nor listen to it . . ." The issue of intellectual freedom vs. censorship is really too significant, I believe, for trivialization.

Recent censorship
literature reviewed
and two lists

9

(The nineteen book reviews [two of one book—to what turned out to be against the rules of two editors!] and two booklists in this chapter cover quite an imposing library of books worth reading in the difficult area of intellectual freedom/censorship. From Marjorie Fiske in 1959 to Ralph McCoy in 1979, the perspective is broad, and the disputes are many. I think I see at least some consistency in the reviewer's attitude, if not necessarily in those of the authors.)

REVIEWS

Book Selection and Censorship: A Study of School and Public Libraries in California. Marjorie Fiske. University of California Press, 1959.

For some time there has been discussion and even apprehension throughout the library world about the Fiske report. Advance news told us that this study, financed by the Ford Fund for the Republic and sponsored by the University of California School of Librarianship, would show that public and school librarians were doing far more actual censoring on their own, quietly, than was even advocated, let alone successfully carried on, by outside pressure groups.

Unfortunately a reading of the actual printed report serves to make the picture a good deal blacker than those who are sincere believers in the freedom to read would like. I say "sincere," because this study points up the interesting finding that although nearly 50% of the librarians interviewed by Miss Fiske and staff "expressed unequivocal freedom-to-read convictions," the sad fact is that in practice, "nearly two-thirds of all librarians who have a say in book selection reported instances where the controversiality of a book or an author resulted in a decision not to buy." Worse yet, almost 20% of those interviewed "*habitually* avoid buying any material which is known to be controversial or which they believe might become controversial. . . ." Even among those with "strong" feelings about the freedom to read, "40 percent take controversiality into account under some circumstances, particularly if another, more 'legitimate,' reason can be found for avoiding a book."

Of course, as all librarians know, there are many ways of restricting circulation, once a book is added. Of the 46 school and 45 county and municipal libraries studied, 82% placed some restrictions on the distribution of controversial books, with 91% of the public librarians so operating. Three out of ten permanently removed from their collection controversial materials "on one occasion or another." Some restricted circulation by transfer to the librarian's office (33%), some put such books on "reserve" so that patrons had to request them (33%), and 27% put the worry-causing volumes "under or behind the front desk." Fifteen percent limited the number of copies bought, 14% used other restrictions (such as labeling books with a symbol on the spines or circulation cards to indicate particular groups), and 7% put the items in locked cases. Miss Fiske states that "the librarian who has President Eisenhower's comment on freedom to read pasted on the glass door of a locked bookcase is probably not conscious of anything untoward about this circumstance."

On the basis of her 1956-58 study, Miss Fiske concludes that in general—at least in California—"an atmosphere of caution" prevails among the library profession. Yes, profession, even though "those with no professional training are more likely to avoid controversial materials habitually (29% as compared with 16%)." Miss Fiske also reveals the somewhat unexpected information that "exposure to professional organizations seems to be conducive to the kinds of compromises in book selection that can be professionally rationalized."

This is an important volume, both in its explicit statements and in the implications its findings have for the library profession, library education, and the future relationships of librarians with the public. As Miss Fiske says, in comparing her state to the rest of the country in its reaction to the various "drives" to restrict library book purchases considered controversial, Californians are "just like other people but perhaps more so . . ."

Look at your own state or province, your own community, your own library, yourself. *Book Selection and Censorship* may turn out to be more of a mirror than a landscape of a scene far away. This is one book that, although controversial, should be bought by 100% of all libraries and restricted by none.

Freedom of Inquiry: Supporting the Library Bill of Rights. American Library Association Intellectual Freedom Committee. American Library Association, 1965.

Of the printing of statements and opinions and facts intended to help those who are on the firing line in the perpetual war against censorship there seems to be no end . . . and this is a very good thing. The enemy is a constantly shifting one, and every responsible, cogent collection, such as this, of materials to help those who are attempting to support the Library Bill of Rights is of great value. This particular collection—reprinting material in the June, 1965 *ALA Bulletin*—is of particular importance because it (and the *Bulletin*) put into print for the first time some very important arguments countering the kind of material that is put out by the thousands of copies by the advocates of censorship.

It is rather refreshing, for once, to see the opinions of others besides librarians included in discussing the freedom to read. Too long have we listened mostly to ourselves, and the perspective afforded by such authorities as Dr. William C. Kvaraceus, Director of Youth Studies, Lincoln Filene Center for Citizenship and Public Affairs at Tufts University, writing on "Can Reading Affect Delinquency?," or Theodore Gill, President of the San Francisco Theological Seminary at San Anselmo, California, telling us about "The Freedom to Read and Religious Problems," is most salutary.

One of the most exciting parts of these proceedings is the reprinting of the inspiring and most informative talk by nationally known attorney Edward de Grazia, who is the attorney of record in several vital Supreme Court cases on censorship. Mr. de Grazia, writing on "Defending the Freedom to Read in the Courts," here makes available the kind of legal opinion and advice that would cost a good deal if done on an individual basis. Perhaps the most important statement that he makes is that "any material selected by a librarian, in the exercise of his function as a librarian, is protected (under the recent Supreme Court decisions—Ed.). The protection extends both to his acquisition and retention of the material, and also precludes any valid prosecution of the librarian for acquiring it or retaining it." Mr. de Grazia makes clear that in general, in his opinion, under the law today "the librarian . . . is absolutely entitled to acquire, and make available to an adult, for library purposes, any book, in confidence that any prosecution of him or injunction against him by state or federal authorities for any of these acts would, if properly presented, be invalidated by the U.S. Supreme Court." This is only a brief portion of a vital article, which alone justifies acquiring this permanent collection of the reporting of the proceedings of the important Conference on Intellectual Freedom held in Washington, D.C., on January 23-24, 1965.

In addition, there is a series of brief statements, by such people as Richard B. Kennan of the National Education Association, Enid M. Olson of the National Council of Teachers of English, Nancy Baker of the Freedom of Information Center, and Peter Jennison of the National Book Committee, on censorship, each of which has its particular claim to notice and deserves attention. Other articles are contributed by Archie L. McNeal, Martha Boaz, Dan Lacy, Lee A. Burress, Jr., Charles Morgan, Jr., and Wesley McCune. Mr. McCune's article, entitled "The Freedom to Read and the Political Problem," is especially important for its compilation of otherwise rather difficult to get in one place items on the extreme right wing and its activities concerning censorship.

All in all, this is the kind of book which should be on the book shelf of every professional librarian, and certainly of which there should be a copy available to the general public in every public library, school library (for the professional shelf), and academic library.

I recommend it without reservation. Just because the Pacific Northwest area has not been very much plagued to date by censorship problems is no sign that this condition will continue for the indefinite future. Anyone who wants to be forewarned and forearmed cannot afford to miss this book.

From Radical Left to Extreme Right: Current Periodicals of Protest, Controversy, or Dissent—U.S.A. Robert H. Muller. Ann Arbor, Michigan: Campus Publishers, 1967.

Dr. Muller has almost written a self-review in his lengthy title and subtitle to his unique and very much worthwhile publication. Since the University of Michigan Library, of which he is the Associate Director, is blessed with the most unusual Labadie Collection, which contains many otherwise not readily available "radical" publications, he was able to do practically all of the research for this work right on the spot. It has been a labor of love for Dr. Muller, which should be paid for by the profession by a widespread purchase of the book.

As he notes in his very clear and explanatory preface, "to purchase all of the periodicals analyzed in this volume would cost a library around $600 per year." Surely, as Dr. Muller says, to obtain these publications would "serve an important educational function in alerting people to the existence of dissenting views in our society that has increasingly been tending toward consensus and conformity."

Typically, publications such as "The Rockwell Report," "American Atheist," "Realist," and "On Target" (the official publication of the Minutemen, an armed secret organization to combat Communism, with the motto ("Words Won't Win—Action Will"), are not made available even in the larger libraries of the United States. The question arises, especially for librarians who give lip-service to the Library Bill of Rights, why? If we are truly professional librarians, and if our purpose is really to provide our patrons with the kinds of publications that they need to have to understand our entire culture, rather than simply parts of it, at least a representative selection from this list should be seriously considered by every librarian who has the space and the funds to house these magazines.

Dr. Muller's objurgation that "when we deal with such publications, the usual criteria of book selection, that is, substance and quality, do not apply" should be remembered. He stresses that "we should not bar them from the public just because we may find them distasteful personally, or uninteresting, or of low quality . . ." He points out that "the library should consider it as an obligation to display as much of the spectrum of dissident opinion as space will allow, so that the library can serve as a sort of 'Hyde Park Corner' where free communications, a clash of ideas, can become a conspicuous new dimension of library service."

Our gratitude as a profession is due to Dr. Muller for this groundbreaking publication. He has informed me that the printer was very doubtful as to whether even as small an edition as was issued would sell. This reviewer hopes that in the Pacific Northwest, alone, the entire first edition may be sold out. It is reasonably priced, carefully edited, and a source of information that is absolutely unavailable without going through the many hours, days, and months and even years of effort that have produced the book.

In his preface Dr. Muller says that he plans a regular updating of this compilation, if demand warrants. If demand does *not* warrant continuance of this kind of publication, we might as well forget about the Library Bill of Rights and admit that we are simply following the conformist pattern which non-librarians often feel is the stereotype for all librarians.

Censorship: For and Against. H. L. Hart. Hart Publishing, 1971. *Perspectives on Pornography.* Douglas A. Hughes. St. Martin's Press, 1970.

When W. S. Gilbert delivered the rhymed (after a fashion) dictum

"That every boy and every girl
That's born into the world alive,
Is either a little Liberal,
Or else a little Conservative!"

he was probably not thinking of the further dictum that "to be liberal is to be against censorship: to be conservative is to be for it."

Reading H. L. Hart's paperback compilation of original* essays on censorship can be fun, if you read the list of contributors, view

*Not quite: Charles Rembar's essay is adapted and updated from portions of his *The End of Obscenity* (Random House, 1968) and his contribution to *Censorship and Freedom of Expression: Essays on Obscenity and the Law* (edited by Harry Clor; Rand McNally, 1971).

their portraits and dossiers, and then try to predict whether they will be "pro" or "con," *before* reading each untitled section. Let's see: Hollis Alpert? Judith Christ? Monsignor Joseph Howard? Charles H. Keating, Jr.? Nat Hentoff? Charles Rembar? Max Lerner? Rebecca West? Eugene McCarthy? Carey McWilliams? Ernest von den Haag? Rabbi Arthur Lelyveld?

Yes—the Catholic priest and the Jewish rabbi are in opposite camps. The liberal U.S. senator, the liberal movie critics, the noted novelist, the liberal lawyer, the liberal journalist—all argue strongly against censorship, in varying degrees and for different reasons. The conservative sociologist and the writer of the *Minority Report* for the Commission on Obscenity and Pornography argue just as vehemently *for* censorship.

The text of the book includes 154 pages against censorship, and only 57 pages for—9 articles against, 3 for. But there is one element of confusion in this tally: Monsignor Joseph Howard, Executive Secretary of the National Office for Decent Literature, concludes his 17-page stint by saying, "So, Mr. Editor, in your *Censorship: For and Against*, put me down with the Against." A careful reading of his arguments would seem to indicate that what he really meant was that he was *for* censorship, and *against* pornography. His chief contribution to the continuing argument, by the way, is what he calls the "Howard Pornographic Principle." Here it is, in the good Father's own capitalization: "THE FURTHER ONE IS REMOVED FROM REAL PORNOGRAPHY, THE MORE PER-MISSIVE HE IS LIKELY TO BE." Or, in other words, *censors* (police, some judges, some school administrators, Catholic priests) are in favor of *censorship!*

It is interesting to librarians to hear from Father Howard that (speaking of the Office for Decent Literature), "we don't worry about what adults were reading; our concern was with youngsters." The long record of NODL's attempts to limit adult reading to a juvenile level certainly confutes this statement.

Father Howard's main arguments are these: 1) "Think of the loss to society if even ONE (Father Howard's emphasis) of a thousand readers is drawn over the threshold of promiscuity, perversion, crime, or violence"; 2) The reason that no "causal connection between crime and pornography has ever been proven," he says, is that "no parent, however depraved, would ever allow his child to participate in such a study"; 3) "Where are we going to draw the line? . . . a few common sense rules are all we need." Somehow one wishes that Monsignor Howard had written down these "few common sense rules." Many people, from librarians to Supreme Court judges, would be grateful if he really does have the magic answers. His climaxing, clinching, superargument "against" censorship, quoted from "the man who has had more experience with crime and criminals than any man in the United States" (J. Edgar Hoover), is that "indecent literature is making criminals faster than we can build jails to house them." This is a fine, sweeping statement; it could stand just a little documentation.

Practicing psychoanalyst and NYU Adjunct Professor of Social Philosophy Ernest Van den Haag makes some quite broad—and rather easily demonstrated as false—generalizations about censorship.

Item: "Censorship has been abolished, with the exception—universal until quite recently—of sexual matters." *True—except that political and religious censorship definitely are still in existence (or what was the Pentagon Papers case all about?)—and sexual censorship has never in history been "universal."*

Item: "In all known societies, people function by controlling their impulses. . . ." *Malinowski and Mead, Levi-Strauss and Radcliffe Brown, why have you bothered?*

Item: ". . . the elimination of legal censorship might well provoke arbitrary and damaging non-legal attempts at repression by private persons and groups. . . ." *And just what are the Citizens for Decent Literature, Inc., and the National Office for Decent Literature, among many others . . . and how do they operate now when there is legal censorship?*

Item: "Censorship inflicts no suffering." *Tell Mark Twain and Tolstoi and D. H. Lawrence—and countless other writers, living and dead, that!*

The third of the pro-censorship trio included in this volume, Charles H. Keating, Jr., has, of course, become nationally famous, both as founder (1956) and legal counsel for the Citizens for Decent Literature, and as President Nixon's only appointee to the Commission on Obscenity and Pornography—the one who wrote the widely publicized "Minority Report" of the COP. Six of the nineteen pages in his whole contribution to this book are exactly the same as a similar six in his Minority Report; the other thirteen pages include such *ex parte*, undocumented statements as this one: "It is apparent that the laws prohibiting obscenity and pornography have played an important role in the creativity and excellence in our society." It should hardly be necessary to refute such outrageous claims as this in a magazine mainly read by educated persons! Most of his other arguments are about on this level of verifiability and acceptability.

As for the nine opponents of censorship, as previously indicated, they are a varied group in background and interest, and certainly in how they face the issue.

Film critic Hollis Alpert (*Saturday Review*) makes clear that he is *not* pro-pornography, even though he is anti-censorship. His main point against censorship is that with improving and changing technology—home videotaping, cassettes, cartridges, and such—"It would require, sooner or later, a vast national (even international) effort and *1984* would be here long before its time." He feels that censorship ". . . in the long run . . . is no more productive than flailing at windmills."

Veteran author and liberal Carey McWilliams is opposed to censorship for many reasons, principally because he is against using the criminal law "to attain purposes for which it is not well-suited." He considers society's social health may well be measurable in an inverse ratio to the degree of public demand for censorship. McWilliams sees censorship as basically "an attempt to suppress fears," specifically those concerned with sexuality.

Senator Eugene McCarthy, as might be expected, deals as much with political as with sexual censorship. He finds governmental control over news and information considerably more dangerous to "the health of American democracy . . . than freedom of expression and publication." As for sex censorship, he sees the crucial question to be the relationship, if any, between pornography and "violent or anti-social behavior," a question he considers "probably unanswerable one way or the other." But he indicates a general anti-censorship feeling.

Novelist and critic Rebecca West has the interesting thought that "the idea of censorship is unworkable but not unthinkable." She is strongly against censorship of books for adults, but even more strongly *for* censorship of sadistic pornography dealing with child-assault, or related themes. Like C. P. Snow's wife, Pamela Hanford Johnson, she feels that reading such material will invariably and inevitably lead to the commission of related sadistic crimes.

Judith Crist, well-known film critic, who ruefully anticipates "the censorious Seventies," in reaction to the new freedom in the arts of the Sixties, calls for only one kind of censorship—"self-censorship on the part of the public and . . . the creator." She feels we are about at the conclusion of what she calls "the era of voyeurism," and that the younger generation has taken sex and the arts "in stride—or couldn't care less."

Jazz and political writer Nat Hentoff not only feels that "censorship in any form is . . . unnecessary . . . and . . . unconstitutional," but states unequivocally that "it is, and it has been, and always will be, so long as any of it lasts, demonstrably harmful." His main point is that censorship feeds the illusions of those who believe that individual morality can be improved via legislation.

To the President of the American Jewish Congress, Rabbi Arthur Lelyveld, the appropriate punishment for "coarseness" is moral rather than legal condemnation. Like several of the others who were on the "Against" side in this book's two-sided presentation, he sees the possibility of a sort of self-cure in the present plethora of pornography, because "after a relatively short time, pornography produces ennui." Incidentally, the Rabbi is *not* for "variable obscenity" laws "defending" children; he favors "faith and good judgment" as a better solution than legislation.

The journalist and political scientist Max Lerner has one of the more thoughtful and original contributions, with his perception that the 60-5 U.S. Senate vote against the Commission on Obscenity and Pornography *Report* was expressing a "world view utterly different from the world view of the Commission." Lerner is not for either of the two views; his feeling is that "other persons, like myself, should have open to them the moral choice about the kind of erotic lives they will live." But he is willing to accept "not intolerable limits" to his own free choice, simply to avoid making life "intolerable" to others.

Lawyer Charles Rembar presents herein his familiar legalistic arguments for ending *all* literary censorship, because of the First Amendment.

Out of all this, can the librarian find some guidance, some help in doing his day-to-day job? Perhaps so, but more likely he will simply find this book "great argument about it and about," and come out by the same door wherein he went, to paraphrase Omar.

The best arguments for and against censorship are not all in this rather narrowly-ranging volume—and just possibly the editor would have done well to include at least one Downs or Shera or Moore or Asheim as "experts." Indeed, it is rather difficult to try to find good reasons why he did not. Surely the librarian who has spent his entire professional life dealing with the censor might well give better counsel than those whose concern with censorship is really only peripheral. Or did Mr. Hart perhaps feel that he and the rest of the general public knew in advance what the librarian would say and wanted and needed to hear from a new (and presumably less prejudiced) group? If so, the results were hardly novel or unbiased enough to justify the exclusion

Quite a different book is *Perspectives on Pornography*, edited by Douglas A. Hughes. The 14 contributors to this collection were not planning to contribute to a two-sided debate; they were, in 1961-69, writing for magazines and their own books. Perhaps that is why there is more strength and less equivocation in these expressions of points of view on both sides of an issue obviously directly related to censorship. Also, the authors make up a somewhat different mix— novelists (Moravia, Burgess), critics (Levin, Hyman, Steiner, Goodman, Elliott, Sontag, Phillips), academicians (Michelson, Mercier, van den Haag), a librarian (Felix Pollak), and the producer of "Oh! Calcutta!," Kenneth Tynan. Only one contributor, van den Haag, appears in both books.

Hughes, from his academic refuge at Washington State University, feels that far from being a signal of moral decline or the ebbing of our vitality, the acceptance of the senses and the thorough-going liberalization of sexual attitudes are "signs of vigor and health." He collected these essays in an attempt to answer what he deems to be "the two fundamental questions surrounding pornography: What are the psychological *effects* of pornographic works on the normal individual, as manifested in moral and social behavior; and to what extent may pornography be judged as legitimate literature rather than merely ersatz eroticism." In other words, his basic concerns are psychology and aesthetics, not morals or censorship or the law. Curiously, very few of the symposiasts find it possible to be quite as narrow in their discussions as Hughes would seem to want. The pornography in our civilization until very recently was identical with the legally censorable, and the complete *bouleversement* of sexual and moral values since World War II is still too recent for definitive, completely discerning views.

Moravia begins this volume with a very brief statement on "Eroticism in Literature," notable chiefly for its clear defense of today's literary writing about the sexual act, so long as it reaches neither extreme of "moralistic horror (or) vulgar hedonism." Anthony Burgess in "What is Pornography?" sees pornography as absolutely separated from literature, but does not condemn it for this. He criticizes censorship as a job for the critic, the individual, not the State, saying, "our souls are ultimately our own, and it is only to God that we pray not to be led into temptation."

Critic Harry Levin, one of those who testified for *Tropic of Cancer* in 1961, stresses, in his "The Unbanning of the Books," that "when everything has been said, we can focus on how it is said." English professor Vivian Mercier contrasts *"Master Percy* and/or *Lady Chatterley"*—explicit mid-Victorian pornography and the Lawrence classic—and calls for a "New Erotics," which "would be a blend of art and science," a sort of mixture of responsible asethetics and revelatory sex education—a rather tall order! Perceptive literary critic Stanley Edgar Hyman, writing "In Defense of Pornography," says "experience and taste will save us, those who want to be saved." Paul Goodman gives a rather lengthy (18½ pages) discussion on "Pornography, Art, and Censorship," claiming that censorship is the *cause*, rather than the *result*, of the prevalence of pornography, and then suggesting the values of an official, judicial point-of-view "that it was not obscene to stir sexual desires and thoughts," but that there must be "a probable social or human utility" to justify pornography in any form.

Peter Michelson, whose ideas on this subject can be read at much greater length in his *The Aesthetics of Pornography* (NY: Herder and Herder, 1971), writes "An Apology for Pornography" (first chapter of his book), calling pornography ". . . the imaginative record of man's sexual will" and averring that "not to explore the

impulse to pornography is a form of denying human sexuality."
George P. Elliott is strongly "Against Pornography," describing it
as "a social evil" and says that "a civilized method of censoring is
feasible" (although his idealistic conception of boards of censors
including judges or lawyers, humanities professors, and "a social
member, psychologist, or clergyman," begs the eternal question set
by Juvenal, "*Quis custodiet ipsos custodes?*").

In an article which has been rather widely cited, "Night Words:
High Pornography and Human Privacy," critic George Steiner
seems to want the "dirty" words to be reserved for sexual reality,
rather than representation. Of all varieties of art, for Steiner, that
dealing with sex alone should not be tolerated—which might well
justify a Freudian study of Steiner!

Drama critic and producer Kenneth Tynan, of course, says
"Dirty Books Can Stay." He defines pornography as "writing that
is exclusively intended to cause sexual pleasure." If one once grants
Tynan's claim that "the aim of pornography is physical enjoy
ment," and further accepts his dictum that "if a writer uses literary
craft to provoke sex and delight, he is doing an artist's job," then it
must logically follow that Tynan's answer to Hughes' two questions are: Pornography does have psychological, even physical
effects, and these are good; and pornography is perfectly legitimate
literature.

Sociologist Ernest van den Haag's point is that "The Case for
Pornography Is the Case for Censorship and Vice Versa." By thus
relating pornography and censorship, he directly (and explicitly)
counters Goodman's arguments; for van den Haag, "If we indulge
in pornography, and do not allow censorship to restrict it, our
society at best will become even more coarse, brutal, anxious, indif-
ferent, de-individualized, hedonistic; at worst its ethos will disinte-
grate altogether."

The cream of this collection is in the last three articles—Susan
Sontag's thoroughgoing examination of "The Pornographic
Imagination," Felix Pollak's sprightly "Pornography: a Trip
Around the Halfworld," and *Partisan Review* editor William
Phillips' brief but perspicacious "Writings About Sex." The Son-
tag *opus* is one of the few examples extant of purely aesthetic and
intellectual, rather than moralistic and simplistic, considerations of

the uses and potential of pornography as a literary *genre*. Pollak's entertaining essay may be epitomized by his final statement, that "the only acceptable view and practice of sex is the hedonistic one." Phillips recommends simply taking sex "for granted like other neutral activities, like, say, eating or swimming," and, as a concomitant, causing writing about sex to be judged by purely literary (rather than moral, political, or social) standards.

Perhaps an insight into what is and has been going on in our society in the way of changing values accorded to censorship and pornography might be afforded by looking at those compendia of the generally accepted dictionaries. The 1967 *Random House Dictionary* defined pornography as "obscene literature, art, or photography, esp. that having little or no artistic merit." The 1969 *American Heritage Dictionary* defined pornography as "written, graphic, or other forms of communication intended to excite lascivious feelings." Only a generation earlier the 1934 *Webster's New International Dictionary* gave these two definitions of pornography: "1. Description or portrayal of prostitutes or of prostitution," and "2. Obscene or licentious writing, painting, or the like." And the 1933 *Shorter Oxford Dictionary*'s definition was, rather similarly, "description of the life, manners, of prostitutes and their patrons; hence the expression or suggestion of obscene or unchaste subjects in literature or art."

Little by little, the cause of intellectual freedom progresses, even if it takes most lexicographers and some critics a long time to acknowledge that progress.

A Question of Judgment: the Fortas Case and the Struggle for the Supreme Court. Robert Shogan. Bobbs-Merrill, 1972.

Abe Fortas, a prominent Washington, D.C. attorney and advisor to at least three presidents, served as a Justice of the U.S. Supreme Court from October 4, 1965 to May 14, 1969. He resigned, under press and political pressure, because of his highly questionable financial relationship with a convicted stock swindler. The author of this book, a *Newsweek* writer, concludes that Fortas was the victim of "a case of non-criminal, non-judicial misbehavior," which the ethics committee of the American Bar Association found to be "clearly contrary to the canons of judicial ethics."

What should be of most interest to readers of the *Newsletter* is what Justice Fortas contributed (or did not contribute) to the continuing battle against censorship. During his nearly four years in office, Fortas was noted as a civil libertarian, nearly of the caliber and force of Justices Black and Douglas—but not quite.

The most famous difference between the Black-Douglas views of freedom of speech and that of Justice Fortas was on the Ralph Ginzburg case. According to Shogan, it was Fortas who "helped develop" the legal principle of "pandering" as a usable legal formula to attack distributors of "questionable" materials. In fact, says Shogan, Fortas "urged" this idea on Justice Brennan, over whose name the *Ginzburg* decision appeared.

Shogan claims that Fortas' justification for this was that "unless the Court imposed some limits on obscenity . . ., public revulsion would be so great that Congress might eventually step in and perhaps even revise the First Amendment." For Fortas, "his approach offered the most realistic defense of free expression." The reasoning behind this view, we are told, was that, by stressing the "pandering" point, those distributors of potentially "questionable" material who wished to avoid prosecution simply would have to do their advertising and promotion in a more circumspect way than did Ralph Ginzburg, with his use of what Justice Brennan called "the leer of the sensualist" in his promotion of his publications.

Justices Black and Douglas, in their minority opinions, differed strongly. Black, in accord with his well-known beliefs on the absoluteness of the right of freedom of speech, wrote, "I believe the Federal government is without any power whatsoever under the Constitution to put any type of burden on speech and expression of ideas of any kind." Indeed, he stated, "sex at least as much as any other aspect of life is so much a part of our society that its discussion should not be made a crime." Justice Douglas wrote in his opinion on *Ginzburg* that "I do not think it permissible to draw lines between the 'good' and the 'bad' and to be true to the constitutional mandate to let all ideas alone."

Fortas' quite acerbic judgment on both Black and Douglas—with whom on many other civil liberties issues he generally agreed—was that they were "whoring after principle" (which Shogan calls a "pungent phrase," but which I would characterize as more excessively rhetorical than "pungent").

Shogan's blow-by-blow description of the rather sad story of Fortas, his overweening ambition, and his poor judgment will probably be of more interest to political scientists than to librarians and library trustees. Actually, only two pages of this 313-page volume are directly concerned with obscenity-pornography-censorship. The minutiae of Fortas' rather unusual life history and personality, as chronicled herein, may be of some interest to those who have a psychological bent.

What Everyone Knew About Sex*: *Explained in the Words of Orson Squire Fowler and Other Victorian Moralists. William M. Dwyer. Payne, 1972.**

This cannot really be classed as anything but a funny book—which it is. Dwyer's work is certainly not a serious effort to review, reflect upon, or explain the sanctimonious, pseudoscientific "fact" books which the Victorians accepted as reliable guides for sexual behavior. The nine-page introduction contains this quite accurate description: ". . . a distillation of what some fifty . . . proper Victorians wrote about such subjects as abortion, courtship, female disorders, prostitution, and venereal disease." While laughing at the obviously stupid notion that masturbation causes acne, consider that our current sex fads may well convulse readers in 2072. For public libraries and academic browsing rooms.

The Supreme Court Under Earl Warren. Leonard W. Levy. Quadrangle Books, 1972.

Out of the once-read, too-soon-forgotten pages of various issues of the *New York Times Magazine* comes this cumulation of well-worth-reading articles by such authorities as Anthony Lewis (6 articles), Fred Rodell (3), Alan Westin (2), Alexander Bickel, Edmond Cahn, Bernard Schwartz, and Supreme Court Justice William J. Brennan, Jr. The editor, himself an authority on constitution history—particularly as related to civil liberties—devotes a good share of his preface and epilog to corroborating the accuracy of the generally high esteem held for the Warren Court by libertar-

---

**Reprinted from *Library Journal Book Review 1976.* Published by R. R. Bowker Co. (a Xerox Company). Copyright © 1976 by Xerox Corporation.

ians, as well as to cleaning up some misapprehensions about that Court.

For example, *did* the Warren Court really open the floodgates to an unprecedented flow of obscenity in our reading? Not really; despite its generally "broad view of the First Amendment rights, enabling obscene literature to escape censorship," the *Roth* decision —and some others—sustain the constitutionality of what are now looked upon by some as rather repressive state and federal obscenity laws. In particular, as Levy stresses, if the rulings on pandering in the *Ginzburg* decision "were applied literally, one might be jailed for hawking . . . even the Bible," if prurient interest was the basis for that sale.

The volume, of course, covers a much broader spectrum than how the Warren Court dealt with the freedom to read, or even with civil liberties in general. But Levy claims that on the whole the Supreme Court under Earl Warren's leadership (1953-1969) was basically dedicated "to passing on to future generations a better Bill of Rights burnished by growing use and imaginatively applied to new situations." And its legacy—as yet not appreciably affected by what might be called the Burger Court or the Nixon Court— depending on the reader's bias or lack of it!—is certainly an outstanding one.

In his epilog, Levy paints a rather dour picture of the first two years of the Burger Court, at least so far as concern with civil liberties is involved. In the 1970-71 term, for example, says Levy, in every single case involving a civil liberty or a civil right, the Court decided *against* such claims.

Still, the main point of this book is not condemnation of the early Burger Court, but general commendation of the Warren Court. Professor Joseph W. Bishop, Jr. of the Yale Law School praises the Warren group with faint damns in the area of their dealing with obscenity. He describes the sum total of the Wareen Court's several decisions which attempted to define obscenity as "verbal murk," asserting that each successive decision in this area "elaborated and augmented the confusion created by its predecessors."

Alexander Bickel, another Yale Law School professor, also criticizes the Warren Court for its lack of consistency in defining obscenity—as witness for the famous (or infamous) *Ginzburg* case, which added the completely gratuitous and non-precedent or even law-based term of "pandering" to the criteria for recognizing obscenity. He goes so far as to plump for letting "the politically responsible institutions" (in which description he obviously does not include the Supreme Court!) find balances "between contending interests and ideologies." For him the Warren Court too often followed the election returns, rather than clear, understandable, constitutional principle.

As was said earlier in this review, the total impression of this volume is definitely favorable to the Warren Court but the strictures on its verdicts in cases involving censorship are many. And this does seem odd, indeed, in the light of the fact that after all it was indubitably the Warren Court which will go down in American libertarian history as the one which made the real breakthrough for American intellectual freedom, via such cases as *Roth, Jacobellis, Lamont* v. *Postmaster General*, and others which effectively revitalized the First Amendment and its application to the freedom to read in our time.

The Law, the Supreme Court, and the People's Rights. Ann Fagan Ginger. Barron, 1974.

This handy household guide for the civil libertarian is a lively collection of what the author, a California constitutional lawyer and law professor, president and founder of the Meiklejohn Civil Liberties Institute in Berkeley, calls "landmarks in human rights law." All of the Supreme Court cases covered are "victories for the proponents of human rights law" during the years Earl Warren was Chief Justice. The book's range is very wide—with the three sections covering cases involving many facets of denials of freedom, justice, and equality. Ms. Ginger devotes only a few pages—one brief chapter out of twenty-nine—to freedom of the press and only a portion of those pages to what she considers—as do many students of the subject—probably the most important single Supreme Court decision on obscenity, *Roth* v. *United States* (1957). Much as *Roth* has been discussed, the Ginger report is useful and fresh. She points out that *Roth* was the very first case in the whole history of the U.S. Supreme Court to face up to the basic constitutionality of and the standards for American obscenity law. After reviewing the essentials of both the majority and dissenting opinions in *Roth*, she concludes this section with an updating paragraph on the implications of the famous—or infamous—1973 Court majority decisions relating to obscenity.

Certainly the Ginger volume is not essential for any library or librarian concerned only with the material it contains directly bearing on intellectual freedom—but its comprehensiveness on civil liberties generally, its up-to-dateness, and the very reasonable price (even for a paperback) combine to make it a valuable volume for all *Newsletter* readers.

Where Do You Draw the Line? Victor B. Cline, ed. Brigham Young University Press, 1974.

A new and disturbing phenomenon is becoming evident in American intellectual life: the role of the defender of the censor is more and more being assumed, not by the Yahoos, the illiterate, the taboo-and-emotion-driven members of what H. L. Mencken used to call the "booboisie," but, to an alarming extent, by our social scientists, psychiatrists, and physicians. Witness a medium-sized bombshell from the pristene ambience of Brigham Young University; out of Provo, Utah, comes a white-jacketed volume (with the cover-page dramatically bespattered with a raw, red, blood-resembling line ending in a crimson blotch of ink), which is subtitled *An Exploration into Media Violence, Pornography, and Censorship.*

No less than twenty savants, ranging from the editor of *Commentary* to the former Surgeon General of the United States, and including law professors, political scientists, psychologists, psychiatrists, psychoanalysts, and physicians, give us the benefit of their individual and collective thinking on such topics as "The Case for Liberal Censorship" (Irving Kristol), "The Impact of Violence and Pornography on the Arts and Morality" (Robert E. Fitch), "Pornography Effects; the State of the Art" (Victor B. Cline), and "Democracy and Pornography" (Ernest van den Haag). Some of the book's contents have previously been published, even widely printed, and some are new; but all do seem to agree that there really is no answer to the question asked in the title. And not one gives a clear and direct answer to the more important query, "*Why* do you draw the line?"—which is nowhere asked in the book's 365 pages.

The 58-page section titled specifically "Where Do You Draw the Line?" includes a statement by a Stanford psychology professor (Dr. Alberta Siegel) on suggested "Alternatives to Direct Censorship"—among which she includes "an independent monitoring agency to provide regular reports on the level of violence in television entertainment," consumer boycotts of "violence vendors" (both by non-purchase of products so advertised and by refusal to buy stock in such firms), "increased support for public television," ". . . travel fellowships to the writers and producers of children's television programs," and the appointment of a "child advocate" to the FCC staff. This is a mixed bag, indeed, of constructive and censorial suggestions.

Dr. James Q. Wilson, Harvard government professor, discusses "Violence, Pornography, and Social Science," concluding, without really proving his conclusions, that "in the cases of violence and obscenity, it is unlikely that social science can either show harmful effects or prove that there are no harmful effects. . . . These are moral issues," he says, "and ultimately all judgments about the acceptability of restrictions on various media will have to rest on political and philosophical considerations." Surely this is a counsel of despair!

Miami (Ohio) University political science professor Reo M. Christenson agrees that "statutory-judicial definitions of pornography are rather vague," but, rather vaguely on his own part, argues that "the same applies to numerous other laws," such as monopoly-definition under the Sherman anti-trust law. Kenyon College political science professor Harry M. Clor comes perhaps the closest to answering the book's title-question in his essay on "Obscenity and Freedom of Expression," but he still blurs any distinction between "soft" and "hard-core" obscenity. Dr. Cline concludes with the quite unsupportable claim that "there is no historical instance where control of obscene or violent media materials has endangered other freedoms"; one among many possible answers is to remind Dr. Cline (and anyone else interested) of the classical case of the British persecution for obscenity of American rebellion-favoring John Wilkes, during the eighteenth century.

But—philosophical, historical, political, and ethical considerations aside—what is more important is that it certainly behooves librarians and library trustees to read this volume, if only in self-defense. With all its imperfections, the volume presents a surface impression of being a seamless web, which the censoriously inclined will undoubtedly welcome for its supply of what look like valid supporting arguments. Those on the other side will find the Goldstein-Kant volume, *Pornography and Sexual Deviance* (University of California Press, 1973) and H. H. Hart's compilation, *Censorship: For & Against* (Hart Pub., 1971), readily available. (My innate modesty forbids more than a brief reference to a recent publication by the writer of this review, which includes an extended anti-censorship bibliography, as well as some detailed arguments which might seem appropriate in refuting presentations in the Cline collection.)

Brigham Young University Press, incidentally, does not know where to draw the line on common ethics in publishers' advertising: their *Publishers' Weekly* advertising for this book quotes a very favorable review by Dr. Fredric Wertham. Unfortunately for one's likelihood to accept his encomia as unbiased, a nineteen-page excerpt from a 1966 book by Dr. Wertham is one of the items reprinted in the very book he recommends.

The Morality of Consent. Alexander M. Bickel. Yale University Press, 1975.

This posthumously published volume, based on lectures delivered at Yale in 1974, is a book that, like Yale law professor Bickel himself, will comfort the afflicted and afflict the comfortable. It may even rearrange—if not completely reverse—your prejudices.

What Bickel, throughout a long writing career (which, a useful bibliography of his writings in *Consent* tells us, included nine books, 154 periodical articles and book chapters, and fifteen book reviews), strove to communicate to his legal colleagues and to justice-minded citizens, was that there is more—much more—to the search for justice and equality than seen by those whom he describes as "disenchanted and embittered simplifiers and moralizers."

To the hard questions he asks in his book, on such vital matters as the proper goals of the U.S. Supreme Court, the duties and responsibilities of a citizen and the proper role of what he calls "domesticated civil disobedience" in a democracy, and the relationship of the intellectual and moral authority, Bickel has no easy answers. But in a comparatively brief space he outlines for the thoughtful the possibilities of at least "an imperfect justice, for there is no other kind" and of a moral authority which will be made strong by arising from "that middle distance where values are prominently held, are tested, and evolve within the legal order. . . ."

Not, I hasten to add, that this kind of reasonable, ratiocinative approach means Bickel was an either-or type, an on-this-side-and-that-side wabbler. He is quite definite and clear as to where he stands on many issues quite significant for civil libertarians. For example, he agrees with a 1971 Supreme Court decision in *Rosenbloom* v. *Metromedia, Inc.*, which he paraphrases as stating "that freedom of expression, if it would fulfill its historic function in this nation, must embrace all issues about which information is needed or appropriate to enable the members of society to cope with the exigencies of this period."

Bickel was clearly on the side of the conservatives as regards obscenity. He sees the role of any law against obscenity as "supportive, tentative, even provisional. It walks a tightrope and runs high risks." He admits that "on occasion, in some corner of the country, some fool finds Chaucer obscene or the lower female leg indecent," but still he feels there needs to be such laws, although they "must avoid tyrannical enforcement of supposed majority tastes, while providing visible support for the diffuse private endeavors of an overwhelming majority of people to sustain the style and quality of life minimally congenial to them."

Clearly Bickel was not an all-out follower of the John Stuart Mill kind of libertarianism; as the first twenty-five pages of this book state unequivocally, he favors Edmund Burke above John Locke and Rousseau. As many passages indicate, he is in disagreement with Justice Hugo Black's all-out, black-and-white reading of the First Amendment's protection of freedom of *all* speech, of "an absolute right to self-expression and to conscience."

There is a good deal in Bickel's book that will irritate, perhaps even inflame, the librarian who sees every word of the Library Bill of Rights as revealed gospel. But, as Bickel reminds us—if the continual recent surprises from the Burger Court when dealing with such matters haven't already—"ambiguity and ambivalence . . . is, if not the theory, at any rate the condition of the First Amendment in the law of our Constitution." There are grounds for agreement with his pronouncement that "one has to believe that no amount of opinion can be eternally certain of the moral righteousness of its preferences, and that whoever is in power in the government is entitled to give effect to his preferences."

Bickel is against "a dictatorship of the self-righteous," and so am I. Yet, writing this review, as I am, on the first day after the resignation of that doughty warrior for the First Amendment and defender of library freedoms, William O. Douglas, I wonder if Bickel was not perhaps a shade *too* cautious, too un-liberal in his Burkean conservative-liberalism. Yet he *was* the chief—and victorious—counsel for the *New York Times* in the Pentagon Papers case. If prior restraint in this "national security" case had been sanctioned by the Supreme Court, we might *never* have gotten rid of Richard Nixon!

This one goes on my shelf of recent "re-readables," alongside John Rawls' *A Theory of Justice*, Robert Nozick's *Anarchy, State, and Utopia*, and James M. Buchanan's *The Limits of Liberty*. Those who favor the recently suggested sweeping revision of the Library Bill of Rights might well read all four before going *too* far on the road to complete Rousseauism.

Freedom of the Press vs. Public Access. Benno C. Schmidt, Jr. Praeger, 1976.

In May, 1976, the American Newspaper Publishers Association formed a committee to talk with judges and lawyers on how to deal with "gag orders" by judges restricting what newspapers can print about court cases. Columbia Law Professor Schmidt, once a law clerk to Chief Justice Warren, herein deals with almost exactly the other side of the coin, that the press *must* give access to opinions contrary to what it prints. (His study was backed initially by the National News Council, "an independent body dedicated to the preservation of the media's rights under the First Amendment, concerned with the public's confidence in the fairness and integrity of the media, providing a forum for ventilation for the public and the media, and opposing government regulation of the media."

That description is from the foreword, written by NCC Chairman Stanley H. Fuld. The other sponsor of Schmidt's work is the Aspen Institute Program on Communications and Society, probably, since its 1971 beginning, the seminal group involved in such studies, with trustees ranging from Attorney General Edward H. Levi to Dr. Karl Menninger, from Robert S. McNamara to Mortimer Adler.)

At first encounter, the idea that the public is entitled to have its dissenting or differing opinions printed in a newspaper or magazine sounds most attractive. Surely free speech is not really free if only one side of a controversial topic is printed in the mass media. But let's see how this would work in a library milieu.

Suppose a public or academic library issued a booklist on a controversial topic, and that list did not enumerate all the possible books—even in that particular library—on the topic considered. Would the author of a book already in the library, but not in the published list, have the right to demand revision of the list to include *his* publication? This hypothetical situation is not really far removed from the *Miami Herald Publishing Co.* v. *Tornillo* Supreme Court decision to deny so-called "guarantee of access"—government-enforced—to individuals or groups.

Consider another—perhaps less hypothetical or unlikely—library-related "access" problem. Suppose the John Birch Society (or the Socialist Labor Party or the National Rifle Association or the Right to Life group), or any of these groups' members, insisted that a public or school or academic library *had* to accept gifts of publications of these highly partisan organizations and make them equally available to library patrons with the publications which were on the other side. Under *Miami Herald*, are you, as the librarian, now protected against such "guaranteed access"?

Surely libraries—just as well as newspapers, magazines, publishers, the electronic media—are promulgators, disseminators of information. Read Schmidt's thorough-going, readable, and fact-full book for its own sake—but (and perhaps more usefully for the library profession) for its implications for the libraries and librarians of America. A similar study along the lines suggested just above might be of profound value to the profession. Any access-law-theory librarians around?

Those libraries stretching out a timid toe to step into the boiling waters of public cable television will benefit from Schmidt's chapter on this already quite important and potentially vital topic. As Schmidt says, "Since 1972, cable television has been the vehicle for the most ambitious and far-reaching access obligations yet attempted in the United States." The continuing debate on traditional broadcasting's access rights and obligations is—so far—a settled question in cable television. But there are many complications: for example, if a cable channel shows teleprinter type from the wire services or an operator holds up pages of printed books for telecast and viewing, does cable television then become a *print* medium, not bound under FCC regulations?

We are in a McLuhanatic world, whether we like it or not. The problems are complex, the solutions are certainly not simple—but read Schmidt for authoritative elucidation and valuable judgments. *Miami Herald* will not be the Supreme Court's last word on media-access—but, as Schmidt says, it may, oddly enough, bring "a commitment to journalistic responsibility," now that—with some qualifications—the media don't *have* to be responsible on a constitutional level. Professional morals and ethics may bring even better access for the public than enforcement by legal regulation.

Literature, Obscenity, & Law. Felice Flanery Lewis. Southern Illinois University Press, 1976.

Academic librarians usually feel themselves above the continuing battle between the censor and the advocate of intellectual freedom. By definition, they say, the academic library is the place where no censor is either welcome or effective. But, upon consideration, it is easy to identify many ways in which the supposedly seamless web of academic librarianship could be—and frequently is—breached. Every type of librarian needs to know as much as possible about the past history and likely future trends of both the publication of and judicial restraints on literary works dealing with sex.

It is rather surprising that Dr. Lewis (Dean of Connolly College, The Brooklyn Center, Long Island University) has herein written the very *first* book to deal with *all* ". . . works of imaginative literature . . . known to have been the subject of obscenity litigation in the United States . . . ," as well as related judicial opinions. Despite what the popular belief seems to be, Dean Lewis stresses the well-documented fact that "... censors have not discriminated between outstanding cultural contributions and ... worthless pornography," although judges usually have, especially at the Supreme Court level.

In highly readable fashion Dean Lewis reminds us that a great many of our leading litterateurs—including Whitman, Dreiser, Cabell, Faulkner, Sinclair, Farrell, Caldwell, Hellman, Edmund Wilson, and O'Hara—have faced the censor's censure. The record is not one to make freedom-loving Americans proud, but it is useful to have it available through this volume. Nearly one-third of the book's text (seventy-eight pages) is devoted to detailed description and/or illustrative quotations from fiction, poetry, and drama involved in American obscenity cases since 1890 (which, the author claims, was the beginning of both a sexual revolution in American fiction and of the first really substantial effort to censor by law and legal action such fiction without regard to literary merit).

Her book is comprehensive and clear but could have profited from more attention to the efforts of those groups and individuals who led the anti-censorship fight—the American Civil Liberties Union (one brief reference) and the American Library Association (unmentioned), for example. There is a great deal included on the efforts of the so-called "anti-vice" groups.

But, as a pioneering and thorough work in a highly significant field for librarians and others devoted to intellectual freedom, it deserves a place on the shelves of every academic librarian and library.

Literature, Obscenity, and Law. Felice Flanery Lewis. Southern Illinois University Press, 1976.

Surprisingly, this appears to be the first book published in America which deals specifically and entirely with the censorship of fiction. There have, of course, been many volumes which concerned themselves with censorship in general, but Dr. Lewis, dean of Connolly College, The Brooklyn Center, Long Island University, has aimed at the heart of the problems confronting American creative writers and tolerant readers. She sees 1890 as the watershed year when there was both "the beginning of a sustained effort to censor fiction, regardless of its literary quality, through legal action." And in 1976, nearly a century later, we still have American fiction dealing explicitly with sex, as well as censors—from local prosecutors all the way up to the Supreme Court—trying to repress and restrain.

First, the book gives a brief but comprehensive review of the history of literary censorship in the colonies and the early United States, as well as of the concomitant development of reputedly sexually frank literature—from Benjamin Franklin's "Advice to a Young Man on the Choice of a Mistress" through Hawthorne's *The Scarlet Letter* and Whitman's *Leaves of Grass*. The study then turns to detailed consideration of such matters as erotic fictional "classics"—the *Decameron* and the *Arabian Nights*, for example, and the turn-of-the-century European novels and plays which were involved in censorship litigation. Somehow, today, Tolstoy's *Kreutzer Sonata*, Shaw's *Mrs. Warren's Profession*, d'Annunzio's *Triumph of Death*, and Elinor Glyn's *Three Weeks* do not seem to present a real menace to American civilization, but they certainly were so reputed in their day. In pre-World War I America, cases involving Dreiser's *The "Genius"* and a forgotten minor "naturalistic" novel (Daniel Carson Goodman's *Hagar Revelly*) are herein highlighted and, along with the transatlantic works earlier discussed, serve as examples of how modern fiction then singled out the mistress and the prostitute as topics "crying out for franker discussion." Next Lewis correlates the wave of postwar freedom in literary expression with an increasing amount of pressure exercised through censorship litigation. Cabell, Dreiser, Schnitzler, D. H. Lawrence all dared the censor's red pencil and won, during the years between 1917 and 1925. The next decade featured James Joyce's unprecedentedly forthright *Ulysses*, approved for importation into America in 1933. Justice Woolsey's decision is still a landmark in American intellectual freedom; without *Ulysses* and Woolsey, there is little question that all American fiction would have been far less free in language and theme.

The 1930s and 1940s again saw some outstanding litterateurs facing the censor, from Farrell and Faulkner to Erskine Caldwell and James M. Cain. Following World War II, trends toward diction using four-letter words and more detailed descriptions of sexual activity brought censorship trials of such works as Edmund Wilson's *Memoirs of Hecate County*, John O'Hara's *Ten North Frederick*, and Calder Willingham's *End as a Man*. The cases involving *Lady Chatterley's Lover*, *Tropic of Cancer*, and *Memoirs of a Woman of Pleasure* are familiar to today's generation of librarians.

What is unusual about this work is its quite detailed summaries, with appropriate quotations, of controversial books in censorship trouble since the 1890s, and its clear presentation of the parallel march of increasingly frank writing and attempts at increasingly strict censorship. The activities of various extra-legal groups such as anti-vice societies receive an appreciable amount of attention. It is unfortunate that the work of anti-censorship groups, such as the American Civil Liberties Union and the American Library Association, is hardly mentioned.

On the whole, this is a trail-blazing, well-researched volume, written in a highly readable style, undoubtedly useful for both authors and their audience, but likely to be particularly helpful to librarians and library trustees. It puts censorship and creativity in such revelatory juxtaposition as has rarely occurred before and illuminates both of these significant features of American life and culture.

Citizens for Decency: Antipornography Crusades As Status Defense. Louis A. Zurcher, Jr., and R. George Kirkpatrick. University of Texas Press, 1976.*

The seemingly inherently cautious nature of most librarians necessarily means that very few librarians give those censorious of pornographic or possibly pornographic materials any opportunity to conduct crusades against them. But it is a different story with those in the pornography-book-and-film business. Although nowhere in this volume is there any reference to libraries or librarians, the study will well repay study by librarians and library

---

*Reprinted from review by Eli M. Oboler in *Journal of Library History*, vol. 12, no. 4 (Fall 1977). Published by University of Texas Press, 1977.

trustees. Zurcher and Kirkpatrick have formulated a sociological construct which can well serve as guidance to those librarians who *do* run into similar "crusades."

According to their research—conducted for the U.S. Commission on Obscenity and Pornography in the early seventies in two "typical" midwestern and southwestern cities—the hunt for pornography and pornographers is a "symbolic crusade," aimed to vent feelings of those in American communities who feel what they describe as "status discontent." This term is defined as "when the individual's prestige is less than he expects as someone who has pledged to a usually prestigious style of life" (p. 7). Or, to put it in less sociologically grounded jargon, the censor is censoring to get social recognition otherwise unobtainable.

This is an inviting hypothesis, which the authors have tested "by analysing data from the natural histories of two antipornography crusades and by citing questionnaire data concerning socio-demographic and attitudinal characteristics of crusaders and their opponents" (pp. 9-10). To at least the authors' satisfaction, this hypothesis was verified and transformed into a theory.

The book is full of insight-packed information on the whys and wherefores of the censors (whom they call "Conporns") and their opponents ("Proporns"). Although the authors disclaim the advisability of any "straightforward extrapolation of (their) findings to other cases" (p. 328), it is still true that much can be learned from them. Perhaps the most useful generalization they offer is that "participation in the crusade allows individuals whose life style is being threatened to reinforce that style and yet not to interfere lastingly or significantly with social change" (p. 347).

Similar research[1] (conducted in 1967-68), although limited to the question of how significant the Supreme Court decisions on erotica under Earl Warren had been in relation to local communities, gives a somewhat different view. Harrell Rodgers found the censorship groups "generally not very effective" until they felt they had the backing of the Court (as they did after the 1973 *Miller*, etc. decisions). Symbolic victories, after all, do not result in actual closing

[1]Harrell R. Rodgers, Jr. "Censorship Campaigns in Eighteen Cities: an Impact Analysis" (*American Politics Quarterly*, v. 2, no. 4, October, 1974), pp. 371-91.

of bookstores or movie houses. And ". . . doubts about the sincerity and motives of the censors probably negated any symbolic successes of the campaigns."

Nevertheless, the Zurcher-Kirkpatrick book belongs on the shelf of anyone interested in the continuing story of the censor in America, alongside Paul S. Boyer's *Purity in Print: The Vice-Society Movement and Book Censorship in America* (New York: Scribner's, 1968) and David J. Pivar's *Purity Crusade: Sexual Morality and Social Control, 1868-1900* (Westport, Conn.: Greenwood Press, 1973).

Freedom in America: a 200-Year Perspective. Norman A. Graebner. Pennsylvania State University Press, 1977.

In these waning years of the eighth decade of the twentieth century, the prospects for freedom in our country are not really encouraging to most observers. The fifteen scholars and activists who led a series of public forums in Pennsylvania from December 1975 to June 1976—out of which this volume emerged—each had individual opinions and perspectives on their important topics— but were in agreement on what the preface-writers refer to as the urgent need for "a reaffirmation of the principles of human dignity and the maintenance of an environment capable of sustaining them."

Pauline Maier defines and clarifies "Freedom, Authority, and Resistance to Authority, 1776-1976," showing that before the American Revolution such rights as freedom of the press or of speech "were traditionally understood as means to assure the people's ability to learn about the wrongful acts of miscreants in power and to resist them." But, from the 1780s on, the rights of free Americans were intrinsic, basic, "separate ends in themselves." And she itemizes the examples throughout American history—such as the Populists of the 1890s and the radicals of the 1960s—of the continuing influence of "the citizen's right and duty to resist authority."

Writing on the constitutional background and history of American freedom, Gordon S. Wood stresses the primacy of *individual* freedom if constitutional democracy is to survive. There is no guarantee, he says, that rule by the majority cannot turn into at least occasional tyrannies over the minority. His is a salutary reminder that "unless the private rights of individuals and minorities (are) protected against the power of majorities . . . no government (can) be truly free."

The period just after the beginning of the Republic (1789-1801) is highlighted by Merrill D. Peterson, discussing the infamous Alien and Sedition Laws of 1798 and their repudiation by the election of Jefferson as president in 1800. In his inaugural address Jefferson called for the continuance of the Union and its republican form "as monuments of the safety with which error may be tolerated where reason is left free to combat it."

In an essay on "The Moral Foundations of American Constitutionalism," Editor Graebner calls for a reconsideration of what "freedom and fairness" mean in today's society; he sees a lack of "any sufficient common core of conviction, purpose, and moral judgment" to achieve the full measure of civic responsibility our constitutional setup requires. Indeed, it is lack of individual and governmental morality—at all levels, but especially in Congress and the Executive Branch—which Graebner finds to be at the heart of our problems with growing governmental authoritarianism.

It is disconcerting to find Abraham Lincoln, of all American leaders, named by Don E. Fehrenbacher, in his comments on "Lincoln and the Paradoxes of Freedom," as the president first to provide the model for the "imperial presidency," so unhappily exemplified by several twentieth-century presidents. Lincoln's suspension of *habeas corpus*, his "presidential decrees, arbitrary arrests, (and) military trials" certainly contribute to Fehrenbacher's characterization of this "somewhat ambiguous figure . . . (who) epitomized democracy, but assumed a considerable measure of autocratic power," a president who helped keep American popular government intact, but who "in the process impaired some of the substance of American liberty."

Robert K. Murray sees as a hopeful sign that "many Americans still believe that a government which most carefully protects and promotes freedom of thought, expression, action, and criticism has the best chance for survival and for achieving progress, security, and happiness." Political theorist Hans J. Morgenthau is more pessimistic, seeing, among other threats to democracy, the possibility that "the forces of the status quo threatened with disintegration will use their vast material powers to try to reintegrate society through totalitarian manipulation of the citizens' minds and the terror of physical compulsion."

Supreme Court specialist Henry J. Abraham—perhaps a little surprisingly to some of us Court-watchers—sees "free speech, both in its symbolic and advocative tenets," as "getting even freer" under the Burger Court than with the Warren Court. He does admit that obscenity and freedom of the press are "possible" exceptions to this, but is optimistic that "in the final analysis the (Burger) Court will . . . ultimately adopt Mr. Justice Brennan's minority position that 'at least in the absence of distribution to juveniles or obtrusive exposure to unconsenting adults, the First and Fourteenth amendments prohibit the state and federal governments from attempting wholly to suppress sexually-oriented materials on the basis of their allegedly "obscene" contents.'"

In the last section of the book, "Freedom, the Economy, and the Environment," are included searching contributions by Paul K. Conkin, Barry Commoner, Thomas C. Cochran, and Victor Ferkiss on various related topics. Conkin reminds us that "today, as in the past, the most active support for specific expressive freedoms comes from eccentrics, from minorities, from those with an immediate stake in a given freedom (*my note:* librarians, for example!) . . . or from a new intellectuals who embrace broad and abstract principles." Commoner sees freedom of the American people "eroding while the government's power, often without the consent of the governed, has increased." Thomas Cochran traces the historical changes in the American concept of economic freedom, delineating today's society as "still the most competitive in the highly industrialized world" despite "some restraints." Futurist Victor Ferkiss sees the traditional American freedoms as needing an added freedom—"social action for common ends," as "an enlargement, not a diminution, of freedom."

This volume is well worth adding to the personal library of any believer in intellectual freedom, perhaps mostly for its trenchant reminders that intellectual freedom cannot flourish in a vacuum, and that for Americans it is an inextricable part of the whole matrix of related freedoms. As Graebner states in his introduction, "What matters . . . is a public of sufficient awareness to encourage its leaders to design and act in the public interest." And surely librarians do not need to be reminded of their key role in creating and serving such a public.

An Intellectual Freedom Primer. Charles Busha. Libraries Unlimited, 1977.

My dictionary tells me a primer is either "an elementary textbook" or "a book that covers the basic elements of any subject." This work is neither, but it is a sound, informed collection of essays on some of the most important phases of intellectual freedom and censorship today. Busha—well-known for his 1972 report on how Middle West librarians feel and act vis-à-vis book-censorship—has contributed both a well-worded introduction and one of the best brief summaries I've ever seen of the state of U.S. freedom in this century.

Library science professor Stephen P. Harter, discussing "Privacy and Security In Automated Personal Data Systems," warns of the dire possibilities of centralized national data centers. Artist and librarian Yvonne Linnert Morse views the role of governments in "Freedom of the Visual Arts," from "September Morn" to today's less-publicized but widespread governmental censorship of pictures, photographs, and sculptures that do not conform to the view of local Comstocks. The former head of the Institute for Sex Research Library, Rebecca Dixon, writing on "Bibliographical Control of Erotica," calls for librarians to "select, acquire, and organize erotica," not only for research and preservation purposes, but because the Library of Congress (for whatever reason) "does not catalog most of these titles. . . ." A possible project for the ALA Intellectual Freedom Round Table or the Intellectual Freedom Committee?

Music professor and humanist Barbara Connally Kaplan has "a review of the issues" in "Censorship and the Performing Arts," which is clearly the high point and the most original chapter of the entire volume. School media specialist Gail Linda Robinson, in describing "Censorship and the Contemporary Cinema," cites many examples of film censorship in America today and finds such activity "useless, ineffective, and . . . indeed a foe of our democratic principles."

College librarian Richard E. McKee's report on "Censorship Research: Its Strengths, Weaknesses, Uses and Misuses" admits that censorship "is truly a difficult matter to treat objectively and precisely" but still laments the lack of "count something" research on the topic. It is clearly as important a field for the wide-ranging humanist as for the data-conscious social scientist.

As a whole, this book is generally provocative, knowledgeable, and worth reading. Perhaps a second edition might include a much-needed index. We are in Dr. Busha's debt for a rather different book in a field that very much needs fresh approaches.

Unmailable: Congress and the Post Office. Dorothy G. Fowler. University of Georgia Press, 1977.

There are three basic varieties of censors: official, unofficial, and self. One of the least written about of the first variety is the U.S. Post Office. Of the sixty volumes listed under "Postal Service" in the *1977-78 Subject Guide to Books in Print*, not one deals entirely with postal censorship. In fact, the only volume written on this topic in many years was the James Paul and Murray Schwartz book, *Federal Censorship: Obscenity in the Mail*, published in 1961, long out of print, and dealing with the censorship of only one type of material.

So, Ms. Fowler's book is very welcome, indeed. It is too bad, incidentally, that the Library of Congress catalogers didn't bother to read or examine the book more carefully. Somehow they managed to assign only three subjects to it: "United States Postal Service"; "United States Congress"; and "Postal service—United States—History." Fine—but what ever happened to "Censorship," which is incontrovertibly the basic theme of the book? When the Paul-Schwartz book appeared in 1961, at least its assigned LC subjects were "Censorship—U.S." and "Obscenity (Law)—U.S."

Now let's look at what the book has to tell us about official censorship, with the sanction of the U.S. Post Office and of Congress and the president. It is not exactly a secret that for over a century the official censors have been hard at work making sure we are not corrupted by bad words and evil pictures of a sexual nature, from the censorship of Tolstoy's "Kreutzer Sonata" to the attempted barring of Larry Flynt's *Hustler*. But Ms. Fowler adds many illuminating facts to our information on how the powers and the duties of the Post Office gradually expanded.

What began in the 1830s as efforts to bar anti-slavery newspapers and pamphlets from transmission to southern States—via proposals by President Andrew Jackson and Senator John Calhoun—developed by the 1970s to include a wide variety of prohibitions. "Nonmailable matter" now includes such items as obscene matter, fraudulent matter (which includes lotteries), and dangerous items. These are described by Fowler as "matter that might do physical damage to Post Office equipment or personnel as well as written matter that might hurt, financially or morally," Post Office users.

Of more significance to the workings of democracy were attempts by the Post Office, Congress, and several presidents to bar from the mails newspapers and magazines containing material contrary to established beliefs. For example, in 1906 President Theodore Roosevelt tried to bar the syndicated weekly *Appeal to Reason* because of one article by Socialist leader Eugene V. Debs. No action was taken, but in 1908 Congress passed a law barring from second-class mailing privileges "anarchistic" (not further defined) publications.

During World War I a law barred "matter of a seditious, anarchistic, or treasonable character" from the mails. Under this law Postmaster General Burleson kept out of the Post Office the handling of several issues of publications which he said contained "articles that might impede recruiting or enlistment." As Ms. Fowler points out, the 1917-1927 decade, "more than any other period in American history, saw immoderate grants of power to the postmaster general, not only over the press but also over correspondence of individuals." And we all know that the Nixon-controlled Postal Service permitted the FBI to keep close surveillance over "enemies" of Nixon.

World War II brought an official Office of Censorship, which existed from 1941 through 1946. Its main target was material of foreign origin which was "inimical to the war effort of the United States or contrary to the interests of the United States or its Allies." A large number of presumably "treasonable" or "seditious" American periodicals were also denied second-class mailing privileges by the postmaster general during this period.

In 1965 the Supreme Court delivered a unanimous opinion (written by Justice William O. Douglas) which for the first time declared an act of Congress concerning mail censorship to be unconstitutional. In ringing, unforgettable words this decision stated: "The United States may give up the post office when it sees fit, but while it carries it on the use of the mails is almost as much a part of free speech as the right to use our tongue."

During the 1950s and 1960s, as Fowler details, many Post Office attempts to censor were prevented or appreciably modified by various court orders—including the famous *Esquire, Roth,* and *Sunshine and Health* cases. Several laws were passed (and are now being observed) which reqire "adults only" labels on ads for so-called adult merchandise, and which permit individuals to file cards with the Post Office to keep out "sexually oriented advertisements."

Little by little, especially in the last few years, the responsibility for deciding what comes into our home mail boxes has been shifted, particularly on printed matter dealing with sex, but even including "junk mail." Whereas in 1865 mail delivery was up to the Post Office, now, as the 1970 Supreme Court decision in *Rowan v. U.S. Post Office Department* stated, current practice permits "the parent to police his own mail box."

Thus, of the three varieties of censor described at the beginning of this review, we are back to the only one which really should be acceptable to the practitioners of intellectual freedom: one's own self or, in the case of the family, the parents. And Ms. Fowler's well-researched, interestingly-written book deserves to be in the library of all students of censorship, its practice and prevention (or, at least, diminution). It fills a great gap in the literature, and should stay in print for many, many years to come.

The Young Adult and Intellectual Freedom. Mary L. Woodworth. University of Wisconsin Library School Publications Committee, 1977.

The school librarian, the children's librarian, the public library trustee—indeed, all who are involved in dealing with young adults —are facing an ever-growing problem in reconciling the censorious efforts of individuals and groups determined to extirpate controversial books from libraries with the increasingly frank writings of popular novelists aiming at the young adult market. In June 1976 the University of Wisconsin conducted an institute aimed to present frankly and forthrightly the issues facing librarians and trustees who must deal on a day-to-day basis with such seemingly simple yet complex questions as "Shall I buy this novel? After all, it uses many four-letter words," or "Shall I show this film? It's bound to annoy some parents of teenagers." This volume includes the proceedings of that 5-day institute.

Although dealing with a 1976 institute and published in 1977, the book is still timely, still useful in 1979. It includes—as any locally-based gathering might be presumed to do—some very localized and not necessarily nationally significant data. But on the whole the material stands up surprisingly well, both for breadth and depth of coverage. The mix of library school and law professors, English teachers, professional educators, State Board of Education members, and Rebecca Mueller, then assistant to the director of the OIF, has produced a book worthy of study on—and being consulted from—the shelf of anyone interested in intellectual freedom, its practice and its defense, today.

To be specific, this book includes a good deal of practical help. For example, there is a Nebraska participant in fighting a typical censorship effort aimed at the MACOS (Man, a Course of Study) film based on social studies courses for fifth and sixth grade students. It has an invaluable set of suggested "Strategies in Working with Administrators and School Boards" that says more in 11 pages than seems otherwise to be available in print on this subject.

Professor Miriam Braverman of Columbia's School of Library Service confronts some vital issues in her discussion on "the Realistic Young Adult Novel," albeit with some not necessarily widely accepted views of her own on what our society really affirms. Wisconsin law professor Mark Tushnet examines "Free Expression and the Young Adult: a Constitutional Framework," emerging with a pessimistic view on just how free young adult students are today to express themselves in print or speech. A useful presentation is included on the highly controversial issues behind the evolutionist-creationist fracas, by a pair of science educators, Richard Bliss and Jerry Rice. And there is much, much more.

I found this institute (and this report of it) unusual in several major respects. It included comparatively few "big names," but it produced some very helpful "big thoughts." It was willing to face the world of reading and education as it really is, in these last years of the disputatious 70s. The participants were not wordy, but informed and explicit.

I highly recommend this book for library schools and for all who must deal with perhaps the most gravelly problem now confronting exponents of intellectual freedom—how can we build our library collections so as to mirror the many conflicting points of view in today's society for our young adults so as to make sure that when they become adults themselves they will help create a better society tomorrow?

Freedom of the Press: a Bibliocyclopedia. Ten-Year Supplement (1967-1977). Ralph E. McCoy. With a foreword by Robert B. Downs. Southern Illinois University Press, 1979.

Although 17/1000 of 1% of this comprehensive annotated bibliography of publications (print and non-print) on censorship and intellectual freedom during the years 1967 through 1976 deals with writings by this reviewer, an attempt will be made to be judicious and fair about the other 99.0083%. Seriously speaking, this is a simply marvelous updating of Dr. McCoy's classic and unique 1968 *Freedom of the Press: an Annotated Bibliography.*

The field is so vast that bibliographical control is a *sine qua non* for the researcher on this important topic, and the various added pieces of information furnished by the author truly make this volume worthy of the term "bibliocyclopedia" (which, as far as I know, is a useful neologism invented by the author for this purpose). In addition to an alphabetical arrangement by author, McCoy has furnished a thorough 39-page index for the 515 pages of text. The index is so complete that it even includes, for instance, a reference to Renata Adler because she was one of a six-member panel which put out a tape-recording in 1970 on the topic of "Theater and Movies: Four Letter Rebellion" (incidentally, with all of this strenuous effort to be scrupulously complete, there are, of course, some gaps. For example, the British Lord Chamberlain is referred to in item 1D28, but this is not mentioned in the index; there are other similar examples which Dr. McCoy will, I'm sure, welcome as suggestions of possible corrections for the "errata sheet" to his clearly forthcoming 1989 supplement, just as he has done in this volume for the original 1968 edition).

More important than the minutiae of perfection or imperfection of this grand enterprise is to try to define what its values are for anyone interested in this important topic. As Dr. Robert Downs says in his useful foreword, "it is refreshing and heartening to note the continued interest in the historical aspects of speech and press freedom." Just as long as there is this much attention paid to what the censor is up to, he (or she) won't get away with anything simply for lack of public notice. Furthermore, the very fact of the existence of this comprehensive compilation will help out in the defense of intellectual freedom, on every level and in every format. For example, there are no less than 41 items listed under the topic "Copyright law (United States)."

It would have been helpful if the bibliography had included more material on the fight for privacy and against governmental secrecy, such as are listed in profusion among the 669 items (1971-76) in Aslib Bibliography no. 1, Maxine MacCafferty's *The Right to Know* (London, Aslib, 1976). The only other even remotely comparable bibliography is the one of over 1300 items prepared by Kenneth Donelson for the February, 1975 issue of the *Arizona English Bulletin,* which is not fully annotated, but does include quite a number of school-library-related censorship items not in the McCoy listing.

But all this kind of criticism is being rather captious. Instead, let those of us and you who are interested in the twin causes of promoting intellectual freedom and fighting censorship be grateful for what we do have. Here is a gigantic, highly-readable publication in a most useful large print format, very well bound and printed, jam-packed with useful information and opinions. It should serve as a unique *vade mecum* to the entire field of freedom of the press for years to come. As just one insight into its massiveness, among the 6500-plus items included are no less than 112 issued by the U.S. Government—Congress, executive offices, etc.—in the period covered.

Combine this book with its 8000-item predecessor (still, happily, very much in print), and any lover of freedom should rejoice. We all owe a deep debt of gratitude to Ralph McCoy for his incredible labors which, in this case, contrary to Greek myth, have brought forth a mountain, not a mouse.

Let me end with one more quotation from Robert Downs' elegant and informative foreword, which is intended to cover—and does, quite handsomely—"vital issues of the past decade" in the area of press freedom. In dealing with such matters as the Pentagon Papers, classified information, prior restraint, press gag orders, fair trial vs. free press, privacy, rights of special groups, obscenity and pornography, the Obscenity and Pornography Commission Report, and textbooks, Downs concludes by saying, "The evidence is overwhelming that censorship and governmental repression is on the increase throughout the world." The torrent of discussion of these matters so ably sourced in the McCoy books can only be of help to the side which is important, and my biased view is that that side is to let people know what their choices are, so they can decide for themselves what they want to see, hear, or read.

FOUR REVIEWS TO BE PLAYED ON THE PORNOGRAPH

(Please bear with us; our reviewer seems to have forgotten completely—if he ever knew!—that Fanny Hill was published in 1749, and seems to be convinced it was first published in 1977. Further, somehow he sent us not one but four reviews—the others clearly intended for *Library Journal*, *School Library Journal*, and *Library Quarterly*. Well, their loss, our gain . . . —Editor's Note)

Fanny Hill. John Cleland. The Erotic Art Book Society, 1977.

This volume tells, in fictional form, the story of a London prostitute in the eighteenth century. Despite its fidelity to life as it then was, it may well encounter some over-prudish readers who will find its realism censorable. It is, however, clearly erotica rather than pornography; as one evidence, there is not one so-called "dirty"

word anywhere in this whole volume, although it deals principally
with sexual activities. Of most importance to *Newsletter* readers in
the fact that *Fanny Hill* has numerous illustrations (Aubrey-
Beardsley-like drawings) which could inspire some difficulties with
the censor. A reference to two Supreme Court cases—*Butler* v.
State of Michigan (1957) and *Sunshine Book Company* v. *Summerfield* (1958)—should be of help: *Butler* for its defense of the rights
of adults not to have their reading standards set to suit youth and
Sunshine (1955), which found nudity *per se* not obscene.

Whether this book goes into any library should depend on taste,
library standards, balance of collection, and other criteria, not on
its admittedly sexual subject matter's morality or immorality.

LIBRARY JOURNAL

A first novel, in epistolary, 18th century style, not at all in the
current vein. The author has euphemistically avoided plain speech,
but, curiously, this does not seem to affect the book's basic aphro-
disiac effect. The setting, the seamy side of 18th century London, is
expertly described, and the heroine receives a well-rounded characterization. A bit anticlimatic after Winsor's *Forever Amber* (*LJ*,
Oct. 15, 1944), but recommended to large public libraries with a
tolerant clientele, and academic library browsing rooms. The illustrations, incidentally, are expertly drawn in the Beardsley style—
uncensored.

SCHOOL LIBRARY JOURNAL

YA — An event-filled story of a young girl who faces perils to
life and limb in 18th century London. Filled with detailed sexual
scenes, but worth considering for any school librarian willing to
support the need for acquainting young adults with the world as it
is. Containing no obscene or scatological words, it is written in
quite an artistic style. The graphic illustrations might well supplement art volumes dealing with Aubrey Beardsley (whose style is
used).

LIBRARY QUARTERLY

Immanuel Kant's concept of *das Dinge an zich* (as cited in Norman Kemp Smith's *A Commentary to Kant's "Critique of Pure Reason"* (New York: Humanities Press, 1950) is intrinsically and extrinsically *apropos* for Cleland's *magnum opus.* This exhaustive—and exhausting—recital of the sexual misadventures of an eighteenth century London hetaira is embellished by rather epicene illustrative material. Despite its repetitive text, it is well-suited to administrative offices of major libraries (if members of the Association of Research Libraries).

THE FREEDOM TO READ: A SELECTED READING LIST

The Censor is Everyman, sometime, everywhere—and to some extent always, he is the man or woman in *your* mirror!
—*Eli M. Oboler*, The Fear of the Word *(1974)*

The list which follows includes only complete works on the freedom to read, book censorship, and related topics (Books out-of-print as of 1979 are marked "O.P."). Many of the books include more inclusive, often annotated, bibliographies. Up-to-date listings are best located in the "Intellectual Freedom Bibliography" in each issue of the *Newsletter on Intellectual Freedom.*

BIBLIOGRAPHIES

Harvey, James A. *Librarians, censorship, and intellectual freedom: an annual annotated bibliography, 1968-69.* Chicago: American Library Association, 1970. O.P.
Harvey, James A. and Patricia R. Harris. *Librarians, censorship, and intellectual freedom: an annual annotated bibliography, 1970.* Chicago: American Library Association, 1972.
MacCafferty, Maxine. *The right to know.* London: Aslib, 1976.
McCoy, Ralph E. *Freedom of the press: an annotated bibliography.* Carbondale: Southern Illinois University Press, 1969.
_____. *Freedom of the press: a bibliocyclopedia.* Ten Year Supplement (1967-1977). Carbondale: Southern Illinois University Press, 1978.

Schroeder, Theodore A. *Free speech bibliography.* New York: Bert Franklin, 1969. Reprint of 1922 edition.
Young Kimball. *Bibliography on censorship and propaganda.* Eugene: University of Oregon, 1928. O.P.

GENERAL

Beman, Lamar T., comp. *Selected articles on censorship of speech and the press.* New York: AMS Press, 1969. Reprint of 1930 edition.
Craig, Alec. *Above all liberties.* New York: Arno, 1970. Reprint of 1942 edition.
Daily, Jay E. *The anatomy of censorship.* New York: Marcel Dekker, 1973.
DeGrazia, Edward. *Censorship landmarks.* New York, Bowker, 1969.
Downs, Robert B., ed. *The first freedom: liberty and justice in the world of books and reading.* Chicago: American Library Association, 1960.
Emerson, Thomas T. *Towards a general theory of the First Amendment.* New York· Vintage Books, 1966.
_____. *The system of freedom of expression.* New York: Random House, 1970.
Fellman, Davis. *The censorship of books.* Madison, Wis.: University of Wisconsin Press, 1957.
Gillett, Charles R. *Burned books: neglected chapters in British history and literature.* Port Washington, New York: Kennikat Press, 1964.
Haight, Anne L. *Banned books: informal notes on some books banned for various reasons at various times and in various places.* 4th edition. New York: Bowker, 1978.
Haney, Robert W. *Comstockery in America; patterns of censorship and control.* New York: Da Capo Press, 1974. Reprint of 1960 edition.
Hart, Harold H., ed. *Censorship: for and against.* New York: Hart Publishing, 1971.
Hewitt, Cecil R., ed. *Books in the dock.* London: Deutsch, 1969.
Hudson, Edward G. *Freedom of speech and press in America.* Washington, D.C.: Public Affairs Press, 1963. O.P.
Jones, Howard M., ed. *Primer of intellectual freedom.* Cambridge: Harvard University Press, 1949. O.P.
Liston, Robert S. *The right to know: censorship in America.* F. Watts, 1973.
McClellan, Grant S., ed. *Censorship in the United States.* New York: Wilson, 1967.

McCormick, John and Mairi MacInnes, eds. *Versions of censorship: an anthology*. New York: Octagon Books, 1979. Reprint of 1962 edition.

Library Trends (July, 1970). Entire issue on intellectual freedom.

Murphy, Paul L. *The meaning of freedom of speech: First Amendment freedoms from Wilson to FDR*. Westport, Conn.: Greenwood Press, 1972.

Perrin, Noel. *Dr. Bowdler's legacy: a history of expurgated books in England and America*. Hanover, N.H.: University Press of New England, 1969.

Phelan, John, ed. *Communications control: readings in the motives and structures of censorship*. New York: Sheed and Ward, 1969. O.P.

Rogge, O. John. *The first and the fifth, with some excursions into others*. New York: Da Capo, 1971. Reprint of 1960 edition.

Schumach, Murray. *The face on the cutting room floor: the story of movie and television censorship*. New York: Da Capo Press, 1974. Reprint of 1956 edition.

Schwartz, Bernard, ed. *Protection of public morals through censorship*. New York: New York University School of Law, 1953. O.P.

Seagle, William. *Cato; or, The future of censorship*. New York: Dutton, 1930. O.P.

Tribe, David H. *Questions of censorship*. New York: St. Martin's Press, 1974.

Worton, Stanley N., comp. *Freedom of speech and press*. Rochelle Park, N.J.: Hayden Books, 1975.

LEGAL ASPECTS

Berns, Walter. *The First Amendment and the future of American democracy*. New York: Basic, 1976.

———. *Freedom, virtue, and the First Amendment*. Baton Rouge: Louisiana State University Press, 1957.

Canada Law Reform Commission. Prohibited and Regulated Conduct Project. *Criminal law: obscenity*. Ottawa: Information Canada, 1973. In English and French.

Clor, Harry, M., ed. *Censorship and freedom of expression: essays on obscenity and the law*. Chicago: Rand McNally, 1971.

DeGrazia, Edward, ed. *Censorship landmarks*. New York: Bowker, 1969.

Devlin, Patrick. *The enforcement of morals*. New York: Oxford University Press, 1968.

Drinker, Henry S. *Some observations on the four freedoms of the First Amendment*. Boston: Boston University Press, 1957. O.P.

Ernst, Morris L. and Alexander Lindey. *The censor marches on: recent milestones in the administration of the obscenity law in the United States.* New York: Da Capo Press, 1971. Reprint of 1940 edition.

Fowler, Dorothy G. *Unmailable: Congress and the Post Office.* Athens, Georgia: University of Georgia Press, 1977.

Gellhorn, Walter. *Individual freedom and governmental restraints.* Westport, Conn.: Greenwood Press, 1968. Reprint of 1956 edition.

Hart, H. L. A. *Law, liberty, and morality.* Stanford: Stanford University Press, 1963.

Hutchinson, E. R. *Tropic of Cancer on trial: a case history of censorship.* New York: Grove Press, 1968. O. P.

Kuh, Richard H. *Foolish figleaves?: pornography in and out of court.* New York: Macmillan, 1967. O.P.

Lewis, Felice Flanery. *Literature, obscenity, & law.* Carbondale: Southern Illinois University Press, 1976.

Paul, James C. and Murray L. Schwartz. *Federal censorship: obscenity in the mail.* Westport, Conn.: Greenwood Press, 1977. Reprint of 1961 edition.

Ringel, William E., ed. *Obscenity law today.* New York: Gould, 1970.

St. John-Stevas, Norman. *Obscenity and the law.* New York: Da Capo Press, 1974. Reprint of 1956 edition.

Schroeder, Theodore A. *"Obscene" literature and constitutional law: a forensic defense of freedom of the press.* New York: Da Capo Press, 1972. Reprint of 1911 edition.

Sobel, Lester A., ed. *Pornography, obscenity, and the law.* New York: Facts on File, 1978.

The Supreme Court obscenity decisions. San Diego: Greenleaf Classics, 1973. O.P.

CENSORSHIP AND SEX

Bosmajian, Haig, ed. *Obscenity and freedom of expression.* New York: Bert Franklin, 1976.

Boyer, Paul S. *Purity in print: the vice-society movement and book censorship in America.* New York: Scribner, 1968. O.P.

Chandos, John, ed. *To deprave and corrupt . . . original studies in the nature and definition of obscenity.* New York: Association Press, 1962. O.P.

Cline, Victor B., ed. *Where do you draw the line?: an exploration into media violence, pornography, and censorship.* Provo, Utah: Brigham Young University Press, 1974.

Clor, Harry M. *Obscenity and public morality: censorship in a liberal society.* Chicago: University of Chicago Press, 1969.

Comstock, Anthony. *Traps for the young.* Cambridge; Harvard University Press, 1967. Reprint of 1883 edition.

Craig, Alec. *The banned books of England.* Westport, Conn.: Greenwood Press, 1977. Reprint of 1962 edition.

————. *Suppressed books: a history of the conception of literary obscenity.* Cleveland: World Publishing Co., 1963. O.P.

Dhavan, Rajeer and Christie Davies, eds. *Censorship and obscenity.* New York: Rowman, 1978.

Ernst, Morris L. and William Seagle. *To the pure . . .: a study of obscenity and its censor.* New York: Kraus, 1969. Reprint of 1928 edition.

Ferlinghetti, Lawrence. *Howl of the censor.* Westport, Conn.: Greenwood Press, 1967. Reprint of 1961 edition.

Gerber, Albert B. *Sex, pornography, and justice.* New York: Lyle Stuart, 1965.

Goldstein, Michael J. and Harold S. Kent. *Pornography and sexual deviance.* Berkeley: University of California Press, 1973.

Haney, Robert W. *Comstockery in America: patterns of censorship and control.* New York: Da Capo Press, 1974. Reprint of 1960 edition.

Hewitt, C.R., ed. *Does pornography matter?* New York: Arno, 1971. Reprint of 1961 edition.

Holbrook, David, ed. *The case against pornography.* LaSalle, Ill.: Open Court, 1973.

Hughes, Douglas A., ed. *Perspectives on pornography.* New York: St. Martin's Press, 1970. O.P.

Kallen, Horace M. *Indecency and the seven arts, and other adventures of a pragmatist in aesthetics.* New York: AMS Press, 1976. Reprint of 1930 edition.

Kerr, Walter. *Criticism and censorship.* Milwaukee, Wisc.: Bruce Publishing Company, 1956. O.P.

Kilpatrick, James J. *The smut peddlers.* Westport, Conn.: Greenwood Press, 1973. Reprint of 1960 edition.

Kronhausen, Eberhard and Phyllis. *Pornography and the law: the psychology of erotic realism and pornography.* New York: Ballantine Books, 1964. Second edition. O.P.

Lawrence, D.H. *Sex, literature, and censorship.* New York: Twayne Publishers, 1953.

Legman, Gershon. *Love and death, a study in censorship.* New York: Hacker, 1949.

Marcus, Steven. *The other Victorians: a study of sexuality and pornography in mid-nineteenth-century England.* New York: Basic Books, 1966.

Michelson, Peter. *The aesthetics of pornography.* New York: Herder and Herder, 1971. O.P.

Murphy, Terence J. *Censorship: government and obscenity.* Baltimore: Helicon Press, 1963. O.P.

National College Competition Winning Essays on the Subject. *Obscenity: censorship or free choice?* San Diego: Greenleaf Classics, 1971. O.P.

Oboler, Eli M. *The fear of the word: censorship and sex.* Metuchen, N.J.: Scarecrow Press, 1974.

Peckham, Morse. *Art and pornography: an experiment in explanation.* New York: Harper & Row, 1971. O.P.

Rembar, Charles. *The end of obscenity: the trials of Lady Chatterley, Tropic of Cancer, and Fanny Hill.* New York: Simon and Schuster, 1968.

Rist, Ray G. *The pornography controversy: changing moral standards in American life.* New Brunswick, N.J.: Transaction Books, 1975.

Roeburt, John. *The wicked and the banned.* New York: MacFadden-Bartell Corp., 1973. O.P.

Rugoff, Milton. *Prudery and passion.* New York: Putnam, 1971. O.P.

Rushdoony, Rousas J. *The politics of pornography.* New Rochelle, N.Y.: Arlington House, 1974. O.P.

Sagarin, Edward. *The anatomy of dirty words.* New York: Lyle Stuart, 1962.

Sharp, Donald B., ed. *Commentaries on obscenity.* Metuchen, N.J.: Scarecrow Press, 1970.

Sunderland, Lane V. *Obscenity: the courts, the Congress, and the President's Commission.* Washington, D.C.: American Enterprise, 1974. O.P.

Thomas, Donald. *A long time burning: the history of literary censorship in England.* New York: Praeger, 1969. O.P.

Uhrhammer, Jerry. *The salacious literature problem.* Eugene, Ore.: Regioter-Guard, 1960. O.P.

U.S. Commission on Obscenity and Pornography. *Report.* New York: Bantam, 1970. O.P.

U.S. Commission on Obscenity and Pornography. *Technical Reports . . .* 9 volumes. Washington, D.C.: Government Printing Office, 1970.

Zurcher, Louis A., Jr. and R. George Kirkpatrick. *Citizens for decency: antipornography crusades as status defense.* Austin: University of Texas Press, 1976.

POLITICS, RELIGION, AND CENSORSHIP

Adams, Michael. *Censorship: the Irish experience.* University, Ala.: University of Alabama Press, 1968.

Barrier, Norman G. *Banned: controversial literature and political control in British India, 1907-1947.* Columbia: University of Missouri Press, 1974.

Burke, Redmond A. *What is the index?* Milwaukee, Wisc.: Bruce, 1952. O.P.

Carmilly-Weinberger, Moshe. *Censorship and freedom of expression in Jewish history.* New York: Herman, 1977.

Coleman, Peter. *Obscenity, blasphemy, sedition: censorship in Australia.* Brisbane: Jacaranda Press, 1963. O.P.

Cotham, Perry C. *Obscenity, pornography, and censorship: where should Christians draw the line?* Grand Rapids, Mich.: Baker Book House, 1973.

Dewhirst, Martin and Robert Farrell, eds. *The Soviet censorship.* Metuchen, N.J.: Scarecrow Press, 1973.

Drakeford, John W. and Jack Hamm. *Pornography: the sexual mirage.* Nashville, Tenn.: T. Nelson, 1973. O.P.

Nikitenko, Aleksandr V. *The diary of a Russian censor.* Amherst: University of Massachusetts Press, 1975. O.P.

Norwich, Kenneth P. *Lobbying for freedom: a citizen's guide to fighting censorship at the state level.* New York: St. Martin's Press, 1975.

Perry, Stuart. *The indecent publications tribunal: a social experiment: with text of the legislation since 1900 and classifications of the Tribunal.* Christmark, N.Z.: Whitcombe and Tombe, 1965. O.P.

Popper, William. *The censorship of Hebrew books.* New York: Bert Franklin, 1968. Reprint of 1899 edition.

Putnam, George H. *The censorship of the Church of Rome and its influence upon the production and distribution of literature.* New York: Arno Press, 1967. Reprint of 1906 edition. 2 volumes.

Summers, Robert E., comp. . . . *Wartime censorship of press and radio.* New York: H. W. Wilson, 1942. O.P.

Swayze, Harold. *Political control of literature in the USSR, 1946-1959.* Cambridge: Harvard University Press, 1962.

Wiest, Donald H. *The precensorship of books (canons 1384-1386, 1392-1394, 2318, paragraph 2): a history and a commentary.* Washington, D.C.: Catholic University of America Press, 1953. O.P.

LIBRARIES, SCHOOLS, AND CENSORSHIP

American Library Association. Committee on Intellectual Freedom. *Freedom of book selection.* Chicago: American Library Association, 1954. O.P.

_____. *Freedom of communication.* New York: Arno, 1971. Reprint of 1954 edition.

Anderson, Arthur J. *Problems in intellectual freedom and censorship.* New York: Bowker, 1974.

Berninghausen, David K. *The flight from reason: essays on intellectual freedom in the academy, the press, and the library.* Chicago: American Library Association, 1975.

Berns, Walter. *The case of the censored librarian.* Chicago: American Foundation for Continuing Education, 1959. O.P.

Busha, Charles H. *Freedom versus suppression and censorship: with a study of the attitude of Midwestern librarians and a bibliography of censorship.* Littleton, Col.: Libraries Unlimited, 1972.

Conference on Intellectual Freedom, Washington, D.C., 1965. *Freedom of inquiry, supporting the Library Bill of Rights; proceedings.* Chicago: American Library Association, 1965.

Davis, James E., ed. *Dealing with censorship.* Urbana, Ill.: National Council of Teachers of English, 1979.

Fiske, Marjorie. *Book selection and censorship: a study of school and public libraries in California.* Berkeley: University of California Press, 1959.

Fowell, Frank and Frank Palmer. *Censorship in England.* New York: Bert Franklin, 1970. Reprint of 1913 edition.

Frank, John P. *Obscenity, the law, and the English teacher.* Champaign, Ill.: National Council of Teachers of English, 1966. O.P.

Fryer, Peter. *Private case—public scandal.* London: Secker and Warburg, 1966. O.P.

Merritt, Leroy C. *Book selection and intellectual freedom.* New York: H. W. Wilson, 1970.

Moon, Eric, ed. *Book selection and censorship in the sixties.* New York: Bowker, 1969.

Moore, Everett T. *Issues of freedom in American libraries.* Chicago: American Library Association, 1964.

National Council of Teachers of English. Committee on the Right to Read. *The student's right to read.* Champaign, Ill.: National Council of Teachers of English, 1962. O.P.

Nelson, Jack and Gene Roberts, Jr. *The censors and the schools.* Westport, Conn.: Greenwood Press, 1977. Reprint of 1963 edition.

Oboler, Eli M. *Defending intellectual freedom: the library and the censor.* Westport, Conn.: Greenwood Press, 1980.

Pope, Michael. *Sex and the undecided librarian: a study of librarians' opinions on sexually oriented literature.* Metuchen, N.J.: Scarecrow Press, 1974. O.P.

Thompson, Anthony H. *Censorship in public libraries in the United Kingdom during the 20th century.* New York: Bowker, 1976.

THE CENSOR'S LIBRARY: WHAT THE OTHER SIDE IS THINKING

The following list, although not inclusive, is representative of many books currently available for the intellectual and emotional reinforcement of the literary censor. A few include *some* arguments on the side of intellectual freedom and tolerance, but most are wholeheartedly antipornography, pro-censorship, or both. Any library which "overlooks" such books is really not being intellectually free; certainly the questions library patrons or trustees or library staff members may ask concerning the rightness or wrongness of being anti-censorship need to be answered out of knowledge of a wide spectrum of facts and opinions on the subject.

There is no question that censors exist; let's read *their* "bibles," as well as our own.

1. Berns, Walter. *Freedom, virtue and the first amendment.* Westport, Conn.: Greenwood Press, 1969. (Reprint of 1957 edition)

"The complete absence of all forms of censorship . . . is theoretically untenable and practically indefensible. Civil Society is impossible if every man retains an absolute freedom of opinion."

*2. Cline, Victor B., comp. *Where do you draw the line? An exploration into media violence, pornography, and censorship.* Provo, Utah: Brigham Young University Press, 1974.

"Whatever limit is placed on speech and artistic expression should reflect the consensus of a majority of our citizenry."

---

*Recommended for a basic list.

*3. Clor, Harry M. *Obscenity and public morality: Censorship in a liberal society.* Chicago: University of Chicago Press, 1969.

"Obscenity, while ineradicable from human affairs, is an evil of sufficient magnitude to require the attention of organized society."

4. Comstock, Anthony. *Traps for the young.* Cambridge: Belknap Press of Harvard University, 1967. (Reprint of 1883 edition)

"I unhesitatingly declare, there is at present no more active agent employed by Satan in civilized communities to ruin the human family and subject the nations to himself than EVIL READING."

5. Cotham, Perry C. *Obscenity, pornography, and censorship.* Grand Rapids, Michigan: Baker Book House, 1973.

"The conservative distaste for pornography and obscenity and the liberal suspicion of public censorship are not very compatible. Some kind of marriage by compromise is essential if they are going to coexist. . . ."

6. Drakeford, John W., and Jack Hamm. *Pornography: the sexual mirage.* Nashville, Tenn.: T. Nelson, 1973.

*7. Hart, Harold H., ed. *Censorship: for and against.* New York: Hart Publishing, 1971.

"Freedom . . . must be limited to continue. Unlimited freedom in communications is as inconsistent with any social order as is unlimited freedom in action."

*8. Holbrook, David, ed. *The case against pornography.* New York: Library Press, 1973.

"I am . . . prepared to accept that obscenity is sometimes necessary within the whole content of a serious work of art. Only I believe those works which really need obscenity are few and far between."

9. Kilpatrick, James J. *The smut peddlers.* Westport, Conn.: Greenwood Press, 1973. (Reprint of 1960 edition)

". . . a free society should find nothing inconsistent with its freedom in seeking to keep from its reservoirs the merchants of filth."

10. Kuh, Richard H. *Foolish figleaves? Pornography in and out of court.* New York: Macmillan, 1967.

*Recommended for a basic list.

"When the law provides no adequate redress, the citizenry may not always be rational in its resort to self-help."

11. Rushdoony, Rousas J. *The politics of pornography.* New Rochelle, N.Y.: Arlington House, 1974.

"The new pornography . . . is . . . a crusade for a new freedom and an all-out war against God and His law."

12. Sunderland, Lane V. *Obscenity: the court, the congress and the president's commission.* Washington, D.C.: American Enterprise Institute, 1975.

". . . resolution of obscenity cases will still depend, finally, on the subtle quality of judicial judgment."

Notes, maxims, and an intellectual freedom creed

10

*(These condensed comments on intellectual freedom and cen-
sorship do not aspire to the pithiness and worldly-wiseness of
a La Rochefoucauld or a Lord Chesterfield, or even the
homely truths of a Thoreau or Franklin; let's settle for the
occasional achievement of something worth saying in a style
worth reading. Nothing in this chapter has been published
previously.)*

SOME NOTES AND MAXIMS

. . . In this postliterate age the freedom to see and hear is more in
danger than the freedom to read, which has had a longer history of
attack and defense. The major battles for the book have all been
fought; only the minor skirmishes, the preliminary maneuvering
have occurred in regards to film and television and all the other
impedimenta of the McLuhan era. The fear of actually looking at
life as it is, of hearing the sounds of reality, far transcends whatever
comparatively slight trepidation comes out of printed pages.

. . . The librarian who selects books on the basis of personal
prejudices is not practicing book selection for his or her library; he
or she is simply buying books for his or her personal library.

. . . Of all the basic requirements for being a truly professional
librarian, the primary one is the ability to differentiate between
book selection and book censorship.

. . . Censorship crusades seem to come in cycles, with their peak coinciding with excesses in political and financial corruption—almost as if they were compensation in lip service to ultrabourgeois morality. Anthony Comstock and the "robber barons" both flourished in the same period of American history; so did Eisenhower's Postmaster General Arthur Summerfield and the post-World-War-II profiteers.

. . . No librarian qua librarian can be a censor; no censor qua censor can be a librarian. Librarianship and censorship are antithetical.

. . . When a censor decides for a librarian whether or not to buy or keep a book, Thomas Jefferson revolves in his grave—one more time!

. . . Let's say that censorship, whether by law or by private efforts, becomes the rule, rather than, as at present, the exception. Then let's also say that the American system of librarianship and libraries is dead—for it will be.

. . . The two basic sources of the Library Bill of Rights are the First Amendment to the U.S. Constitution and the Golden Rule. The only thing the intellectual practitioner asks is that he or she get to be treated just as the individual or group who is attempting to control his or her would like to be treated—at least regarding access to print or nonprint. Unfortunately, the censor's version of the Golden Rule seems to be: treat others as you would hate to be treated yourself. We know this because the ultraright and the ultraleft are equally censorious, but insist that libraries hold every scrap of print expressing their particular views.

. . . It is easy to overestimate the potential role of the academic or public library, and particularly of the library which is an official depository for U.S. government documents, in assisting the enemies of this country to find out significant information of a national security nature. The theory seems to be that it is perfectly all right for U.S. bureaus to write and to publish revealing information, but somehow wrong of the depository library to circulate them to an individual who can use that information deleteriously. It is as if a grocery store were held criminally responsible for unknowingly selling sugar to a diabetic.

. . . Censoring books considered by a jury to be obscene is now (since the 1973 Supreme Court *Miller*, *Kaplan*, etc. decisions) legal; local communities decide for themselves. How chilling an effect have such rulings had on library book selection, on book publishing, on book writing? There is really no way to tell.

. . . If a librarian assents to censorship, is he or she still a librarian? If a censor agrees to intellectual freedom, there is no question that he or she is no longer a censor.

. . . The censorship of books because they include words or pictures which bother the censor's sexual mores almost inevitably will lead to the censorship of books because they offend the censor's social/political/religious/economic mores.

. . . It is a matter of fact that more books were printed in the first half-century after Gutenberg brought printing to Western civilization than there were copies in all of Western civilization's monasteries in the millennium before Gutenberg. Now, with over 100 new books published every single day in America, why should anyone worry about free access to knowledge? Unfortunately, quantity is not what matters; there is no way of predicting in advance which book or books will be of significance in intellectual history. The closer we come to absolute intellectual freedom, the closer we will come to achieving both the ends and means of democracy.

. . . Scratch a censor, and you'll find an authoritarian's blood flows forth.

. . . The love and practice of intellectual freedom cannot be taught in library school, but no library school which ignores it deserves to be accredited or respected.

. . . Long ago Walter Lippmann drew a clear line for the sincere believer in freedom of the press: simply fighting the censor is not enough. Freedom of speech, he wrote in *The Public Philosophy* (1955), ". . . can be maintained only by promoting debate."

. . . Every censor knows what's best for everyone else; librarians should try to think of what is really wanted by their patrons.

. . . If the library patron thinks a book should not be in a library, naturally the librarian will keep the book in and congratulate himself on his constancy to intellectual freedom. But what if that library patron is the mayor of the city or the president of the college or the principal or superintendent of the school?

. . . Set up a scale: on one side, put all the traditional arguments against the promulgation of ideas with which the censor disagrees and wants to silence. On the other, only one idea is needed to tip the scale inevitably: freedom.

. . . Librarians have usually been stereotyped as individuals who, afraid to face reality, hide behind books in the sanctuary of the library. If there is one cause which every librarian should actively fight for—within or without the library—it is, of course, the right of all to intellectual freedom. Unfortunately, it very often happens that that right comes in messy, untidy guises, and requires approval of the promulgation of what many would find immoral, indecent, or certainly highly controversial.

. . . There are still too many libraries with locked cases or closed closets containing censored books, but whose doors flaunt the Library Bill of Rights.

. . . One of the distinguishing marks of a profession is its followers' strict adherence to a strict code of practices. Librarians who willfully violate the Library Bill of Rights thereby violate their professionalism.

. . . It is curious how many critics of "pure" intellectual freedom equate censorship with protection of the highest qualities of civilization. Yet it should be obvious that civilization as we know it can only survive in today's world if there is the greatest possible freedom of the mind, because without it civilization, which requires constant change, creativity, and progress, will become stagnant and stale.

. . . Every democrat believes in freeing the minds of all the people of their shackles, self-imposed or exterior; every despot believes in constant, continual denial of freedom to his subjects' minds.

. . . Give the censor the one book he or she wants out of the library's collection today, and he or she will be back tomorrow for another one. Every censor's appetite is inexhaustible.

. . . More library schools should teach fewer courses in how to manipulate a computer and more courses in how to deal with censorship through intellectual freedom. The computer is a current gadget; censorship is perennial.

. . . Hobbes's love of authority and Mill's longing for individual freedom are only philosophical expressions of points of view which live and flourish today. Democracy needs both to some extent, for without respect for authority there is only anarchy; without individual freedom, there is only tyranny. And the key to individual freedom is the freedom to speak, to read, to dissent, and to dispute.

. . . Never tell a newspaper editor, "My library is threatened by censors." Get him or her into the act by saying, "Freedom of speech and the press are under attack in the library." After all, you and the editor are both defending the same basic principles.

. . . The First Amendment, to some, is an abstract legalism; make it live by frequent reminders to your community of what its violation would mean to both the community's intellectual and social life.

. . . When a librarian decides to buy a particular book for a library, he or she is making a commitment. That book is, or should be, a book which deserves to be in that particular library only because it will be of some value to some patron of that library—or, preferably, patrons. It is not there to suit the personal predilections of the librarian, to prove a point—even about intellectual freedom—and, most of all, it should not be there by accident. Every book in every library should be there as a selected book, a deliberate choice made among similar books if any, or, perhaps, even because of its uniqueness. But it should not be there as an act of defiance—whether of the community, of authority, or of all possible future censors.

. . . The censors are organized under constantly changing group names—Morality in Media, Citizens for Decency, etc.—but all these groups agree on one thing: it is their job to mind your business. No such group ever represents a majority; it is up to the librarian to find the group or groups in his or her community which favor intellectual freedom.

. . . If you ever doubt the value of intellectual freedom, as far as achieving democracy is concerned, check on the prevalence of that right in countries under a dictatorship.

. . . The obvious impossibility of ever knowing all the truth about everything does not vitiate the necessity of giving all possible opportunity to citizens to come as close as possible to that ideal goal.

. . . There is no such thing as absolute intellectual freedom, just as there has never been nor could there ever be absolute censorship.

Those who argue in terms of the stupidity of absolutism are flogging a horse that never lived. The debate should center on who does what to whom and why, in relation to the freedom of speech and the press.

. . . There are so many natural obstacles to ascertaining the truth on any issue that governmental restrictions and partisan or sectarian obfuscations seem to be acts of supererogation.

. . . The thoughts that are not permitted to be expressed may be the very ones that most need to be expressed. Unless they are printed or otherwise made available for mass consideration, how are we going to know?

. . . Let us face up to the censor as, in most cases, the representative of others; the lone censor is usually about as effective, or as common, as the lone defender of intellectual freedom. There may not always be victory in numbers, but solid backing helps in a democracy.

. . . It does not take a conspiracy of silence to stop listeners or readers or viewers from finding something out; all it takes is unconcerted ignoring of the book or film or cassette or videotape which tells what should be known. The worst restriction on the freedom of the mind is not censorship but ignorance.

. . . No censor ever admitted he was himself liable to the corruption he considers likely to come from a particular book or film. He is so pure, he is impervious to sinful immoralities. Everyone else, however, is weak and defenseless before the onslaughts of the Devil.

. . . One of the most difficult portions of the Library Bill of Rights to carry out is the one which involves making the library available as a public forum. Such normally minority organizations in America as the Ku Klux Klan, the American Nazi Party, or the local atheists' club deserve their reasonable share of whatever facilities are available just as much as Establishment groups do. No one wants to encourage or stimulate rioting—but freedom of association and freedom of speech are often indivisible.

. . . Tell the Censor he cannot possibly stop the Truth from marching on; he will still persist in trying.

. . . When the intellect is free, it can create. When it is confined, it imitates.

. . . One of the most difficult tasks for any librarian is to recognize his or her own censorship proclivities. It is very easy to rationalize a single censorship action or even a series of them, and, in many cases, only the lone librarian performs the actual act or acts —without any cross-check whatsoever. The very best safeguard is the professional conscience of the librarian. If he or she has none, then he or she isn't a librarian, anyway, but simply someone who happens to work in a library.

. . . In his second inaugural address, Thomas Jefferson viewed the United States in 1805 as ". . . an experiment . . . whether freedom of discussion, unaided by power, is not sufficient for the propagation and protection of truth." Nearly 200 years later this is still in the experimental stage. But such monumental national self-cleansings as Teapot Dome, Watergate, and the *Credit Mobilier* revelations serve to make most of us optimistic that the experiment will ultimately succeed. However, power gets more powerful all the time!

. . . Jefferson saw the best guard against excessive freedom of the press in what he called (in his second inaugural address) "the censorship of public opinion." The question of whether public opinion is a sufficient censor to deter an unbridled press—or rather media these days—is still moot.

. . . George Washington once said that "until there was some infallible criterion of reason, a difference of opinion must be tolerated." Obviously, he didn't know about the groups and individuals who wanted to silence the ALA film, *The Speaker*. Either those individuals and groups disagreed with Washington, or perhaps they found "some infallible criterion of reason" which was far beyond the average person's comprehension.

. . . In Jefferson's *Notes of the State of Virginia* (1781) he wrote, "It is error alone which needs the support of government. Truth can stand by itself." He continued, "Subject opinion to coercion: whom will you make your inquisitors? Fallible men; men governed by bad passions, by private as well as public reasons. And why subject it to coercion? To produce uniformity. But is uniformity of opinion desirable? No more than of face and stature." Jefferson's queries, made so long ago, remain unanswerable today in any other way than what he implies. Indeed, they are still provocative today, but, one hopes, will lead most of us to the same conclusions about the value of truth, as opposed to error.

. . . When a governmental censor manages to find still another way of stiffling criticism of the government, the cause of the captive mind has won another victory.

. . . The ocean of Truth has drowned many mariners, but censor-locked landsmen never even get the chance to try its dangers.

. . . What can a librarian do to help the cause of intellectual freedom? Most of all, he or she can set an example. The free mind, for the librarian, is best exemplified in book selection—but there are plenty of other obvious possibilities. Just posting the Library Bill of Rights on a public bulletin board is really not enough.

A LIBRARIAN'S INTELLECTUAL FREEDOM CREED

1. I believe in the absolute freedom of the mind as an ideal, if not a a practical goal.
2. In order to achieve the freedom of the mind, I believe in the freedom of all communications media, and especially in the freedom of the press.
3. I believe in the freedom of the individual to express his or her own opinion through every possible medium.
4. I believe in the right of society to protect itself against destruction by enemies, foreign and domestic, but I do not believe in the right of society to silence dissent, as long as that dissent is not expressed in violent acts.
5. I believe in the right of the individual to his own privacy, but I do not believe in using that right to deny society its own rights to protect itself against crime, especially treason and insurrection.
6. If society must choose between the individual's freedom to speak, to read, to hear, and to view the widest possible variety of points of view on social, religious, and economic matters and society's right to self-protection, I believe the rights of society must always be paramount—but only after careful judicial determination that those rights are truly in danger.
7. I believe no description or representation of a sexual act in any artistic medium can ipso facto be deemed obscene, any more than human nudity per se is obscene.
8. I believe that no group in society has any special rights to intellectual freedom as compared to any other group.

9. I believe that librarianship as a profession is as much based on the freedom of the mind as the profession of medicine is based on its responsibility for the care of the body or the profession of law for equitable determination of the relative rights of individuals, or of the individual and society. If universal health is the proper goal of the doctor and universal justice the appropriate aim of the lawyer, then, equally, universal intellectual freedom is unquestionably the right target for the librarian.

10. I believe that the librarian who sacrifices his or her library's intellectual freedom for personal interest or gain has lost his or her right to be a librarian.

Index

About the Author

ELI M. OBOLER is university librarian at Idaho State University in Pocatello. He is the author of *The Fear of the Word: Censorship* and *Sex and Ideas and the University Librarian* (Greenwood Press, 1977), as well as of numerous articles in journals and newspapers. For 1979-80 he is vice-president of the Freedom to Read Foundation, vice-chairman (chairman-elect) of the ALA Intellectual Freedom Round Table, and a member of the ALA Council.